THE CITIES OF SELEUKID
SYRIA

THE CITIES
OF
SELEUKID SYRIA

JOHN D. GRAINGER.

CLARENDON PRESS · OXFORD
1990

Oxford University Press, Walton Street, Oxford OX2 6DP

Oxford New York Toronto
Delhi Bombay Calcutta Madras Karachi
Petaling Jaya Singapore Hong Kong Tokyo
Nairobi Dar es Salaam Cape Town
Melbourne Auckland

and associated companies in
Berlin Ibadan

Oxford is a trade mark of Oxford University Press

Published in the United States
by Oxford University Press, New York

British Library Cataloguing in Publication Data
Grainger, John D.
The Cities of Seleukid Syria.
1. Syria, Cities, ancient period
I. Title
939'.4'009732
ISBN 0–19–814694–9

Library of Congress Cataloging in Publication Data
Data available

Typeset by Pentacor Ltd, High Wycombe, Bucks
Printed in Great Britain by
Courier International Ltd,
Tiptree, Essex

PREFACE

THE Hellenistic world has usually been studied from the viewpoint of the state, or thematically, as in its architecture, literature, and so on. Only rarely has a geographical section been isolated for detailed study, and such parts are usually detached from the rest for reasons other than the study of Hellenistic history. So Judaea is studied in its Hellenistic period for religious reasons above all, Athens because it is Athens, Baktria for its mystery and its coins, Egypt for its papyri. In this book, based on my Ph.D. thesis, I aim to look at a part of the Hellenistic world which was geographically central, rich economically, and therefore, for both of those reasons, a centre of power. The source of its power was partly due to its position, partly to the rule of a succession of able and busy kings, but above all because it was the site of the foundation of an extraordinary quantity of large cities. Hence the essential content of the study is an investigation into the size, history, geography, foundation, rise, and decline of those cities, and in particular their relationship with their kings.

The original study on which this book is based was done between 1981 and 1986 while I was an external student of Birmingham University. In the course of my studies I incurred debts of gratitude to my employers, Hereford and Worcester Education Committee, who generously funded my studies, to my headmaster, Mr J. J. Smith, for timely support and for not flinching when I asked for leave of absence to visit Syria, to many friends in Syria and Turkey who smoothed my travelling path, to my examiners, Professor R. A. Tomlinson of Birmingham and Professor J. K. Davies of Liverpool, for their comments and encouragement, to the never failing resources of the Ashmolean Library in Oxford, to my friends whose enquiries as to my progress spurred me on to be able to answer honestly that I was making some, and above all to my tutor at Birmingham, Martin Goodman, patient and rigorous at the same time, who deflected my dafter notions with a sure touch.

J.D.G

CONTENTS

List of Maps and Plans   viii

Abbreviations   ix

Introduction   1

I. SELEUKOS NIKATOR

1. *Seleukos' Acquisition*   7
2. *The Work of Seleukos Nikator*   31
3. *Seleukos' Cities: Sites and Situations*   67

II. AFTER SELEUKOS

4. *The Cities and the Villages*   91
5. *The Evolution of the Urban Hierarchy*   120
6. *The Kings and the Cities*   137
7. *The Survival of the Cities*   170

Appendices

1. *Concordance of City-Names*   201
2. *Hellenistic Kings of Syria*   202
3. *Evidence for Persian and Hellenistic Period Occupation*   204

Bibliography.   211

Maps and plans   229

Index   247

LIST OF MAPS AND PLANS

1. Syria in 301 BC
2. The Cities of Seleukos
3. The Southern Frontier Zone
4. Syria in 66 BC
5 (a). The North-West
   (b). The North-East
   (c). The South
6 (a). Antioch
   (b). Apamea
   (c). Laodikeia-ad-Mare
   (d). Seleukeia-in-Pieria
   (e). Beroia, Chalkis
   (f). Kyrrhos, Seleukeia-Zeugma
   (g). Arados, Arethusa, Epiphaneia-Hamath, Laodikeia-ad-Libanum, Europos-Carchemish
   (h). Rome, Miletos, Cosa

ABBREVIATIONS

AAAS, AAS	*Annales archélogiques (arabes) syriennes.*
AASOR	*Annual of the American School of Oriental Research.*
Admiralty, *Syria*	Admiralty, *Syria and Palestine*, Geographical Handbooks Series (1943).
Admiralty, *Turkey*	Admiralty, *Turkey*, Geographical Handbooks Series (1942).
AJA	*American Journal of Archaeology.*
ANRW	*Aufstieg und Niedergang des Romischen Welt.*
Antioch-on-the-Orontes	R. Stillwell *et al.* (eds.), *Antioch-on-the-Orontes*, 6 vols. Princeton, NJ., 1933–54.
App. *Syr.*	Appian, *The Syrian Wars*
App. *Mith.*	Appian, *The Mithridatic Wars*
Arr.	Arrian, *Anabasis of Alexander*
BAR	British Archaeological Reports
BASOR	*Bulletin of the American School of Oriental Research*
Bellinger, 'End'	A. R. Bellinger, 'The End of the Seleucids', *Transactions of the Connecticut Academy of Arts and Sciences* 38 (1949).
Bevan, *House*	E. R. Bevan, *The House of Seleucos*, 2 vols., (1902).
CAH	*Cambridge Ancient History*
Cl. Ph.	*Classical Philology*
CRAI	*Comptes rendus de l'Académie des Inscriptions et des Belles Lettres*
Curt.	Curtius Rufus, *History of Alexander*
Diod.	Diodoros Sikulos, *Histories*
Downey, *Antioch*	G. R. Downey, *A History of Antioch in Syria* (Princeton, NJ, 1961)
Dussaud, *Top. hist.*	R. Dussaud, *Topographie historique de la Syrie ancienne and médiévale* (Paris, 1927)
FGH	Jacoby (ed.), *Die Fragmente des Griechischen Historiker* (Berlin and Leiden, 1923–58)
Head, *HN*	B. V. Head, *Historia Numorum* (1911)
Honigmann, 'Hist. Top.'	E. Honigmann, 'Historische Topographie von Nordsyrien in Altertum', *ZDPV* 46 (1923) and 47 (1924)
IGLS	*Inscriptions grecque et latine de la Syrie*

JNES	*Journal of Near Eastern Studies*
Jones, *CERP*	A. H. M. Jones, *The Cities of the Eastern Roman Provinces*, 2nd edn. (1971)
Jos. *AJ*	Josephus, *Antiquitates Judaicae*
JRS	*Journal of Roman Studies*
Lib.	Libanios
LIEAO	*Lettre d'information européenne archéologique orientale*
Mal.	Johannes Malalas, *Chronographia*
Morkholm, *Antiochus IV*	O. Morkholm, *Antiochus IV of Syria* (Copenhagen, 1966)
MUSJ	*Mélanges de l'Université Saint-Josèphe*
Newell, *WSM*	E. T. Newell, *Western Seleucid Mints* (New York, 194), and 2nd edn., revised by O. Morkholm (New York, 1977)
OGIS	*Orientis Graeci Inscriptiones Selectae*
P. Gurob	Papyrus Gurob, trans. in N. M. Austin, *The Hellenistic World from Alexander to the Roman Conquest* (Cambridge, 1981), no. 220
Pliny, *NH*	Pliny, *Natural History*
Plut. *Dem.*	Plutarch, *Life of Demetrius*
Pol.	Polybios, *Histories*
Ptol.	Claudius Ptolemy, *Geography*
PW	Pauly, Wissowa, Kroll, *Realencyclopadie der Klassischen Altertumswissemschaft*
Rev. num.	*Revue numismatique*
Rey-Coquais, *Arados*	J. P. Rey-Coquais, *Arados et sa Perée*, (Paris, 1974)
Sauvaget, *Alep*	J. Sauvaget, *Alep* (Paris, 1941)
Sauvaget, 'Plan'	J. Sauvaget, 'Le Plan de Laodicée-sur-Mer', *Bulletin des études orientales*, 4, (1934) 81–114 and 6 (1936) 51–2
Seyrig, 'Aradus'	H. Seyrig, 'Aradus et sa Perée sous les Rois séleucides', *Syria* 28 (1951) 206–17
Seyrig, 'Ères'	H. Seyrig, 'Ères de quelques villes de Syrie', *Syria* 27 (1950), 5–50
Seyrig, 'Séleucos I'	H. Seyrig, 'Séleucos I et la fondation de la monarchie syrienne', *Syria* 47 (1970) 290–311
Str.	Strabo, *Geography*
TAPA	*Transactions of the American Philological Association*
Wagner, *Zeugma*	J. Wagner, *Seleukeia am Euphrat/Zeugma* (Wiesbaden 1974)

Will, *Hist. pol.*	E. Will, *Histoire politique du monde hellénistique*, 2nd edn. (Nancy 1979–82)
Xen.	Xenophon, *Anabasis*
ZDPV	*Zeitschrift für Deutsche Palaestina-Vereins*

INTRODUCTION

AFTER their victory at the battle of Ipsos in 301 BC, the three winners, Kassandros, Lysimachos, and Seleukos, divided the spoils, each taking a section of the kingdom of their defeated rivals Antigonos and Demetrios. Seleukos took two adjacent lands, Mesopotamia and Syria,[1] which were thus added to his existing empire which stretched away to the east as far as the borders of India. It was not quite so rich an acquisition as he had perhaps hoped for when he had joined in the war against Antigonos and Demetrios. Even more galling, he found that his erstwhile colleague Ptolemy had already seized control of Phoenicia and Palestine now and refused to leave, even though he had not been present at the decisive fight[2]. Seleukos' expected gains were in effect halved. This dispute between Seleukos and Ptolemy set in process the long sequence of 'Syrian Wars' which plagued both kingdoms for the next two hundred years.

The Syrian land which Seleukos annexed in 301 is the setting for the subject of this study. Other lands in all directions came at some time under Seleukid rule—Kilikia and Asia Minor, Phoenicia and Palestine, Mesopotamia—but only Syria remained under the rule of the Seleukids from Ipsos to the final Roman annexation. By the 140s those peripheral areas were becoming separated from the rule of the dynasty, but Syria remained under Seleukid control for a further eighty years. It was, in fact, the land that the dynasty ruled longest: 237 years from acquisition to the Roman annexation. More, by his actions right at the beginning of the period, in the years 300 to 298, Seleukos I ensured that Syria became, from the first, one of the major centres of Seleukid power. Eventually it was their major power base, so that the Seleukids could be seen, in the Roman period, as kings of Syria above all else, and Appian could call his account of Romano-Seleukid relations the 'Syrian' wars. In the same way, in this study the term

---

[1] Diod. 21. 1.5.
[2] Ibid.

'Syria' will refer to this land, bounded by the Taurus mountains on the north, the Euphrates river and the sea to east and west, and the Eleutheros river on the south. The clear-cut boundaries delimit it neatly from its neighbours. With a southern extension into Palestine, these bounds defined also the great Roman province of Syria for several more centuries after the end of the Seleukid dynasty[3].

It is Seleukos' actions in Syria in his first years which mark out that land as important in itself; those actions and their consequences in Syria are my subject here. The land he acquired will be investigated first, since only by having a clear view of what he got can we see the effects of his actions. This is by no means an easy problem, for a number of assumptions need to be cleared away, and the main evidence is archae-ological, a peculiarly intractable type of source.

Having cleared the undergrowth, then the actions of Seleukos himself can be looked at. His main activity was to found a set of cities, and this demands an investigation into why he did so, what sites he chose for the cities, what the cities were like and how Seleukos ordered the government of the area—a more difficult and intricate matter once cities existed than when there were none. These are large matters and will need extended treatment, both from the historical viewpoint and then from the geographical.

Once founded, the cities remained closely tied to the dynasty. They certainly altered, in size and population, though this was less their own doing than the dynasty's. By applying the Central Place Theory to the pattern of Syrian cities (in Chapter 5) some explanations can be given of this process—and some light is thrown also on the theory. The failure of the dynasty, first in bouts of civil warfare, then in the débâcle of the generation after *c*. 100 BC, forced the cities to look elsewhere for support. This problem had been inherent in their situation from the start, and the history of Arados, a city not founded by Seleukos but in his kingdom, is an instructive contrast to those he did found. Many of the cities survived, ultimately, by accepting Roman domination, which ensured their continuance for seven more centuries.

---

[3] Syria's boundaries are, of course, one of the modern world's problems too: see T. Petran, *Syria, a Modern History* (1972), especially the map on page 267.

This study is quite deliberately focused on this narrow area. It is one of the temptations, and one of the problems, of Hellenistic history, to make up for the paucity of evidence in certain areas (of which Syria is emphatically one) by referring to other places and drawing parallels. In the case of cities, the practice exists of referring to old Greece for information on subjects for which Syrian sources are lacking. It is my contention that this procedure is wrong, that it is bad historical practice, and that it should not be indulged in. Thus in this study I confine my sources to those within Syria, and any comparisons with other areas are deliberately very limited. The urban development of Syria took place in a Syrian context above all, and references to the history of Egypt or Asia Minor or old Greece can only mislead and distort, as well as discounting the individuality of all these areas.

Yet at the same time, if the study is not to be mere local history, with only a local relevance, it must be placed in a larger context. It is a study of some three centuries of the history of a small country, after all. Yet this is a country with a great importance. It has been a land of cities since the third millennium BC It has more than once been the stage of events of world-historical importance—it was the centre of the Ummayyad dynasty's power, the origin of a dynasty of Roman emperors, to give only two examples. It has been the neighbour of Palestine and of Babylonia, sharing many experiences with those lands, but also experiencing them in subtly different ways. It is only when the history of Syria itself has been unravelled that all this, and more, can be understood and seen in a proper context. This study is a step in that direction.

PART I

Seleukos Nikator

I

SELEUKOS' ACQUISITION.

WHEN Seleukos Nikator's army occupied Syria in 301 BC, it was only the latest in a long series of such armies. In the last hundred years, Syria had been repeatedly traversed by military forces, both hostile and friendly, though the difference between the two was probably not clear to the suffering peasantry. And before that, the land had been ruled by a succession of alien governors sent from ever more distant imperial capitals, first Assur, then Babylon, then Persepolis. None of these governors or rulers or military commanders had shown any interest in Syria itself or the Syrians themselves, except as a source of taxes and provisions. This was true, also, of the Macedonians, the latest alien conquerors, who had ruled since Alexander's conquest in 333, but these, for the first time in four centuries, had shown some interest in taking measures to increase the resources of Syria; this process was to culminate in Seleukos' spectacular series of urban foundations, soon after he arrived.

The result of four centuries of alien conquest, alien rule, and extractive taxation had been to leave Syria devastated, and at the same time to prevent its recovery. When Seleukos took over there was only one actual city on the mainland, only a few years old, and one more on a small offshore island. The population of Seleukos' new acquisition was not merely mainly rural, it was all but exclusively rural. This was in a country which had been thickly sown with cities four centuries before. It was foreign conquest and rule which had brought about the devastation.

There are, however, alternative possible explanations for the state of affairs Seleukos inherited in Syria. There are also alternative accounts of the actual Syrian situation which would admit the existence of cities when Alexander conquered the land. These alternatives must therefore be considered before the evidence on which the above statements are based is presented. It could be, for instance, that the climate had changed, thus enforcing depopulation, and so this possibility needs to be considered. This requires, in turn, a preliminary account of the physical geography of Syria.[1]

The physical boundaries of the Syria which Seleukos acquired are obvious enough: the sea on the west, the desert to the east; in the north-east the Euphrates river, along the north the Taurus and Amanus mountain zone, and to the south the Eleutheros river (Nahr el-Kebir) which divided the Bargylos from the Lebanon mountains. But on closer examination these boundaries are seen actually to be zones of transition rather than precise lines. On the west, the apparently clear line of the coast is in fact a zone in which there are, successively, offshore islands, beaches, cliffs, and coastal dunes, in all up to a mile in width. The river boundaries have a similarly zonal nature, for often the rivers unite the opposing banks rather than separate them; in particular the Euphrates, for all its size and power, has only very rarely been useful as a boundary line; more frequently, as in Seleukid times, both banks have been controlled by one power. The mountains to the north are a succession of ranges with intervening valleys, up to 100 kilometres wide in places. And to travel due east is to move from cultivated land to pasture to steppe to desert, the changes at times almost imperceptible, at times abrupt, and shifting with the seasons: another zone.

The land itself is divided into a series of long, narrow, north–south zones. The coast is both inhospitable to the sailor and difficult of access from inland. It has rocky and cliff-bound sections, alternating with open beaches which all too often are backed by extensive sand dunes.[2] Along the coast are a series of rich fertile plains, separated from one another by mountains reaching the sea. Those in the north around Iskenderun and at the mouth of the Orontes are narrow and short; in the centre is the large and wealthy plain centred on Lattakia, in the south is the largest and richest of them all,

---

[1] The main accounts of Syrian geography are Admiralty, *Turkey* and *Syria*, and E. Wirth *Syrien* (Darmstadt, 1972), which has greater detail but is confined to the modern republic's area.

[2] The coast is described, from a seaman's point of view, in Admiralty, *Turkey*, pp. 100–2, and *Syria*, pp. 57–9.

around Arad and Tartus, which stretches on south into the modern Lebanon. Behind these coastal plains is a line of mountains, the Amanus in the north and the Bargylos in the south, and continuing south as the Lebanon range. These mountains are a formidable obstacle to communications, and are the country's major geographical feature.[3] The Bargylos mountains are occupied up to their (fairly gentle) summits, but the Amanus are higher and more rugged, and are still in part heavily forested. Both ranges rise relatively gently from the sea and the coastal plains, but their eastern, inland, slopes are very steep. It is this inland scarp which limits east–west communications: the Bargylos range is crossed today by only two major routes, though there are also a number of minor tracks which were more important in the days before motor transport,[4] and the Amanus is also crossed by only two major routes, the Beilan and the Bagche passes.[5] It is easier to travel through the two valley routes which split the mountains into sections: between the Amanus and the Bargylos is a fault-line gap through which the Orontes river reaches the sea, and south of the Bargylos the Eleutheros river gap forms a similar route. Thus in the whole line of the mountains, well over 300 kilometres in length, there are only six major routes and only two of these are low-lying.

The physical effects of these mountains extend well beyond the problem of communications, for their existence is the determining factor in the climate of all the land to the east. Rainfall is brought by weather-systems from the west,[6] which are intercepted by the mountains, which catch most of the rainfall. This reduces inland Syria to a rainfall regime which in many areas is incapable of supporting agriculture except on a marginal basis. Thus the water supplied by the Orontes river, which flows northwards east of the Bargylos mountains, is crucial to agriculture along the whole of its length; in the

[3] E. de Vaumas, 'Montagnes du Proche Orient: L'Amanus et le Djebel Ansarieh', étude morphologique', *Revue de géographie alpine* 42 (1954) 111–42.

[4] P. J. Riis, *Sukas* i (Copenhagen 1970) 156, discusses pre-motor age routes from Jeblé to Hama.

[5] U. Bahadur Alkim, 'The Amanus Region in Turkey', *Archaeology* 22 (1969), 280–9, and in more detail, 'The Road from Samal to Asitawandawa', *Anadolu Arastirmalari* 2 (1965), 1–45, which is a translation by G. E. Bean of the Turkish original in *Belleten* 24 (1960), 349–401.

[6] Wirth (note 1) ch. 2, pp. 68–106.

north and west, where rainfall is strongly affected—that is,
encouraged—by the Taurus mountains, the rivers which flow
southwards from those mountains—the Kara, the Afrin, the
Qoueiq, the Sajur, the Euphrates—are similarly vital to the
lands they water.

Two of these rivers, the Kara and the Orontes, occupy a
long valley east of the mountains. They meet in the Amuq
basin near Antioch and their joint waters empty into the
Mediterranean through the gap between Amanus and Bargylos. The whole valley is actually a tectonic formation, a
northern extension of the Great Rift Valley, and both rivers'
courses are entirely determined by fault lines and basalt flows
rather than the weathering action of water.[7]

The eastern edge of this valley is formed by a line of
limestone hills, lower and drier than the greater mountains to
the west, and again discontinuous. From north to south these
hills are: the Kurd Dagh, parallel to the Amanus; the tangle of
hills with a variety of names around Dana and Sermeda, east
of the Amuq basin; finally the Jebel Zawiye, which reaches
almost as far south as Apamea.[8] These hills have their scarp
slopes on the west and dip gently away to the east to merge
almost imperceptibly into the plateau which slopes southwards from the Taurus foothills, and which is desert in the
south.

In the north rainfall is adequate, thanks to the passage of
winter depressions, which travel eastwards from the Mediterranean, parallel to the Taurus, penetrating along the Orontes
gap. In the southern part of the plateau, in the rain-shadow of
the Bargylos, rainfall is very much less, and the land becomes
desert not very far to the east of the Orontes. The rivers which
flow from the Taurus southwards tend to end in evaporating
inland basins. The Kara and the Afrin flow into the Amuq
Lake, which in turn drains into the Orontes. Further east the
southward-flowing Qoueiq and some minor streams end in

---

[7] J. Weulersse, *L'Oronte* (Tours 1940); C. Voute 'Climate or Tectonics; some
Remarks on the Evolution of the Valley of the Orontes (Nahr el Aassi) between Homs
and the marshy plain of the Ghab (Syria)', *Geologie en Mijnbouw* NS 17, no. 9 (Aug
1955), 197–206.
    [8] E. de Vaumas, 'Plateaux, plaines et depressions de la Syrie intérieure
septentrionale, étude morphologique', *Bulletin de la Société Géographique d'Égypte* 30,
(1957), 97–235.

the two salt lakes and marshes, the Madkh and the Jabboul. The Sajur drains into the Euphrates. The Euphrates valley itself forms another north–south zone, a narrow valley which is an eye-resting green in the harsher red and brown of the surrounding land. It is only two or three miles wide, a flat flood plain within which the river meanders between cliffs. The use of the river's water for irrigation is thus difficult, and the power of the river, fed by the melting snows of eastern Anatolia, makes the use of the valley land itself a hazardous enterprise.[9]

The land throughout Syria, where it is watered by rain or by irrigation, is generally fertile. Even the summit of the Bargylos has carefully tended terraced fields. The soils formed on the limestone of the hills, on the basalt, and on the Tertiary plateaux are fertile—when they are watered. Always it is water which is the limiting factor in agriculture. One account of the soils of Syria says roundly that the only real difference between the rich fertile soils of the Orontes valley and the desert soils to the east is the absence of moisture.[10] Where rainfall is insufficient and irrigation is not possible, crops are not grown. But even a rainfall which is insufficient for arable agriculture may suffice for animal husbandry, particularly sheep and goats (cattle tend to be confined to the coastal plains and the wetter valleys). The concentration of rainfall in the winter months also means that there can be a joint use of the land by grain-growing farmers who allow sheep-herding nomads to pasture their animals on the stubble in the summer. This in turn fertilizes the ground and allows the animals to be moved out of the desert during the summer heat, and towards the west and north into the comparative coolness of the arable lands.[11]

---

[9] This has now changed as the result of the barrage built across the river at al-Raqqa, which has formed Lake Assad, and which in turn is the source for a major irrigation scheme.

[10] The comment is by A. Reifenberg, 'The Soils of Syria and the Lebanon', *Journal of Soil Science* 3 (1952), 68–88. Also useful are A. Muir, 'Notes on the Soils of Syria', *Journal of Soil Science* 2 (1951), 163–82 and, for an explanation of the technical aspects and the potentialities of different soils, S. Limbrey, *Soil Science and Archaeology* (1975), especially on the soils of the Mediterranean area (pp. 211–14) and the soils of arid regions (p. 224).

[11] D. G. Bates, *Nomads and Farmers, a Study of the Yoruk of Southeastern Turkey*, University of Michigan Museum of Anthropology, Anthropological Papers 52 (1973),

The rainfall regime determines agriculture unless supplemented by irrigation (or in the case of the marshes, drainage).
The most easily recognized measure of the extent of agriculture is in plotting the boundary between nomadic and sedentary
agriculture along the edge of the desert. Today, after a century
and more of expansion, agriculture is at its most extensive. In
the past there have been at least two periods when agriculture
has been almost equally dominant, the Bronze Age and the
Byzantine period. In between have been periods of exceptional
contraction. One was the Ottoman period, another was the
Persian. These fluctuations are best explained by reference to
human action, but before this is accepted it is necessary to
dispose of the climatic-change possibility, and then to examine
evidence for the changes in occupation.

First, climatic change. Syria is an area where singularly
little research on historical meteorology has taken place.[12]
Conclusions can, however, be drawn from the more intensive
work which has taken place in surrounding lands, but in the
nature of the problem, such conclusions can be no more than
tentative. The latest authorities are almost unanimous in
claiming, as K. W. Butzer says, that 'seen as a long-term
condition, climate in the better-watered parts of the Fertile
Crescent has not fluctuated significantly during post glacial
times'.[13] The real difficulty here is that, as Butzer goes on to
remark, it does not need a large fluctuation in climate to have
a major effect on the possibilities of land utilization all along
the boundary of the Syrian desert. A small increase in
precipitation can have large local effects.[14] Another variable

documents this process of double land use, but B. C. Aswad, *Property Control and Social
Strategies: Settlers on a Middle Eastern Plain*, Anthropological Papers 54 (1971), dealing
with the same area, shows how a larger nomadic group has been forcibly
sedentarized. The Yoruk survive as nomads partly because of their small numbers,
and partly due to their great care in dealing with the villagers. Their practice of
negotiating grazing on the stubble has such benefits for both groups that it is likely to
be an old practice.

[12] See the preliminary remarks by K. W. Butzer in his chapter 'The Late
Prehistoric Environmental History of the Near East', in W. C. Brice (ed.), *The
Environmental History of the Near and Middle East since the Last Ice Age* (1978), 5–6.

[13] K. W. Butzer, 'Physical Conditions ... before ... Agricultural and Urban
Settlement', *CAH*, 2nd edn. (1970), vol. i, part 1, p. 57.

[14] Two small sketch maps in P. Sanlaville (ed.), *Holocene Settlement in North Syria*,
BAR S 238 (Oxford, 1985), fig. 7, p. 23, illustrate the wide variation in rainfall
possible today.

which is difficult to quantify at present is the effect of human land use, and in particular the effects of grazing animals on the vegetation cover.[15]

In North Africa, it is just possible that the first millennium BC saw 'a southward shift of climatic conditions and a local increase in rainfall'.[16] In Syria this might have brought a greater rainfall as well. This is not at all certain yet, but if it can be demonstrated, it would make the changes which are observable in Syria in that millennium all the more startling, since it is in that millennium that agriculture in Syria shrank.[17] However, the evidence at present available, such as it is, suggests that it is not climatic change which is at the root of any of the land-occupation changes. These changes are not easy to estimate, for the evidence for them is almost entirely archaeological. There are some fragments of information in the literary sources of the Hellenistic and Roman periods, but these are quite disjointed and unsystematic and can do little to help elucidate the evidence of the archaeology.

Intensity of occupation is one of the factors which will affect the general history of any country. It lies at the root of any consideration of production, of communal or individual wealth, and of political power. Put simply, low intensity means a poor society and lack of power; the more people the greater wealth and power. But too many people willl enforce poverty in a different way. Thus, in a land like Syria, which in many areas is marginal for agriculture, the estimate of the degree of land occupation is a useful clue to other aspects, if such an estimate can be arrived at. Hence the concentration

[15] J. T. Bintliff, 'Palaeoclimatic Modelling of Environmental Changes in the East Mediterranean Region since the Last Glaciation', in J. T. Bintliff and W. von Zeist, *Palaeoclimate, Palaeoenvironments and Human Communities in the Eastern Mediterranean in later Prehistory*, BAR S 133 (1982), part II, pp. 485–527, comments on the difficulty of distinguishing, in the whole period from 750 BC to the present day, between the effects of human actions and those of 'minor climatic oscillation' (p. 512).

[16] W. C. Brice, 'Conclusion', in the essays in note 12, at page 356. The evidence is that of Ptol. in the second century AD, supplemented by work on the Anatolian climate by S. Erinc (references in Brice's conclusion.)

[17] There are fluctuations in the Nile valley between 3000 and 2000 BC, according to B. Lenz, 'Palaeoclimatic Interpretation of the last 20,000 years; record of deep-sea cores around the Middle East', in Bintliff and von Zeist (note 15), p. 51; and the 'Southern Levant' (i.e. Palestine) is said to have been 'moister' than at present about 9000 BC (the Natufian period), and in the fifth and fourth millenia BC, by Butzer in *CAH* (note 13). Such fluctuations are also to be expected in Syria and will no doubt emerge when the record is available.

on archaeological evidence, which is the only source which can be used to compare one period with another, and so suggest changes.

The way such alterations to the occupation of the land can be detected very largely boils down to examining the fluctuations on the frontier of settlement along the desert margin. There are also two other areas which might produce information: the coastlands and the plains of the interior. (No archaeological investigation has been made in the Syrian mountains, though they are probably another sensitive area.) Clearly the lands along the desert edge are more difficult to cultivate, the crops are more likely to fail, drought is more common, than in the more favoured lands to the north or the west. Hence of the three environments the most sensitive measure is the fluctuation on the desert frontier. Even here, however, the evidence is such that it is only possible to compare occupation in the whole of the Persian period (539–333 BC) with that of the Hellenistic as a whole (i.e. 333–64 BC). This is, of course, very crude, though a provisional conclusion is certainly possible.

The measurement of occupation along the desert frontier is certainly the most telling of the three, but it is not simply a question of occupation or not, though since the evidence is archaeological, it will appear to be so. That is, a site producing evidence of Persian period occupation will be assumed to be occupied in that period. But the land itself was not therefore necessarily out of use when occupation cannot be detected. The joint use of land by both farmers and nomads, noted above, is one of the possible alternatives; another is purely nomadic use, which would leave little or no archaeological evidence. Yet it is possible, by archaeological means, to indicate the general area in which arable farming was being carried on, since the existence of a settled population, living in permanent villages, presupposes such farming. The absence of a sedentary population implies, not the absence of people or of economic activity altogether, but only the absence of arable farming. An area which can support arable farming can instead be used for pastoral farming alone. There is a wide band of Syrian territory where these alternatives exist, where today arable is in the ascendant, with pastoralism as an additional pursuit. This area has been re-colonized by sedentary farmers only in the past century and a half.[18] It can be defined as a zone west of the Orontes and south of Aleppo as far as the 200 mm. isohyet, which marks the practicable limit of rain-fed agriculture.[19] Within this zone, archaeological evidence can be used to determine broadly whether or not arable agriculture was carried on during the broad periods of Persian or Seleukid rule, by determining whether or not a particular site was occupied, since occupation necessarily implies farming and not nomadism.

The archaeological evidence is in two forms, ground surveys and excavations, and within each type the evidence is widely variable. Surveys have been conducted over much of the northern and central part of Seleukid Syria, but there are none for the coastlands, the mountains, or the southern area, and a good half of the surveys are of little use for the present purpose. Similarly the excavations, which produce much more evidence, are almost infinitely variable in their methods, results, and reliability. The best results come when survey and excavation are combined, but only in two areas has this occurred.

The findings of the surveys and the discoveries of the excavators, in so far as they apply in this study, are detailed in tabular form in Appendix 3 and in maps 5*a–c*. This is an extremely tedious business, and one which is always incomplete in that new reports are appearing annually, each adding its mite to the heap of detail. Those who wish can check the following conclusions against the detail in the Appendix, and further in the references there. Here only the conclusions will be presented.[20]

In the Persian period (539–333 BC) the coastal plains were all occupied along the whole length of the coast from the Eleutheros river north to the plain of Iskenderun, but the intensity and permanence of that occupation clearly varied. In the southern area, about Arados, occupation is known at all

[18] N. N. Lewis, *Settlers and Nomads in Syria and Jordan, 1800–1980* (Cambridge, 1987), and, earlier and more briefly, 'The Frontier of Settlement in Syria, 1800–1950', *International Affairs* 31 (1955), 48–60.

[19] Wirth (note 1), Map 3, opposite p. 93, and Sanlaville (note 14), fig. 7, p. 23.

[20] Detailed references will be found in Appendix 3 and will not be repeated here.

the sites so far investigated by excavation, and at two of these sites, Marathos and Sheikh Zenad, it seems to have actually begun during the Persian period, which suggests that an expansion of settlement was taking place. In the Lattakia area, however, several of the excavated sites show breaks in occupation in that period: Tell Sukas was deserted during the fifth century, while Paltos and Ras el-Basit suffered desertion in the fourth; Ras Shamra was occupied all through but nearby Ras Ibn Hani was not. These were all actually on the coast. On the other hand, Tell Durak was occupied all through the period without interruption and it may be significant that it is a few kilometres inland. In addition to all this, there is literary evidence that there were two villages, Mazabda and Ramitha, on the later site of the city of Lattakia, in 300.[21] In the northern coastal plains the dual site of al Mina-Sabouni, near the mouth of the Orontes, was occupied all through the Persian period, but in the Iskenderun plain archaeologically attested occupation is lacking. Other evidence does show, however, that there were Persian fortifications on the coast to the north; Myriandros was the site of a Persian mint for part of the fourth century,[22] and it was also the appointed rendezvous for supply ships to meet the army of Kyros the Younger in 404,[23] all of which implies permanent inhabitation; Rhosos was the scene of an exploit of Harpalos in 324,[24] and it was an active port in 298,[25] so it would seem reasonable to assume its active existence in the earlier part of the fourth century.

Taking the coastal area as a whole, there is stability and expansion in the Arados area and continuity of occupation at the Orontes estuary. By contrast, the instability in the central region is notable. Arados was a maritime Phoenician city, with a large and active fleet,[26] and it exercised control over its adjacent mainland, the Aradian *peraia*. In the Lattakia area,

---

[21] Mal. 203.

[22] E. T. Newell, *Myriandrus kat' Isson* (New York 1920).

[23] Xen. 1. 4.

[24] Theopompos, *On the Chian Letter*, quoted by Athenaeus XIII, 595. Harpalos erected statues there.

[25] Plut. *Dem.* 32; Demetrios landed at Rhosos on his way to meet Seleukos.

[26] Arados, Byblos, and Sidon had 80 ships between them in the Persian expedition under Pharnabazos in the Aegean in 333–332 and these ships were used against Tyre in 332 (Arr. 2. 20. 1).

on the other hand, there was no such maritime or political protection, and the settlements there were all villages with relatively small populations. Both areas were in maritime contact with Cyprus, Rhodes, and the Aegean, and, later, with Athens, according to the evidence of imported Greek pottery. The excavators at al Mina-Sabouni, at Tell Sukas, and at Ras el-Basit were or are also convinced that Greeks were actually settled at those places.[27] The smallness of these settlements made them all very vulnerable, and two of them, Sukas and Ras el-Basit, were actually destroyed during the Persian period; their subsequent desertion for long periods indicates that the destruction was more than a local accident, and presumably involved the removal, in one way or another, of the inhabitants. No doubt the Atheno-Persian war was to blame.

There is also a wider geographical point to be made. The stable areas of continuous occupation—al Mina-Sabouni and the Aradian *peraia*—were also the places which had the easiest communications with the transmontane interior. The Orontes formed a natural route inland from al Mina-Sabouni towards northern Syria, the Euphrates, and Babylonia, and it seems reasonable to assume that it was by this route that fifth- and fourth-century Greek pottery reached the Amuq plain and the area of Aleppo.[28] It is relevant here to note that the name given by 'Pseudo-Scylax' to the Orontes is the 'Thapsakos' river,[29] by which he presumably meant that it was the route by which the crossing of the Euphrates at Thapsakos was reached. Similarly, the towns and villages of the Aradian area were also in contact with the interior, through the gap formed by the Eleutheros river; in 333, when Alexander dealt with the city of Arados from his camp at Marathos, the authority of

[27] P. J. Riis, 'The North-East Sanctuary and the First Settling of Greeks in Syria and Palestine', *Sukas* i, pp. 126–75; P. Courbin, 'Rapport sur la sixième Campagne de Fouilles (1976) à Ras el Bassit (Syrie)', *AAAS* 27–8 (1977–78), 29–39; C. L. Woolley, *A Forgotten Kingdom*, 1953, ch. 10.

[28] Both Antakya and Aleppo museums have on display locally found examples of Greek pottery of the Persian period. The Jabboul survey noted Greek pottery at several sites along the Aleppo–Bab road; C. Clairmont, 'Greek Pottery from the Near East', *Berytus* 11 (1955), 85–141 and 12 (1956–1957), 1–34, and 'Poterie grecque provenant de Ras Shamra', *Ugaritica* 4 (Paris 1962), 631–36.

[29] C. Muller, *Geographi Graeci Minores*, vol. i (Paris, 1855), 77: Scylax 'Periplus', 102.

Arados was said to extend through that mountain gap to Mariamme on the eastern side.[30] For the settlements in the Lattakia area, on the other hand, communications with the interior were much more difficult, and possibly non-existent at the time. The coincidence of occupation and communication does suggest that more protection was available for trading centres on the coast than for agricultural villages, if such a distinction is valid. Whether that protection came from the interior or, in the case of Arados, was locally inspired, is not clear.

In the interior of the country, east of the mountains, the evidence suggests a different conclusion. Every survey expedition in the interior failed to recognize any distinctive pottery for the Persian period. This cannot simply be ascribed to a lack of interest in the period on the part of the investigators, though that is one factor of the problem. (Most surveys are mainly interested in the Bronze Age remains; none show more than incidental interest in the Persian or Hellenistic periods.) The simplest explanation of the absence of Persian period pottery is that the pottery did not exist in large or distinctive quantities. Some pottery of the period has been found, such as the Greek imports found along the line of the road from Bab to Membij, but only fragments or single pots are known. Now, if pottery of local manufacture is scarce, as the survey evidence appears to suggest, and imported pottery is even scarcer, one of two conclusions thereby suggest themselves: that the population in Persian Syria was very small or that the people were very poor.

As it happens one of the few pieces of literary evidence, Xenophon's account of the expedition of Kyros, suggests that the villages he saw in Syria were relatively prosperous.[31] Kyros' army certainly had no apparent problem with supplies, and later military expeditions seem also to have fared well. The tentative conclusion of this evidence is thus that the population was small but relatively prosperous.

If this is an accurate deduction, it follows that marginal land will have gone out of production, and in Syria this means

[30] Arr. 2. 13. 8.
[31] Xen. 1. 4.

the desert frontier zone. Conversely, the extension of sedentary occupation into the steppelands bordering the desert is clearly a function of the increase of population in the better-watered land. Thus the evidence of occupation or its absence in the borderlands can be taken as evidence also of a relatively high or low population in the rest of Syria. As it happens, the results of the excavations in the borderlands provide quite striking evidence of desertion in the Persian period.

This desert margin can be divided into two parts, the strip between the Euphrates and the Madkh marsh, and that south of the Madkh and east of the Orontes valley. In each case there are sections which show no evidence of occupation at all, and areas where the occupation is clearly evidenced. To some extent this difference must be due to the absence or presence of excavations, but the surveys do tend to tell the same story.

In the northern section Neirab was occupied in the Persian period, but a string of sites eastwards, north of the Jabboul Lake, were all deserted during the period: Tell Abu Danne and Umm el-Mara had clear breaks in occupation between the Iron Age and the Hellenistic periods, and the same thing seems to be the case at Tell en-Naam. To the north of this area of desertion, however, there is a series of occupied sites, spread along the road from Aleppo to the Euphrates at the site of Carchemish, all of which have produced Greek pottery of the Persian period. A line representing the limit of sedentary occupation at the time can thus be drawn between these two groups of sites. Further east the same result obtains in the Euphrates valley, where only one site had occupation of Persian date, Tell el-Abd, near the northern edge of the surveyed area.

To the southern part of the zone there is a line of sites which show very similar characteristics. Tell Mardikh had a limited occupation in the Persian period but not afterwards, thus implying that desertion took place during that period. Tell Afis had been occupied into the Assyrian period, but was then deserted. Tell Mastuma had occupation to the Iron Age, then no more. Only at Tell Tuqun was there continued occupation through the Persian and Hellenistic periods. Its closeness to the Madkh marsh, a source of salt, may explain this continued occupation.

Further south still, there is another line of excavated sites
which exhibit the same characteristics of occupation until the
Assyrian or Persian periods, followed by desertion. Hama was
destroyed by the Assyrians in 720, and archaeological
evidence is quite definite that the site remained deserted
until *c*.200. Tell Hana and el-Mishrife were both deserted by
the end of the fifth century, and the four sites in and about the
Lake of Homs were deserted, except for a 'Greco-Perse' layer
detected at Tell Nebi Mend by Pezard which may show
occupation in the Persian period, though the site was certainly
deserted by its end.

This evidence is quite consistent. A whole series of
settlements within the marginal land became deserted in or
before the Persian period. The conclusion must be that the
boundary between sedentary and nomadic agriculture was
moving north and east, so that more of the land was in use
exclusively by nomads—or not at all—than had been the case
before.

This pattern can also be detected elsewhere in the Fertile
Crescent at the time. South of the part of Syria under study
here, Damascus and its oasis were certainly occupied all
through the Persian period, since it was the seat of the Persian
governor right through to 332.[32] Further south again, in the
lands to the east of the Jordan river, a retreat of settlement has
been detected, just as in the north. J. R. Bartlett, for example,
in discussing the evidence for continuity between Iron Age
Edomites and Hellenistic Nabataeans, summarized the position in the Persian period: 'The Nabataeans, in process of
extending their pasturage over the Edomite hills . . . came
across and in effect surrounded the small, scattered peasant
farming communities located by the springs',[33] no doubt with
disastrous effects on the peasants and their ability to grow
sufficient food. This essentially literary evidence is borne out
by a detailed archaeological survey of the lands of ancient
Ammon and Moab, to the north of Edom. S. Mittmann
surveyed 346 sites and discovered 53 with pottery of the later
Iron Age (the Assyrian and Babylonian periods, more or less),

[32] Curt. 3. 13. 1: a satrap in Damascus when Parmenio approached.
[33] J. R. Bartlett, 'From Edomites to Nabataeans: A Study in Continuity', *Palestine
Exploration Quarterly* 111 (1979), 53–66, at p. 65.

none of the Persian period, 51 of the Hellenistic, and 130 of the Roman.[34] Clearly the total absence of Persian period remains cannot be accepted as final and definitive, but the impression of a discontinuity of occupation provided by these figures is confirmed by the fact that only 18 sites have both later Iron Age and Hellenistic occupation.

The eastern part of the Fertile Crescent does not, at first sight, show the same pattern, but in fact the difference only emphasizes the pattern discerned in the west. R. McC. Adams has made an intensive study of a section of Babylonia between the two rivers north of Babylon covering changes in settlement over five thousand years.[35] He showed that the lowest point of human occupation was in the Middle Babylonian period, which was contemporary with the period of Assyrian domination in Syria. Recovery began in the Neo-Babylonian period (sixth century BC), after the destruction of the Assyrian military power, and continued into the Persian and subsequent periods, reaching its culmination in the intensive and extensive land occupation of the Sassanid and Early Islamic periods (c.AD 250–750). The land under consideration is in its natural state a mixture of marsh, meandering rivers, desert, and steppe. An extension of land occupation meant drainage and irrigation of the marshland first, and then irrigation of the steppeland.

The 'early' recovery pattern (compared with Syria) can be explained by the political situation which followed the Assyrian collapse. Peaceful conditions, returning refugees, and displaced persons, as well as forced migration, all contributed to the repeopling and redevelopment of the area, which had suffered badly in the Assyro-Babylonian wars. The successor empire based at Babylon will have required a substantial population in this area, partly to help feed its capital city. The replacement of the Neo-Babylonian Empire by that of the Persians in 539 caused very little disturbance, and recovery was more or less constant. From a total of 134 sites in the Middle Babylonian period (the lowest point),

[34] S. Mittmann, *Beitrage zur Siedlungs- und Territorialgeschichte des Nordlichen Ostjordanlandes* (Wiesbaden 1970). These calculations have been made from the catalogue of sites on pp. 256–64, omitting doubtful cases.

[35] R. McC. Adams, *Heartland of Cities* (Chicago 1981): see pp. 3–14 and 175–8 for what follows.

occupation expanded to 182 in the Neo-Babylonian, to 221 in the Persian and then to 415 in the Seleukid-Parthian period.[36] This sequence in Babylonia above all brings out the role of the great city in revitalizing the agriculture of its immediate surroundings. Without Babylon and other cities in the area, the peasantry will have had no incentive to expand production. But it is also the case that peaceful conditions returned more speedily to Babylonia than to Syria. In Syria the domination of the Assyrians was followed by the Neo-Babylonian Empire, and both used imperial terror methods of destruction and deportation to enforce their rule.[37] In particular these methods resulted in the almost complete de-urbanization of Syria. Thus by the time peaceful conditions were enforced in Syria, during the early Persian period (539–404) the cities had been eliminated. That time of peace may have allowed a certain recovery to begin. In Palestine it was in that period that Jerusalem was refounded by Ezra and Nehemiah. Yet that episode emphasizes the difficulties involved, ranging from the need to import a new urban population to suspicion and enmity from the local peasantry and nearby governors.[38] In Syria there is no source which suggests any recovery—which is not to say that it did not

[36] Ibid. Table 15, p. 178. Adams can also estimate the size of his settlements, and shows that in the Middle Babylonian period there were only 6 sites of over 10 hectares, but in the Neo-Babylonian-Achaemenid period there were 30, and in the Seleukid-Parthian period 55. That is, size as well as density increased.

[37] A. Leo Oppenheim,. *Ancient Mesopotamia*, 2nd edn. (Chicago 1977), 168–70, summarizes Assyrian methods, whose savagery is only enhanced by the surrounding social history. A. T. Olmstead, *History of Assyria* (Chicago 1923), ch. 44, protests too much. H. W. F Saggs, *The Might that was Assyria* (1984), ch. 16, is explanatory.

The known deportations are listed by B. Oded, *Mass Deportations and Deportees in the Neo-Assyrian Empire* (Wiesbaden 1979). It is clear that some areas were treated very harshly indeed: Kommagene, for instance, must have been virtually emptied of people. It then became an Assyrian military base, which could scarcely have survived the end of the empire. This is the basic explanation for the unimportance of the region later, for it will have taken a very long time for the population to recover.

D. J. Wiseman, *Chronicles of the Chaldaean Kings in the British Museum* (1956), shows Babylonian campaigns in Syria every year but one between 605 and 594, and in Kilikia in 557–556. Other campaigns are known in 588–587 and 555–553 (R. Campbell Thompson, 'The New Babylonian Empire', *CAH*, 1st edn. (Cambridge, 192), vol. ii, ch. 10). These in fact are the only years for which we have information on the political doings of the empire; it is a formidable body of evidence for Syrian discontent.

[38] Neh. 3: 1–32. V. Tcherikover, *Hellenistic Civilisation and the Jews* (New York 1970), 41–50; M. Hengel, *Jews, Greeks and Barbarians* (1980), pp. 6–7.

occur. But it is certain that the next two generations, 404–333, were so disturbed that any recovery would be dashed. There were no less than twelve military expeditions to or through Syria in that period, not including Alexander's conquest, and some of those expeditions lasted for years.[39] Any chance of urban growth was impossible under the circumstances.

By the time of the Macedonian conquest in 333–331—yet another military expedition—there were, therefore, only faint sparks of urban life in Syria. This has not been the impression given by other commentators, who tend to assume the continued existence of cities through from earlier, less destructive times. The assumption was apparently proved correct by the work of A. H. M. Jones, who is the only historian to have considered in detail the extent of urban settlement in Syria in the fourth century BC.[40] He based his argument on linguistic evidence, noting the common survival of many city names from the pre-Greek through to the post-Roman periods, so that, for example, Greek and Roman Beroia had earlier been Halab and later became Halep (i.e. Aleppo), and Epiphaneia had been Hamath and became Hama.[41] This led him to accept that such places were cities continuously, and that Syria was an urbanized land when

---

[39] Armies marched through Syria on the following occasions in the late fifth and fourth centuries:

404	Kyros' expedition from Kilikia to the Euphrates; Abrocomas' force retreated from Phoenicia to the Euphrates before him.
397–396	Phoenician and Cypriot fleet gathered by Konon.
385–383	Persian campaign against Egypt and Evagoras of Salamis.
379–373	Pharnabazos collected an army, slowly, and unsuccessfully attacked Egypt.
369	Datames' unsuccessful attack on Egypt.
362	Revolt headed by Aroandas.
360–359	Fighting between Persians and Egyptians.
351–350	Artaxerxes III Ochus' unsuccessful attack on Egypt.
349	Revolt of Sidon.
345	Ochus' conquest of Sidon.
344–343	Ochus' conquest of Egypt.
335–334	Dareios III's reconquest of Egypt.
333–331	Alexander's conquest.

These are from A.T. Olmstead, *History of the Persian Empire* (Chicago 1948), ch. 27–30 and pp. 491–3 and R.M. Cook, *The Persian Empire* (1984), ch. 18.

[40] Jones, *CERP*, ch. 10. U. Kahrstedt, *Syrische Territorien in Hellenistischer Zeit* (Göttingen 1923), is more concerned with political control, and no more than four of his chapters (5, 7, 8, and 9) are devoted to Syria, as opposed to Palestine.

[41] Jones, *CERP* 231.

Alexander conquered it. Yet it was surprising that none of these places, some of which at all times have been notable fortresses, played any part in Alexander's campaigns,[42] and do not appear in any of the accounts of the Alexander-historians. In fact, the linguistic evidence can be explained in another way. The old city-names survived, not because of their continued use by the inhabitants of the cities, but because the rural population in the areas round about used them to refer to the cities, using Aramaic, in which language the old names were originally expressed. In this situation, therefore, place-name evidence is not sufficient to show the continued existence of an urban community, and it is necessary to consider the literary and archaeological evidence.

When Alexander the Great conquered Syria in 333–332 BC there were only five places which were of sufficient size to be called urban: Myriandros on the coast south of the battlefield of Issos, Thapsakos at the Euphrates crossing, possibly Bambyke nearby, Arados on its island, and Marathos on the coast nearby.

Myriandros was called a *polis* by Xenophon,[43] and by Arrian[44] in his account of the manœuvres before Issos. Xenophon's account makes it clear that it was on the coast, since 200 ships met Kyros' army there, and in Arrian a thirty-oar ship was available to use to reconnoitre the Persian position to the north.[45] Since, in the list of Claudius Ptolemy of the second century AD,[46] Myriandros is named separately from Alexandria and Rhosos, the two main ports along that coast, it must be on a different site. Ada Tepe, ten kilometres or so south of modern Iskenderun, has been suggested as the site; Williams surveyed it in 1951 and marked it as a 'town site' on his map of Hellenistic and Roman sites, based on the extent of the remains.[47] He discounted the suggested identification but only on the grounds that no Persian period remains were found on the site. Since it is clear from his account that the site was covered by remains of the

---

[42] For example, N. G. L. Hammond, *Alexander the Great* (1980), assumes the existence of Aleppo and Homs on his map, p. 113, though neither are mentioned in the sources and neither can be shown to be a city at the time.

[43] Xen. 1. 4. [44] Arr. 2. 6. 2.

[45] Arr. 2. 7. 2. [46] Ptol. 5. 14. 3.

[47] M. V. Seton Williams, 'Cilician Survey', *Anatolian Studies* 4 (1954), p. 139, fig. 6.

Hellenistic, Roman, and Byzantine periods, this cannot be decisive. According to the campaign reports in Xenophon and Arrian the place must be within a few miles of the coastal pass north of Iskenderun, for the armies of both Kyros and Alexander turned towards the Beilan Pass across the Amanus, and the road heads for that pass after reaching the plain. The site is lost because the settlement withered in the face of the growth of Alexandria in the Hellenistic period. It was called a *polis* by both Xenophon and Arrian and this must imply a certain urban size, but, without a precise location and archaeological survey and excavation, precision is impossible.

After crossing the Amanus mountains, Alexander took his main force southwards, but sent a cavalry detachment to guard the Euphrates-crossing at Thapsakos.[48] It was also at Thapsakos that Kyros' army had crossed the river.[49] The crossing was normally by boat, but Alexander's engineers built two bridges.[50] Xenophon calls the place a *polis*, but none of the Alexander-historians do more than record the name. Above all, like Myriandros, it has not yet been exactly located on the ground. The almost complete absence of Persian period remains in the area of the Tabqa Dam survey of the Euphrates Valley sites is strong negative evidence that the site of the crossing lay elsewhere; that is, given the geography of routes, it was either in the area of al-Raqqa, or in the area of the modern crossing at Birejik. Al-Raqqa seems to be too far eastwards since, when Alexander crossed the river, he then marched his army along the foot of the mountains to the north. The Birejik area has usually contained the normal crossing point, for it has the Iron Age city of Carchemish, to the south of the modern crossing, and the Hellenistic and Roman bridge at Zeugma to the north, while Birejik itself has been the crossing place since about AD 1200, under the protection of the Mamluk and later Ottoman castle there. The indications which the ancient sources provide of the position of Thapsakos are confused, but the fact that this confusion

---

[48] This is the implication of the appointment of Menon son of Kerdimmas to guard Syria with a force of cavalry (Arr. 2. 13. 7). He is clearly intended to watch for any possible Persian move from across the Euphrates—which means Thapsakos, as well as holding down Syria itself.

[49] Xen. 1. 4.

[50] Boats in Xen. 1. 4; bridges in Arr. 3. 7. 1–2.

exists indicates that in the Hellenistic period, Thapsakos was small and unimportant. In the Persian period, it was the normal crossing point, and this would suggest that the essential geographical conditions for an urban settlement did exist. It may thus be assumed that something in the way of buildings existed at the site and, since Xenophon called it a *polis*, he presumably recognized it as something greater in size and importance than the villages he had passed through since leaving the coast.

The third site is Bambyke, which is now Membij, and was Hellenistic and Roman Hierapolis. The Hellenistic and Persian remains at the site are buried under Roman and modern debris and buildings,[51] but it seems clear that the place was occupied at the time of Alexander's conquest. The evidence is numismatic. A number of coins have been found, minted in the name of Abd-Hadad at Bambyke, and are dated to 332.[52] The political implications of the coins—in silver, with Abd-Hadad claiming the title of king—are intriguing enough, for they were produced when Dareios III had fled eastwards and while Alexander was stuck at the siege of Tyre, but the implications for the place itself are just as important here. The coins show that Abd-Hadad had a certain political authority, as well as the wealth to finance the coinage. His name implies that he was chief priest of the temple, for Hadad was the consort of Atargatis, whose cult was centred at Bambyke.[53] Again, as at Thapsakos, there are elements present at Bambyke which suggest that the place had an urban nature: a large temple, wealth (as the coins suggest), and an ambitious ruler. A generation later Bambyke was renamed Hierapolis by Seleukos I,[54] and the name again suggests that there was a settlement grouped round the temple. In the absence of further evidence, particularly archaeological, one can go no further.

Bambyke, Myriandros, and Thapsakos are perhaps not

---

[51] D. G. Hogarth, 'Hierapolis Syriae', *Annual of the British School at Athens* 14 (1908), 186.

[52] S. Ronzevalle, 'Les Monnaies de la dynastie de Abd-Hadad et les cultes de Hierapolis-Bambyke', *MUSJ* 23 (1940), 1–82; H. Seyrig, 'Le Monnayage de Hierapolis de Syrie à l'époque d'Alexandre', *Rev. Num.* 11 (1971), 11–21.

[53] See especially the description by Lucian, *De Dea Syria*.

[54] Aelian, *De Natura Animali*, 12. 2; Jones, *CERP* 245–7 and 250; G. Goossens, *Hierapolis de Syrie* (Louvain, 1943), 180–192.

wholly convincing as urban sites in 333 BC, but of the urban nature of Arados and Marathos there is no doubt. Arados' king led his navy in the Persian service in the Aegean campaign in 334–332, while his son surrendered the whole coastland and the island of Arados itself to Alexander, as the latter approached overland.[55] Alexander camped at Marathos for some time.[56] Although Arados on its island and Marathos on the mainland were separate settlements, they formed part of a single polity under the king of the island. There are considerable visible remains at the site today to confirm the size and populousness of both places. On the island, the sea defences were already old by this time, and repairs of both Persian and Hellenistic date have been noted.[57] At Marathos a temple of the Persian period has been excavated, together with a considerable quantity of statuary,[58] and there are several large tombs still visible in the area.[59]

These five sites are the only settlements which seem to be of a size to be classed as urban in Syria in 333. All other possible sites which have been investigated prove to have been desolate or minuscule at that date: Carchemish,[60] Tell Rifaat,[61] Aleppo,[62] Hama,[63] Tell Nebi Mend,[64] were all deserted or were no more than villages. Thus Syria was, in urban terms,

[55] Arr. 2. 13. 7–8.

[56] Arr. 2 13. 8–15. 6.

[57] H. Frost, 'The Arwad Plans, 1964, A Photogrammetric Survey of Marine Installations', *AAAS* 16 (1966), 17.

[58] M. Dunand, N. Saliby and A. Khirichian, 'Les Fouilles d'Amrith en 1954: rapport préliminaire', *AAS* 4–5, (1954–1955), 181–204; M. Dunand and N. Saliby, 'Rapport préliminaire sur les Fouilles d'Amrith en 1955', *AAS* 6 (1956), 3–8; M. Dunand and N. Saliby, 'Le Sanctuaire d'Amrith: rapport préliminaire', *AAS* 11 (1961–62), 3–12; M. Dunand, 'Les Sculptures de la Favissa du Temple d'Amrith', *Bulletin du Musée de Beyrouth* 7 (1944–45), 99–107 and plates XIb—XXIX, and vol. 8 (1946–48), 81–107 and plates XXX—XLII; S. Abdul-Hak, 'Découvertes archéologiques récentes dans les sites greco-romains de Syrie', *Atti del VII Congreso Internazionale di Archeologia Classica*, vol. iii (Rome 1961), 32–33.

[59] The only available map of the Marathos site is by N. Saliby in 'Essai de restitution du Temple d'Amrit', *AAAS* 21 (1971), 284; it is a sketch only, but accurate enough. It is possible, however, that the shoreline has changed since Hellenistic times.

[60] C. L. Woolley, *Carchemish*, ii (1954).

[61] Preliminary reports on excavations at Tell Rifaat by M. V. Seton Williams are in *Iraq* 23 (1961), 15–67 and *AAAS* 17 (1967), 69–84.

[62] J. Sauvaget, *Alep* (Paris 1940), ch. 4.

[63] H. Ingholt, *Rapport préliminaire sur sept campagnes de fouilles à Hama en Syrie (1932–1938)* (Copenhagen 1940), 'Niveau C.'

[64] M. Pezard, *Qadesh* (Paris 1930).

almost a blank when Alexander's army invaded. Further, two
of these sites, Myriandros and Thapsakos, were to be rapidly
superseded by new foundations. Only Bambyke and Arados-
Marathos provided any urban continuity between the Persian
and the Hellenistic period.

This is by no means an unusual situation. The absence of
urban settlements in Syria was repeated in the surrounding
lands. Palestine's cities were in ruins after the Babylonian and
Assyrian period and only Jerusalem had recovered. The
Phoenician cities of Tyre, Sidon, Byblos, Tripolis and Arados
existed, and Tripolis, in fact, was new in the fourth century,[65]
though Sidon had been destroyed by Artaxerxes II in 345.[66]
To the eastwards of Syria, in Mesopotamia, Alexander found
no cities at all in the long stretch between the Euphrates and
the Tigris. City-life in Kilikia seems positively vigorous by
comparison, and it is significant that these cities, Mopsuestia,
Mallos, and others, laid claim to a Greek ancestry.[67] This
meant a rather stronger connection with the sea, and Kilikia is
rather more open to the sea than is Syria, whose mountains
block ingress. The two areas of city-life—the Phoenician coast
and Kilikia—were restricted in size, had strong sea-connec-
tions, and had each retained a strong tincture of independence
in their relations with Persia. The de-urbanized nature of
Syria, therefore, was the normal state for the whole sweep of
lands from the Tigris to the River of Egypt.

The Persian period in Syria is thus characterized by two
phenomena: an absence of urban settlements and the regression of the desert frontier. These two together imply
further that the total population of Syria was low, and it is a
reasonable assumption that the density of the rural population
was also low.

The connection between the existence or absence of cities
and the expansion or regression of the rural population and
the desert frontier is clear. The existence of cities expands
demand for rural produce, and an expanding demand
increases rural wealth and stimulates the cultivation of more
land, thus pushing the margin of cultivation into the desert.

---

[65] Jones, *CERP*, 230–1.
[66] Diod. 16. 45. 4–5.
[67] Jones, *CERP*, 192–3.

The situation was repeated in the same area in the Ottoman period.[68]

The Persians had acquired Syria as part of their conquest of the Neo-Babylonian Empire in 539 and that state had been the successor to the Assyrian Empire. Those states' methods of destruction and deportation had controlled the restless and rebellious Syrian population by eliminating the cities and the local aristocracies. In the process the peasantry would suffer the usual short-term disasters associated with military occupation, but this was not the deliberate government policy which destroyed the cities. The subsequent absence of urban centres and of a consuming aristocracy wrecked the local economy by removing the market for the rural surplus, where one existed, and by removing the skills of the urban craftsmen, but it did not remove the extractive tax system. Thus, whereas in the local economy of the kingdoms of Iron Age Syria the peasantry could expect to receive something in return for paying taxes to the local royal government—doles, a market, protection, craftsmen's products—the elimination of the urban centres meant that such economic compensations vanished. The local defences along the steppe margin ceased to exist, the nomads encroached, taking their own tithe of the peasantry's produce, and the satrapal government in Nineveh or Babylon or even Damascus was not interested, still less was the imperial government based at Persepolis or Ekbatana. All these governments took their taxes and spent them elsewhere. The result was a general impoverishment in Syria, a contraction of the settlement area, and a contraction of the tax base, so that the Persian assessment of Syria (including Phoenicia and Palestine) was no more than 350 talents, less than that of Kilikia.[69]

(It is relevant to note that the next period of regression of population in Syria was also preceded by a time of invasion, conquest, and destruction. Turks, Egyptians, Kurds and Persians were all involved in repelling the European Crusaders between AD 1097 and 1291. All of these were foreign to the long-suffering Arab and Jewish population. In the end the ultimate conquerors, the Mamluk Sultanate of Egypt, deliberately destroyed cities and castles along the coast in order to

[68] N. N. Lewis, *Settlers and Nomads in Syria and Jordan, 1800–1980* (Cambridge 1987).
[69] Herodotus 3. 92.

deny them to any European invader. The inland cities
survived in reduced circumstances because they were necessary to the provisioning of the Hajj, and were out of reach of
the coast, behind the mountains. The period from 1260 to
1800 is one of Syrian decay and depopulation, with a
regression of the desert frontier and large areas of fertile land
going out of cultivation.[70])

The structure of Syrian society at the time of Alexander's
conquest was, thus, almost entirely of a rural type. The
influence of Arados extended along the adjacent coast, its
peraia, and inland to Mariamme,[71] but not further. Myriandros and Bambyke and Thapsakos were equally local. The
rest of the land was one of villages exclusively, inhabited by a
peasantry taxed by the Persian governors. There was also a
stratum of men who, for want of a better word, may be called
chiefs. These are the men who remained loyal to the Persian
king until Gaugamela, two years after the conquest of Syria by
the Macedonians. They appear as Syrian cavalry in that great
battle.[72] The possession of horses marks them out as wealthy
and therefore powerful men. Their role no doubt was one of
intermediaries between the governors and the peasantry. This
simple society of agriculturalists was one which was incapable
of resisting conquest with any hope of success, but it was one
which was admirably suited to survive the troubles of the
fourth century.

That warfare which had washed over Syria during the last
seventy years of the Persian period continued during the first
thirty years of the Hellenistic, first under Alexander, then
Antigonos. Seleukos' acquisition of Syria, however, inaugur-
ated a much longer period of peace than Syria had seen for a
century, and this was closely connected with the re-urban-
ization of the land which he undertook. In two years he
reversed the steady decay of five centuries.

[70] For the destruction by the Mamluks, especially by Sultan Baibars, see S. R.
Runciman, *History of the Crusades*, voll iii (1954), book III, ch. 4; for conditions
afterwards see T. Petran, *Syria, a Modern History* (1972), 39–43, and E. Ashtor, *A Social
and Economic History of the Near East in the Middle Ages* (1976), ch. 8; R. Owen, *The
Middle East in the World Economy, 1800–1914* (1981), ch. 1, does not wholly agree with
the decadence theory.

[71] Arr. 2. 13. 8.

[72] Arr. 3. 11. 4.

2

THE WORK OF SELEUKOS NIKATOR

By the time Seleukos came to Syria as its ruler, in 301, that land had been under Macedonian rule for a full generation, since its conquest by Alexander in 333. Alexander had occupied it without opposition in the exploitation of his victory at Issos. The only substantial political authority in Syria at the time, apart from the Persian governor, had been the city-kingdom of Arados, which had been speedily surrendered to him as he approached; in return he allowed the kingship to continue. A detachment of Macedonian troops was sent to Thapsakos on the Euphrates to block any Persian attempt to recover Syria and to prepare two bridges to allow Alexander's army to cross over in pursuit of further conquests.[1]

In the following years Syria flits in and out of the historical limelight. Its geographical function as a land bridge connecting Asia Minor and Egypt and Mesopotamia ensured that it was the scene of conferences, coups, and marching armies, though only very rarely was Syria itself anything but a passive victim.

Syrian passivity should not necessarily be taken as a sign of Syrian welcome for the Macedonians. Quite the reverse. During Alexander's conquest several incidents showed that the Syrian population as a whole was hostile, even actively hostile, to the Macedonians. In the preliminary moves before Issos Dareios was well informed by Syrians of Alexander's moves,[2] yet Alexander gained no information at all. Arados' acquiescence[3] was not followed by that of Tyre, where the notorious siege[4] was accompanied by raids by mountain

---

[1] Arr. 3. 7. 1–2.
[2] This follows from Dareios' and Alexander's movements; Dareios knew where the Macedonians were all the time; Alexander dallied in Kilikia and then marched to Myriandros in ignorance of Dareios' position: Arr. 2. 6.
[3] Arr. 2. 13. 8; Curt. 4. 1. 6.
[4] Arr. 2. 16–24; Curt. 4. 2–4.

peoples against the Macedonian camp.[5] Alexander had to fight for Gaza too,[6] and Samaria rose in a short-lived rebellion later.[7] Even after all this fighting was over, and all Syria had been occupied, there were still Syrians in the fight against Alexander: at Gaugamela a Syrian contingent fought valiantly for Dareios till the end.[8]

It was thus fully necessary for Alexander to leave a garrison scattered through Syria. There is more precise evidence. The governor placed in charge of Syria and Kilikia in 329, Menes son of Dionysios,[9] replaced two or three other governors and was instructed to see that troops were transferred eastwards from Syria for the hard fighting in Baktria,[10] thus showing that Syria had a considerable garrison until then. There were clearly vital communication nodes within Syria which had to be guarded, such as the bridge at Thapsakos, and the disembarkation ports on the coast.[11]

A gap in the evidence follows, but scattered items in the period following Alexander's death indicate again the presence of detachments of troops. Eumenes of Kardia was able to recruit troops in Syria in 318,[12] and when he was expelled eastwards, it was Syria which became the central bastion of Antigonos' power, from which he was able to attack Babylon (in 317–316, 311, and 302) and Egypt (in 315 and 312),[13] and eventually to retreat to Asia Minor (in 302).[14] Control in these circumstances meant military control, and it is clear that the Syrian population will have got used to Greek and Macedonian troops living amongst them. So when Seleukos arrived

---

[5] Arr. 2. 20. 4–5; Curt. 4. 2. 24–3. 1.

[6] Arr. 2. 25. 4–27, 7; Curt. 4. 6. 7–31.

[7] Curt. 4. 8. 9–10.

[8] Arr. 3. 11. 4.

[9] Arr. 3. 16. 9–10. O. Leuze, *Die Satrapieneinteilung in Syrien und in Zweitromsland von 520–320* (Königsberg 1935), was the main authority on these satraps until A. B. Bosworth, 'The Government of Syria under Alexander the Great', *Classical Quarterly* 24 (1974), 46–64, undermined parts of the structure.

[10] Arr. 4. 7. 1, with amendments as suggested, among others, by Bosworth (previous note).

[11] Rey-Coquais, *Arados*, pp 151–153, suggests that Alexander left a Macedonian garrison at Marathos.

[12] Diod. 18. 61. 4 and 63. 6.

[13] Babylon: Diod. 19. 55. 1–2; 100. 5–7; W. W. Tarn, 'The Proposed New Date for Ipsus', *Classical Review* 40 (1926), 13–15; Egypt: Diod. 19. 64. 8 and 80. 3–5.

[14] Diod. 20. 108. 3.

he will have found that groups of Greeks and Macedonians had been established for a full generation in Syria.

The precise location of any of these garrisons is not clear from any of the sources, although informed guesses, such as the Thapsakos bridges, can easily be made. On the other hand, some evidence does exist as to where Greeks and Macedonians were settled in Syria at this time, and these settlements in many cases may have included garrisons even if that was not their primary purpose. In turn these places, whether they included garrisons or not, contained Greek-speaking populations when Seleukos acquired Syria in 301, and inevitably they became one of the bases for his work. These places conveniently fall into three groups, according to the antiquity of their existence.

In the first place there were already in existence, as noted in the last chapter, a number of villages along the coast which had included Greeks in their populations long before the Macedonian conquest. In the thirty years between Alexander's conquest and the arrival of Seleukos, these settlements seem to have enjoyed a certain prosperity. The majority of the coins found at Minet el-Beida, close to Ras Shamra, were of the last third of the fourth century,[15] and at Sabouni, Woolley detected prosperity when 'the world-wide currency of Macedon replaced the old coins of Athens' in the merchants' cash-boxes.[16] Sabouni, at the mouth of the Orontes, is one of the obvious disembarkation points for troops heading east from Greece. Tell Sukas and Ras el-Basit continued to be occupied and to trade until c.300.[17] In the southern coastal area, Marathos was another obvious point of disembarkation. It is the only one of all these places to have been of urban size, for none of the others was any larger than a village, and none, with the possible exception of al Mina-Sabouni, was more than partly Greek. All of them, however, are possible sites of Macedonian garrisons and transit camps.

[15] B. Zoudhi, 'Monnaies antiques et plus récentes trouvées à Ras Shamra et dans les environs', *Ugaritica* 7 (1968), 183–4.

[16] C. L. Woolley, *A Forgotten Kingdom* (1953), 180.

[17] Sukas: P. J. Riis, 'The North-East Sanctuary and the First Settling of Greeks in Syria and Palestine', *Sukas* i (Copenhagen 1970), 126–75; Ras el-Basit: P. Courbin, 'Rapport sur la sixiène campagne de fouilles (1976) à Ras el Bassit (Syrie)', *AAAS* 27–8, (1977–8), 29–39.

Inevitably there are places—three of them altogether—
which claimed to have been founded by Alexander, which
would put their origins in 333 or 331, if it were true. So the
claims need to be investigated. As it turns out, in none of these
cases can the claim be accepted. All three are in the north-
west corner of Syria: Antioch, Nikopolis, and Alexandria-by-
Issos.

Antioch is claimed to have pre-Alexandrian Greek settlement in some of the ancient sources, but those sources are
distinctly late and unreliable.[18] Three names are cited in
evidence. Iopolis was said to be a settlement of Greeks on
Mount Silpion, which towers over Antioch proper, and which
is the site of the ancient and medieval citadel. The citizens of
the later Antioch elaborated a long myth about the arrival of
Io in the area, based upon this name.[19] E. R. Bevan, however,
pointed out a better explanation:[20] that 'Ione' is more likely to
refer to the 'city of the Greeks' (that is, Antioch itself) among
the countrymen of Syrian speech, in whose language a
corruption of 'Ionia' designated Greeks, and so the name
Iopolis was applied only after Antioch was founded. The two
other names are Bottia and Emathia, both of Macedonian
origin, and are attested within the city. Bottia is claimed to be
either a pre-Alexandrian Greek village,[21] or a village of
Alexander's veterans founded by Alexander himself,[22] and
was also the site of an altar to Zeus Bottiaios at which either
Alexander[23] or Seleukos[24] is said to have sacrificed. The
contradictions are due, no doubt, to the lateness of the
sources—Libanios and Malalas. The most reasonable account would seem to be the last, Alexander's altar. One
method used by city founders to settle a heterogeneous new
population into a new city was to establish altars and temples

---

[18] Lib. (late fourth century AD) is, as he says (Oration 11. 1–10), concerned to
glorify his city; Mal. (sixth century AD) is actuated by similar motives and is even less .
discriminatory.

[19] Lib. Oration 11. 44–52; Mal. 199; Str. 16. 2. 5.

[20] Bevan, *House*, p. 212.

[21] Downey, *Antioch*, pp. 52–3.

[22] N. G. L. Hammond, *Alexander the Great* (1982), 119 says 'probably', and Downey
Antioch, p. 55, says there 'may' have been such a settlement, but there is no evidence
other than Lib. (next note).

[23] Lib. Or. 2. 76.

[24] Mal. 200.

to the gods of the various groups of inhabitants. Thus Zeus Bottiaios would be one of a number of 'foreign' gods being domesticated.[25] Emathia is said by Libanios[26] to be another name for the citadel on Mount Silpion. This is not evidence for an early date, for the name could easily have been bestowed later. The alternative notion that Bottia was a village of Greeks established there before Alexander's arrival is to be explained in a similar way, and may be rejected also.

It is just possible that these stories are an indication of a Greek presence in the Persian period. There were certainly Greeks at al-Mina at the mouth of the Orontes, and Greek goods certainly did penetrate inland along the trade route which led to the Euphrates crossing at Thapsakos. But none of this is evidence for a settlement of Greeks on the site of the future city of Antioch. Perhaps the easiest explanation is that there was a Syrian village on the site whose name sounded to Macedonians like Bottia, though even that is only a theory. The elaboration of the account may be taken to be an expression of the popular desire of Antiochenes to give their city an equal, or even older, antiquity with its great rival Alexandria.[27] One might expect the story, in fact, to develop fairly early, perhaps even by the mid-third century BC, when Antioch was beginning to be seen as a capital of sorts. But the point here is not later conjecture but the fact that none of this is evidence for any settlement at the site of Antioch before Seleukos' foundation of the city.

Nikopolis, in the Kara valley between the Amanus and the Kurd Dagh, has been claimed to be a foundation of Alexander's to commemorate the victory of Issos.[28] But it is nowhere near Issos, nor is it a place Alexander went to,[29] and it is separated from the battlefield by the whole range of the

---

[25] The statue of the *Tyche of Antigoneia* was transferred with (at least some of) that city's colonists to Antioch (Mal. 201), and temples are known of Athena (for the Athenians) (Mal. 201), and Cypriot gods (Lib. Or. 11. 110–13 and Downey, *Antioch*, pp. 88–9). This whole process is, of course, well known, and in most modern cases it is almost automatic. The establishment of mosques and Hindu and Sikh temples in modern British cities is a contemporary example.

[26] Lib. Or. 11. 72–7.

[27] Downey, *Antioch*, p. 55.

[28] Stephanos of Byzantium, s.v. 'Nikopolis'.

[29] Jones *CERP* 244 and 452 n. 24.

Amanus. These objections are quite overwhelming: the attribution to Alexander is clearly wrong.[30]

Alexandria-by-Issos is the only one of these three whose attribution to Alexander is at all plausible. On examination, however, it also fails. The evidence in favour of Alexander as its founder consists solely of the city's name. Tarn, for instance, was convinced solely on that ground.[31] Jones, relying on Appian,[32] suggested that Seleukos founded the city in honour of Alexander,[33] but Appian's word is not good enough in this;[34] some stronger evidence is needed for conviction. It is in fact first mentioned by Strabo, three centuries after its supposed foundation.[35] Neither Arrian nor Curtius Rufus mentions it as one of Alexander's cities, though the latter reports that Alexander put up three altars to commemorate the victory,[36] and both are careful in other instances to record the foundation of such places by Alexander. The city did exist, however, by the reign of Antiochos IV Epiphanes (175–164 BC), for it was one of those which issued a city coinage at that time.[37]

It will be argued later that this city was never formally founded at all, but was one which simply grew as a result of economic forces. My concern here is simply to disprove its foundation by Alexander. In the nature of the evidence this is difficult, indeed virtually impossible. All that can be done is to point out the absence of evidence, which, but for the name of the city, would never induce any historian to suggest an Alexandrian foundation for it. Geographically it had no

---

[30] The existence of a statue of 'Alexander, son of Philip' of the second century AD, of which the base survives, found at Islahiyé (Nikopolis) (*IGLS* 163), which the editors of *IGLS* bring forward as evidence for an Alexandrine date for the city's origin, is not evidence of anything except the existence of a statue of a man called Alexander.

[31] W. W. Tarn, *Alexander the Great* (1948), vol. ii, Appendix 8, p. 239.

[32] App. *Syr.* 57.

[33] Jones *CERP* 197.

[34] App. *Syr.* 57 provides a summary list of cities founded by Seleukos, but it is neither reliable nor really useful. It includes cities which must have been founded by others, for instance Sotera must be Antiochos I's foundation or possibly that of Demetrios I, and Alexandreschate was Alexander's. By simply summarizing ('four Laodikeias'), Appian has reduced research to name-spotting.

[35] Str. 16. 5. 19.

[36] Curt. 3. 12. 27. They were still there in Cicero's time (Cicero, *Ad Familiares*, 15. 4). Had they been maintained by the city of Alexandria, which had appropriated the king's name?

[37] Head, *HN* 716.

significance for Alexander; militarily it is irrelevant; for commemorative purposes it is in the wrong place (just as Nikopolis was), since the battle of Issos was fought twenty or thirty kilometres away, in a place which was as suitable for such a foundation as Alexandria. The evidence, as Tarn realized, is wholly the name, and that name is first attested over a century and a half after Alexander's death. The name does not need to have been 'awarded'; it could simply have been annexed by the citizenry to publicize their city. There is as much, and as little, evidence for that conjecture as for a foundation by Alexander.

The evidence for Greeks living in Syria in Alexander's time and before is therefore of villages only, where the evidence is acceptable. Thus the first Greek or Macedonian settlement which can be called a city in Syria is the city of Antigoneia, founded by Antigonos Monophthalamos. Characteristically, for Syria, the information comes obliquely, as a side-comment by Diodoros in his account of events following the battle of Salamis in 306.[38] On receiving the news of his son's victory at Salamis, Antigonos proclaimed himself king, the first king since the death of Alexander IV in 310; incidental to this, Diodoros remarks that Antigonos was in the process of founding a new city in Syria, by which he appears to mean supervising the layout and the building. How long the process of foundation had already been going on is unknown. Antigonos' movements are not clear for the years preceding 306. His son Demetrios did all the campaigning, while Antigonos gave the orders,[39] so it is possible that he had been seeing to the construction of the city for some time. It had reached an advanced enough stage by 302 for Antigonos to hold celebratory games, which were interrupted by the news of war.[40] This does not imply that construction was in any way complete, though. Seleukos had no compunction about demolishing it next year.

The precise location of Antigoneia is not known, largely because of Seleukos' action. One theory places it on the coast,

[38] Diod. 20. 47.
[39] For example, Demetrios sailed from Athens to Cyprus on instructions from Antigonos (Plut. *Dem.* 15; Diod. 20. 46. 5).
[40] Diod. 20. 108. 1.

at the site of the later Seleukeia-in-Pieria, but the evidence
contained in an anecdote of Antigonos suggests a site inland.

Aristodemos of Miletos brought the message of the victory
at Salamis to Antigonos, who was at Antigoneia. He moved
with gravity and dignity, studiedly refusing to impart his news
until he met Antigonos personally, and so infuriating Antigonos that the old king rushed out to meet the messenger at
the city gate.[41] Honigmann interpreted the story as demonstrating that the city was near the coast, since Aristodemos
walked from the landing-place to the city,[42] but this does not
follow. There must have been a considerable distance
involved, for, as Aristodemos walked gravely and self-
importantly on, Antigonos had the time to receive the news of
his approach and to send several men in succession to ask for
the news before he received it himself at the city gate.[43] The
approximate location of the city was also provided by Dio
Cassius, who mentioned it in his account of the retreat of the
Parthians after their attack on Antioch in 51 BC, as a village of
Antioch[44]—and they were retreating eastwards. The cur-
rently accepted location is on the Orontes, as Diodoros had
said,[45] at the confluence of that river with the Kara Su, which
flows from the Amuq lake, though it has to be admitted that
this is no better than an educated guess, since no actual
remains now exist.

When Seleukos Nikator acquired north Syria in 301,
therefore, there existed in his new territory one Phoenician
city, Arados, with its mainland offshoot at Marathos, possibly

---

[41] Plut. *Dem.* 17.

[42] Honigmann wrote the account of Seleukeia-in-Pieria in the *PW* Supp., in which
he interpreted Plut.'s story as showing *Antigoneia* near the coast; Benzinger, in the
very brief notice of Antigoneia itself (*PW* i. 2404) said nothing of this.

[43] Plut. has Antigonos sending 'messenger after messenger, friend after friend, to
enquire what news' (Plut. *Dem.* 17), before going down himself to the city gate. If this
is to be taken literally, and is not just Plut.'s literary elaboration, then Aristodemos
must have walked many miles. On the other hand, he had deliberately walked slowly,
and there is no sign that his journey took more than the hours of daylight of one day.
How far does a fit man march in a maximum of, say, twelve hours? The distance can
scarcely be less than ten miles, but perhaps not more than twenty. Antigoneia was
only a little farther from the coast than Antioch, which could be reached in a day. But
Aristodemos' landing place is unknown, and it could be three or four miles into the
Orontes, which is navigable for about that distance.

[44] Dio Cassius 11. 29.

[45] Diod. 20. 47. 5; Downey, *Antioch*, p. 56.

towns at Bambyke, Thapsakos, and Myriandros, and a new and unfinished Greek city at Antigoneia. Along the coast there were several small communities which included Greeks among their inhabitants, but none were larger than villages or small ports, such as al Mina-Sabouni, Ras Shamra or Tell Sukas. These settlements were basically those which had existed before Alexander, with the addition of Antigoneia. There were also other places where Greeks and Macedonians had settled down since Alexander's conquest. Some at least of these places can be identified.

There were, by the time of Seleukos' arrival, a considerable number of places which had been given names which derived from Greece and Macedonia. Those names will have been awarded by people who were familiar with the Greek or Macedonian originals. Further, since the names continued to be used in Syria, it is reasonable to assume that people of Greek or Macedonian speech continued to use them. It is my contention, however, that these names date from the generation before the annexation by Seleukos. This can be done plausibly, in fact, in two cases, and in two others with reasonable likelihood.

Seleukos founded his new city of Apamea at a place which already had a Macedonian name, Pella,[46] which it retained in parallel with Apamea for some time. Apamea's foundation took place within a year or so of Seleukos' acquisition of the land. Given the short time between Seleukos' annexation and the foundation of Apamea, the name Pella clearly dates from before Seleukos' foundation; it is therefore the name given to the place by pre-Seleukid Macedonian settlers.

The second place was Larissa, south of Apamea, on the Orontes. Its people always remembered that they were descended from a regiment of Thessalian cavalry,[47] which can only have been one of Alexander's regiments. Neither Antigonos nor Seleukos could have recruited troops in Thessaly, the former because it was under the control of his enemy Kassandros all during his reign, the latter because he

---

[46] Plut. *Dem.* 50 and 52, speaking of 285–283, reports this name and another, 'Pharnake', which is also recorded by Eustathius 918. Chersonesos—clearly a reference to the peninsular-like setting of the acropolis of Apamea—is also reported by Plut.

[47] Diod. 33. 4a.

was too far away from Thessaly until 301, after which it was
under the control of one or other of his enemies.[48] Alexander's
Thessalians were a tough, élite corps, often in the forefront of
his battles,[49] and they can only have survived by a cast-iron
esprit de corps. By the time peace returned to Syria they had
been away from their homeland for twenty years;[50] a
communal settlement by the whole regiment will have been
agreeable to all parties: the soldiers received homes and land,
the ruler (probably Antigonos[51]) acquired a stable settlement
on a major communications route, and he also deprived his
competitors of their services and those of their children.

Thus these two Greco-Macedonian place-names can be
traced back to before 301 with confidence. For two others the
evidence is less certain, but is most suggestive: Kyrrhos and
Chalkis, both in the northern part of Syria. Both of these cities
gave their names to geographical areas—Kyrrhestike and
Chalkidene—of which they were the respective centres. The
order of naming was clearly cities first, then the region. There
is nothing about the dry, flat, inland region of Chalkidene in
Syria to provoke its naming for the sea-girt, multi-peninsular,
mountainous Macedonian area of Chalkidike, but Chalkis'
name may reflect the existence of copper mines in the area.[52]
Thus it would seem reasonable to conclude that Chalkidene
was so named because it was the region around Chalkis.

Kyrrhestike is recorded as an area earlier than was

[48] It is, of course, quite possible that individual Thessalians were recruited, but it
is inconceivable that a whole regiment could have been recruited for Antigonos'
service from lands under Kassander's control. Seleukos was confined east of the
Tigris until 302, and from 296 to 288 Thessaly was ruled by Demetrios. The
possibility of recruitment in Thessaly by Seleukos does exist, but it can scarcely be
more than that: a possibility only. It would seem, anyway, that by this time
recruitment was on an individual basis, not a national one: G.T. Griffith, *The
Mercenaries of the Hellenistic World* (Cambridge, 1935), pp. 254–63.

[49] For example, at Issos, they were the unit switched from one flank to another to
give the greatest weight there (Arr. 2. 9. 1); they went with Parmenio in the dash for
Damascus (Plut. *Alexander* 24); at Gaugamela, again with Parmenio, they bore the
great burden of the defence of the left wing (Arr. 3. 11. 10).

[50] They had left Macedonia in 335; they may, of course, have been on active
service for ten or more years before that, since Philip had ruled Thessaly since 352.

[51] Antigonos seems more likely than Seleukos because of the age which the men
will have reached—by the time of Seleukos' arrival they will have been at least fifty-
plus. But Seleukos is not wholly excluded, I suppose.

[52] R. J. Forbes, *Metallurgy in Antiquity* (Leiden 1950), 300; O. Herzfeld, *The Persian
Empire* (Wiesbaden, 1968), 88–9.

Chalkidene, but its origin is presumably similar: first the place, Kyrrhos, then the region around it. It is recorded as the scene of the confrontation between the forces of Seleukos Nikator and Demetrios Poliorketes in 285. The source for this information is Plutarch.[53] It is possible that he was using a current geographical term anachronistically, but it is more likely that he simply took the name from the source he was using, and that Kyrrhestike was the term current in 285. This would therefore mean that the name Kyrrhos (and thus Chalkis as well) was in use before that date.

In fact it may be possible to go further. The areas named Kyrrhestike and Chalkidene cover all the land between the Euphrates and the Amuq lake, and between the desert to the south and the northern hills, though their precise boundaries are vague; Kyrrhestike faces north and north-west, and Chalkidene faces south. Strabo records that Seleukid Syria was divided into four satrapies,[54] and it is clear from his account that the whole area was called Seleukis, and that Kyrrhestike was one of the satrapies.[55] Chalkidene will have been a second, and probably the others were centred at Antioch and Apamea. This whole scheme must date from the reign of Seleukos I, for, apart from the overall name of Seleukis, it is only at that time that such a scheme makes strategic sense. After 294 Kyrrhos was no longer a border town, for Seleukos acquired Kilikia in that year,[56] and so pushed his boundary forward from the Amanus to the Taurus. The formation of these four satrapies thus took place between 301 and 294, and presumably nearer to the former date than the latter, since the governmental system of his new province must have been one of Seleukos' first priorities. And since the satrapies were named for their centres, Kyrrhos and Chalkis may well have been in existence before 301. The matter is not proved, but it is a good deal easier to accept a foundation date for these cities before 301 than one between 301 and 294.

[53] Plut. *Dem.* 32.

[54] Str. 16. 2. 2.

[55] These four satrapies are a contentious issue. The latest examination is by E. Frézouls, 'Sur les divisions de la Séleukide à propos de Strabon XVI, 2', *MUSJ* 37 (1960). Here I am not concerned with the precise geographical boundaries, which at present are unknowable. G. L. Downey's remarks in 'Strabo on Antioch: Notes on his Method', *TAPA* 72 (1941), 85–95 are worth remembering in this context.

[56] Plut. *Dem.* 32.

There are thus two Greco-Macedonian place-names in
Syria (Pella and Larissa) which certainly date from before
Seleukos' acquisition of the land, and two others (Kyrrhos
and Chalkis) which were also probably in use before 301. This
is as far as the written sources, exiguous as they are, can
provide information. It is time, therefore, to make a broader
consideration of the places with such names.

Many of these imported names were applied to places
whose geographical characteristics were broadly similar to
their old Greek and Macedonian exemplars. The main Syrian
river is the Orontes—which seems to be the Greek version of
the local name[57]—and it was named Axios from the main
river which flows through Macedonia. Pieria was a mountainous area facing the sea in Macedonia, and was applied to a
similar area in Syria. Exact precision was clearly not required,
and both of these examples are in fact reversed—the Axios
flows south but the Orontes north, Pieria in Macedonia faces
eastwards to the sea but in Syria westwards. It is thus only the
broad similarities which apply. Larissa is on a major river;
Kyrrhos was a town in the hills to the north of the main
plains; Emathia was a district name of an inland plain; Beroia
is a central town on a river; Pella was sited by a lake and by a
major river—these broad descriptions could apply to both the
Syrian and the Macedonian places.

On the other hand, some names seem more likely to be
originally native Syrian names which have taken on a Greek
guise. Doliche seems to have been an adaptation of the local
name, Duluk, to a familiar Greek sound.[58] Somewhere in the
Apamene was a place called Megara, which is probably a
graecizing of Maarra, a common Syrian name.[59] An Apollonia was in the Apamean area as well,[60] which Mouterde

---

[57] E. Frézouls, 'La Toponymie de l'Orient Syrien et l'apport des elements
macedoniens', in *La Toponymie antique* (Strasbourg, 1977), 239; Honigmann, 'Hist.
Top.', no 83.

[58] This seems more likely than that a Macedonian name would stick to an old local
shrine. It has Hittite elements about it, and is perhaps also connected with the cult of
sacred fish, which Xen. noted in this area. Cf. F. Cumont, 'Doliché et le Zeus
Dolichenus', *Études syriennes* (Paris 1917), 173. It was one of the four cities of
Kommagene when that kingdom was divided by the Romans after their annexation in
AD 72.

[59] This is the general assumption. Dussaud, *Top. hist.* 204 is followed by later
authorities: Jones *CERP* 243; E. Frézouls (note 57), p. 226.

[60] Str. 16. 2. 10; Stephanos of Byzantium, s.v. 'Apollonia [8]'.

suggested was at Mesta Blouné, due west of Apamea at the foot of the Bargylos.[61] Even less locatable is Ainos, which is no doubt Ain (Arabic, 'a source or spring') with a Greek ending.[62] Maroneia may be an imported name, from the city on the Thracian coast,[63] though the Syrian place of that name was certainly well inland, and corruption of a local name is perhaps more likely.[64]

It is perhaps significant that three of these four cannot be located with confidence; their insignificance suggests casual naming rather than the deliberate adoption of an imported name. Doliche, however, deserves further consideration, for its actual location is known. It was on the main route for travellers moving between the Euphrates and the Mediterranean. It is at the road's most northerly point, and faces the Taurus hills to the north,[65] an area which had been poorly peopled in the Persian period,[66] and which became, later, the satrapy and then the kingdom of Kommagene.[67] It is roughly

---

[61] R. Mouterde, 'A travers l'Apamène: II, Mesta Blouné, Apollonia?', *MUSJ* 27 (1949–50), 16–21.

[62] Honigmann, 'Hist. Top.', no. 19ᵃ, suggested the graecization of Ain, a very common element in local place names. Maroneia is listed by App. *Syr.* 57, and by Ptol. 5. 14. 18.

[63] Maroneia and Ainos were acquired by Philip II in his Thracian campaign (N. G. L. Hammond and G. T. Griffith, *History of Macedonia*, vol. ii (Oxford 1979), 379–82), and were part of Lysimachos' kingdom (Diod. 18. 3. 2), from whom they briefly passed to Seleukos (Justin, 17. 2). They returned to the dynasty when Antiochos III extended his power into Europe in the troubled 190s (Livy, 37. 60. 7). For most of the third century they were Ptolemaic outposts (R. S. Bagnall, *The Administration of the Ptolemaic Possessions outside Egypt* (Leiden, 1976)). It is just possible to imagine that the Syrian Ainos and Maroneia were founded for refugees from the Romans after the battle of Magnesia in 189; others from Euboea and Aetolia were settled in Syria about then (Lib. Or. 11. 119), so it is not totally out of the question. It is less difficult to think of them as graecizations of local names, though.

[65] Cumont in *Études syriennes* (note 58), pp. 182–3, describes well the surprisingly outstanding position of the hill. It is now wooded.

[66] Archi, *Gaziantep, passim*, and the comments in Appendix 3. Persian period occupation is no doubt understated in the expedition's findings, but the general impression of emptiness and poverty may well be correct.

[67] This is the Assyrian province of Khummukh, previously the kingdom of that name. Its repeated rebellions led to a peculiarly thorough process of massacre and deportation (B. Oded, *Mass Deportations and Deportees in the Neo-Assyrian Empire* (Wiesbaden, 1979)); it had recovered sufficiently to provide the basis for an independent kingdom by *c.*162 (Diod. 31. 19ᵃ; H. Seyrig, 'Sur quelques ères syriennes: I. l'ère des rois de Kommagene', *Rev. Num.* 4 (1964) 51–5) though the royal title and full independence is later, perhaps *c.*130, in the aftermath of Antiochus VII's disaster (R. D. Sullivan, 'The Dynasty of Kommagene', *ANRW* 2/8 (1977), 732–98). The land was wealthy enough to support the pretensions of the builder of the sepulchre at Nemrut Dagh two centuries later. The kings extended their rule

halfway between Zeugma on the river and Kyrrhos, both of which were garrisoned. It is a site which would commend itself to a military governor, seeking to control an important military and commercial highway. Proof is lacking, of course, but military sense suggests the likelihood of a garrison being posted there. The corruption of the local name to a Macedonian sound-alike would not be surprising in such circumstances.

These names, which are adaptations of local Syrian names, can best be explained as local corruptions, with the Syrian name triggering a similar sound in the minds of Macedonians there. Thus they perhaps developed spontaneously, before being adopted officially. Other names, in particular the use of the name Pella, were perhaps imposed by the king or the governor. Larissa, with its Thessalian connection, may be a mixture of both, the king perhaps awarding the name in specific acknowledgement of the origin of the men settled there, though the adoption of the name could equally have been the deliberate choice of the first settlers. It appears that Beroia in Macedonia was the home of the ancestors of Antigonos, and this may explain the naming of Beroia in Syria.[68] At the same time, the name Larissa would be the obvious one for a set of Thessalian colonists to choose for themselves, and the adoption of the name of home towns is not a surprising development: royal imposition is not a requirement.

The general similarity in geographical terms, which can be detected between original and new versions in a number of cases, does suggest that this naming was partly spontaneous, but at the same time, the application of Macedonian names to mountain ranges has a very artificial ring to it, as though an attempt was being made to make the land more homelike for exiled Macedonians. It was in the interests of both Antigonos and Seleukos to persuade Macedonians to settle in Syria, but

southwards during the Seleukid collapse in the first half of the first century BC. At the time of Alexander and Seleukos, Kommagene will have been in the process of recovering from Assyrian depredations; a guard over it would be more appropriate than anything more active.

[68] C. F. Edson, 'The Antigonids, Heracles and Beroea', *Harvard Studies in Classical Philology* 41 (1934), 213–46.

Antigonos had the greater resources, and it is altogether likely and reasonable that many men will have already settled there before Seleukos arrived. After 301 BC there can have been few Macedonians available for colonizing new lands, so devastated did Macedonia itself become.[69] These pre-Seleukid settlers must, in many cases, have been soldiers, at least originally, who had been posted in garrisons in Syria. These garrisons will have fluctuated in size and number, depending on the political and diplomatic situation, but some at least would have been permanent. Army bureaucracy would then ensure that the new names became equally permanent.

This *genre* of name exists also in the surrounding lands: Aigai in Kilikia; Dion and Pella in Transjordan; Anthedon in Palestine; Edessa, Anthemos, Amphipolis, Ichnai, and Europos in Mesopotamia. There were also several cities which later claimed to have been founded by Alexander or Perdikkas, but none of the claims stands up to serious examination.[70] The one place where Alexander is virtually certain to have placed a garrison is Samaria, where a rebellion had taken place while he was in Egypt.[71] Of the other places, military considerations are the best explanation for their foundation, but would sit best with a rather later date. Dion and Pella seem to guard the northern Jordan crossing against Arab nomad attacks;[72] perhaps Antigonos, in the aftermath of Demetrios' raid on the Nabataeans,[73] is the most likely founder here. Amphipolis, Anthemos, and Edessa are strung along the road from the Euphrates eastwards, and again it

---

[69] The drain on Macedonian manpower caused by Alexander's campaigns was bad enough, but repeated invasions after 300 BC (by Demetrios in 296, by Pyrrhos several times in the 290s and 280s, and eventually and most devastatingly by the Celts in 279) prevented recovery. Demetrios, in fact, was expelled by the Macedonians in 288 precisely because it was his intention to take the Macedonian levy overseas (Plut. *Dem.* 44).

[70] The claims are all late; the only one which has been taken seriously is for Gerasa (by N. G. L. Hammond, *Alexander the Great*, pp. 119–20; H. Seyrig, 'Alexandre le Grand, fondateur de Gerasa', *Syria* 42 (1965) 25–28) but proof has not been found and the claim is best disbelieved until it is. The excavators of the city suggested Antiochos IV (C.H. Kraeling (ed.), *Gerasa, City of the Decapolis* (New Haven, 1938), 30).

[71] Curt. 4. 8. 9; M. Hengel, *Jews, Greeks and Barbarians* (1980), 8–9. Fourth century BC fortifications were recognized by the excavators: J. W. Crowfoot, K. M. Kenyon, E. L. Sukenik, *The Buildings at Samaria* (1942), 24–7.

[72] M. Hengel, *Jews, Greeks and Barbarians*, p. 16.

[73] Diod. 19. 94–100.

seems best to credit Antigonos with these, since the route towards the bridge from the east would clearly need guarding in the face of the hostility of Seleukos, who was established in Babylon from 312 BC, and in Media soon after. Europos, definitely Seleukid in origin, is obviously connected with the defence of Babylon, and would be Seleukos' own reply to the Antigonid fortifications to the north. Ichnai and Europos look very much like opposing sentinels.[74] Aigai is on the road through Kilikia, and may be seen as the equivalent of the later Alexandria-by-Issos, the next post along the road. It could also be Antigonid in origin. Many of these places are generally attributed to Seleukos Nikator, on no evidence other than Appian[75] whose account is so general that it can be used to prove anything, and so proves nothing. The one certain case is that of Europos, which is out on a limb geographically and has no real connection with Syria. In all these names, that is, there is nothing *against* the theory of pre-Seleukid origins for many of the places in Syria with Macedonian and Greek names; at the same time their geographical distribution suggests that the preoccupations of Antigonos are most likely to have been the decisive ones in their location and establishment. Seleukos after 301 had very different priorities and concerns.

These conclusions, tentative though they must be, do now permit a general summary to be made of the nature and process of the initial settlement of Greeks and Macedonians in Syria. Before 333 there had been a few, small, trading colonies on the coast, whose populations were only partly Greek, but there were no purely Greek settlements anywhere in Syria. After Alexander's conquest, garrisons were established at important points, and there was also a satrapal bodyguard; none of these groups of soldiers were necessarily in fixed or permanent posts or were especially large, and in 330 many of the men were undoubtedly transferred to the east. There were, however, enough troops in northern Syria in 318 and 317 to make it worth while for Antigonos and Eumenes both to recruit there, and after Antigonos' return in 316 garrisons of a relatively permanant nature must be assumed because of the political stakes involved. By that date also Alexander's

[74] M. Rostovtzeff, *Dura-Europus and its Art* (Oxford, 1938), 10 and 'The Foundation of Dura-Europus', *Annales de l'Institut Kondakov* 10 (1938), 99–106.

[75] App. *Syr.* 57.

veterans were seriously looking for places to settle down. Antigonos could not let them leave his lands and return to Macedonia for fear of strengthening his encircling enemies; some were, thus, settled in Syria. These were the originators of some at least of the Greek and Thessalian and Macedonian and Thracian names in northern Syria (and in Palestine as well, presumably). Finally Antigonos founded and peopled his new city of Antigoneia.

When Seleukos Nikator arrived in Syria in 301, fresh from his victory over Antigonos and Demetrios at Ipsos, his new dominion was thus already partly 'Hellenized' and the elements of a new urban network were already in existence in the interior. The old-established, mixed Greek-and-Phoenician communities along the coast had been supplemented by the military posts containing Greek and Macedonian soldiers, which would also, no doubt, contain equally mixed populations. The whole was crowned by the new city of his erstwhile opponent, Antigoneia. Apart from this last, and Arados on its island, none of these settlements need be thought to be at all large, though they were perhaps somewhat larger than the villages among which they were established.

Seleukos, therefore, was not faced with a land which was unfamiliar with Greeks, nor with a land with which Greeks and Macedonians were themselves unfamiliar. It was a land in which compatriots of his had been sinking steadily deeper roots for a full generation, and this circumstance was not one he could ignore, any more than the Norman presence in England could be ignored in AD 1100, after a comparable length of occupation. Yet his actions in Syria in the two years after he acquired the rule over that land were effectively revolutionary, and irrevocably wrenched the developing Syrian–Greek relationship into an entirely new position, with large effects on both peoples, on the land, and on his own power and prospects and the future of his family.

First, his actions; then, his reasons.

One of his first acts when he reached his new territory of Syria in 301 was to destroy the only Greek city in the land. Antigoneia was physically destroyed and its people removed elsewhere.[76] This was the first of a series of actions, which

[76] Mal. 201.

resulted in the establishment of a whole network of cities in Syria in a very short time. The precise sequence of events is not clear, and this is probably not a serious loss, since it is the totality of his deeds which is important. The most detailed description of Seleukos' activities in 301–299 is also the latest in time: that of Johannes Malalas, a patriotic Antiochene of the sixth century AD. His account[77] contains firm dates for the foundations of both Antioch and Seleukeia-in-Pieria, which have been generally accepted, though there is no corroboration. He portrays Seleukos as first founding Seleukeia, then deciding Antigoneia's fate, and then founding Antioch. All this took about a month, from the foundation of Seleukeia on 23 Xanthikos to the foundation of Antioch on 22 Artemisios. No doubt these dates were well attested locally, the occasions for local celebrations. Another Antiochene, Libanios, two centuries earlier, does not add anything of importance.[78] Diodoros Sikulos, however, in the first century BC, said that Seleukos destroyed Antigoneia and then founded Seleukeia.[79] The precise sequence is not recoverable, and perhaps not important; what does emerge clearly is the close interconnection of the decisions to eliminate Antigoneia and to build the two new cities, one to replace Antigoneia and one on the coast.

Malalas reports that Seleukos went on to found a third city, called Laodikeia, distinguished from others as 'on the Sea', immediately after founding Antioch.[80] A physical connection between the two cities has also been suggested, in that the *insulae* within the grid of streets are almost the same. At Antioch they are 112 metres by 58, and at Laodikeia 112 by 57.[81] This is hardly conclusive evidence for contemporaneity, and Malalas' testimony is much more valuable.

Apamea, by the Orontes, is the fourth of the cities which are said to have been founded by Seleukos in a single sequence. The evidence here is much poorer than that for the other three. Strabo in the first century BC described them as 'sister-cities',[82] but Downey has sapped confidence in Strabo at this

---

[77] Mal. 201.

[78] Lib. Or. 11. 85–93.

[79] Diod. 20. 47.

[80] Mal. 203.

[81] Downey, *Antioch*, pp. 70–1; Sauvaget, 'Plan', p. 105.

[82] Str 16. 2. 4. He rather spoils the effect by explaining that the term was due to 'their concord with one another', of which there is precious little evidence, and plenty to suggest the very opposite.

point by bringing out that here he seems to be more concerned to fit the evidence into a pattern than (perhaps) to be quite accurate and comprehensive;[83] thus it is possible that Strabo has distorted his evidence by imposing the pattern on it, to establish the symmetry of four quarters of Antioch, four satrapies in Seleukis, and the four 'sister-cities'. So, in this instance the inference drawn from his words is not wholly convincing. Further, Diodoros mentions that Apamea was also called Pella, and this tends to suggest that in 285, the date of Demetrios' imprisonment there (which is what Diodoros was writing about) the name Apamea had not yet been fully accepted, or even perhaps imposed.[84] These items are the nearest to formal evidence for the city's early origin that we have, and they are not very good. However, there are other indications, which suggest that Seleukos was the founder, and that this took place early in his rule in Syria. The names of all four of these cities are dynastic and all the names are of people close to Seleukos himself—Seleukeia for himself, Antioch and Laodikeia for his parents, and Apamea for his wife;[85] yet Seleukos remarried in 298, his new wife being Stratonike,[86] and it would scarcely be tactful to name a new city for her predecessor. This implies a foundation before 298. The city itself became the seat of the satrap of Apamene,[87] which was thus named for the city, just as Chalkidene and Kyrrhestike in the north were. The only occasion for the organisation of north Syria into these satrapies is in the year or so following Seleukos' acquisition. It follows that Apamea was founded in that same period, that is, in 301–299.

It is unfortunate that the quality of the numismatic evidence for these cities parallels rather than complements that of the literary evidence. Both Seleukeia and Antioch produced an abundant coinage under Seleukos I which is well attested and which was produced right through his reign. Seleukeia's first coinage can be linked with the earlier coins of Antigoneia, while Antioch's are connected with previous issues of Seleukeia-on-the-Tigris.[88] Further, there are also

[83] G. Downey, 'Strabo on Antioch: Notes on his Method', *TAPA* 72 (1941), 85–95.

[84] Diod. 21. 20. Plut. *Dem.* 50 and 52 says he was imprisoned at 'the Syrian Chersonesos', which name would suit the acropolis of Apamea very well.

[85] Str. 16. 2. 4. [86] Plut. *Dem.* 39.

[87] *OGIS* 262. [88] Newell, *WSM* 88–9.

municipal issues as well as royal ones for both of the new
cities.[89] For Laodikeia the coinage is less prolific and
artistically cruder, but quite distinctive—and it continued
with the same design (a dolphin) for seventy years or so.[90]
Apamea, by contrast, never seems to have been a prolific
source of coins, although some coins have been attributed to
it. In particular its production was discontinuous. Newell[91]
recognized a 'possible' coinage of Seleukos I, an early 'short-
lived' issue of Antiochos I, and also one of bronze which was
not of 'certain attribution', and to Antiochos II he allocated
two issues of poor quality silver which were only 'probably'
issued at Apamea. There is thus no help from the coins in
determining Apamea's foundation date, and it must be
accepted that the foundation of Apamea in the reign of
Seleukos I can only be called probable. There is not even the
minimal evidence of *insula*-sizes to cling to, for Apamea's are
105 metres by 57—different from those known for both
Laodikeia and Antioch, although similarly oblong in shape.[92]
On the whole, it seems best to accept the traditional
attribution to Seleukos, even though it is not fully proved, if
only because the satrapy of which it was the head must also be
early, and must certainly be pre–285, which, given the
'argument from tact' concerning his second marriage, de-
ployed above, means pre–298 as well.

Within a year or so, therefore, Seleukos founded these four
cities, all large, and all named for his own family. Another city
is almost certainly as early as this, on sheer grounds of
geographical and strategic likelihood: Seleukeia-Zeugma,
Seleukeia 'the Bridge'. Alexander's bridge over the Euphrates
had been built at Thapsakos, and had been there for over
thirty years,[93] but there is no record of it after Alexander's

---

[89] Ibid.   [90] Ibid. 188.

[91] Ibid. 155–62. Apamea, according to Newell, produced only 16 coins between
300 and 246. Hardly a busy mint.

[92] J.-C. Balty, 'Les Grandes Étapes de l'urbanisme d'Apamée- sur-l'Oronte',
Ktema (1977), 3–16; the *insula* size is reported on p. 5; it is difficult to accept that
approximate 2 : 1 ratios are sufficient to demonstrate any contemporaneity of design
and foundation. F. E. Winter, 'Hellenistic Townplanning' *CAH*, 2nd edn., vol. vii,
part i, p. 372, suggests that there was here a 'regional school' of townplanning, but he
does not take into consideration the fact of the cities' contemporaneity.

[93] Built in 332–331, according to the sources (e.g. Arr. 3. 7. 1–2). Presumably
routine maintenance had kept it going since then.

crossing in 331. Presumably Antigonos needed a bridge, and presumably it was Alexander's which he maintained. In 302, however, Seleukos advanced against Antigonos through Kappadokia,[94] that is, north of the Taurus range. This may have been because Syria was Ptolemy's sector of activity, or because Antigonos could either defeat Seleukos in isolation or simply retreat before him to block the Kilikian Gates, and then deal with Lysimachos and Kassandros in isolation. Antigonos sent a raid to Babylon during the course of the war,[95] which presumably emanated from Syria, and would thus have used the bridge. But Antigonos' forces were concentrated in Asia Minor by the time of Ipsos and so Syria will have been largely evacuated, possibly after the bridge was broken.

At all events it seems that, when he annexed Syria, Seleukos found that a new bridge was required. For him, ruling Babylonia, Mesopotamia and Syria, a bridge was essential. Thus Seleukos is credited in some sources with building the bridge,[96] though elsewhere there is a continued attribution to Alexander.[97] It seems certain that Seleukos abandoned Alexander's site at Thapsakos (wherever that was) in favour of one of his own. At the bridge he established another city called Seleukeia, on the western bank of the river, with a suburb called Apamea on the east bank.[98] This bridge will have been an urgent priority, and its guardian city will have been just as urgent: again a foundation in the first couple of years of Seleukos' rule is required by these considerations.

Six other cities in Syria can, by a variety of arguments, be assigned to Seleukos Nikator as founder. Of these, four had imported Greek or Macedonian names, which indicates that they already existed as centres of Greek settlement when Seleukos arrived. Two of them, Chalkis and Kyrrhos, were the

[94] Diod. twice (20. 108. 5 and 109. 5) says that Seleukos came 'down from the Upper Satrapies' to fight at Ipsos; presumably therefore from Media into Kappadokia.

[95] W. W. Tarn, 'The Proposed New Date for Ipsus', *Classical Review* (1926), 13–15. Tarn also uses a reference in Arrian's *Indica* (43. 4–5) to suggest that Seleukos had been in Babylon early in 302, but the reference is not in fact dated.

[96] Pliny, *NH* 5. 82, for example.

[97] Pliny, *NH* 34. 150 and Dio Cassius 40. 17. 3 both refer to Alexander as the builder of the bridge.

[98] Pliny, *NH*, 5. 86; also called 'Seleukeia-on-the-Euphrates' at 5. 82.

seats of satraps. Their probable existence at the time of
Seleukos' arrival means that for him to be the founder,
Seleukos must have performed some act symbolizing that
status, perhaps by providing a formal recognition as a *polis*
and a provision of detailed planning and some public
buildings. We have no details. Two further places, Europos
and Beroia, are in the same geographical area, and have
names which suggest that they may well be pre-Seleukid.
Europos is said by Stephanos[99] to have been one of Seleukos'
foundations; it occupied the site of Carchemish, one of the
crossing points of the Euphrates.[100] For Beroia, there is not
even the flimsy evidence of Stephanos, and its assignment to
Seleukos I rests on its name, its geographical position, and its
appearance in the list of Seleukos' cities in Appian.[101]

Appian included this list in his long digression on Seleukid
history in his account of Rome's 'Syrian' Wars, but it is of
little use in specific cases. Of the cities which Appian actually
names, he only locates the four great cities clearly in Syria,
while the others are placed in Syria and upper Asia. He does
name Beroia, Arethusa, Chalkis, and Larissa of the known
Syrian cities, but Zeugma is hidden among the nine which are
named after the king himself. So Appian cannot be relied on
for detail about Syria, for, after all, he refers to the whole
Seleukid kingdom. It seems likely from the form of his list that
he is summarizing another source or sources where there were
more details, but this does not help us now.

In one case, however, Appian is quite specific. He said the
Nikopolis 'in Armenia very near Kappadokia' was founded to
commemorate one of Seleukos' victories.[102] Nikopolis, the
present Islahiyé in the Kara valley, was actually in Armenia
later.[103]. The victory which the city's name commemorates is

---

[99] Stephanos of Byzantium, s.v. 'Oropos'; Stephanos does not actually mention an
'Europos' in Syria, but he does include an 'Oropos'; since Europos certainly existed,
and no other indication exists of an Oropos, it seems best to conflate the two,
assuming a mistake by Stephanos or his source.

[100] Europos has been credited to Seleukos by evidence of its name, for the
Macedonian Europos was the king's birthplace (Stephanos, s.v. 'Oropos'). However,
if that is accepted, then Beroia has to be similarly attributed to Antigonos, since he
had been born at the Macedonian Beroia (C. F. Edson, note 68 above).

[101] App. *Syr.* 57.

[102] App. *Syr.* 57.

[103] Jones, *CERP* 452, n. 24.

perhaps that over Demetrios in 285 in the Amanus mountains, which overlook the site. This in turn would place the foundation in the year or so following 285. However, this is the only evidence we have for such an early date. The city does not reappear in any other source until the Roman period.

Seleukos is also credited with renaming Bambyke as Hierapolis. The source, Aelian[104] is late, but the very casualness of the mention carries some conviction. The renaming must indicate—though this is assumption—that the Semitic temple-town adopted a Hellenic guise. Since its chief priest Abd-Hadad had claimed the title of king a generation earlier, it would clearly be worthwhile for Seleukos to keep some control over the place. Conversion to a *polis*, which is clearly indicated by the new name, presumably also indicates the presence of Greek-speaking inhabitants in addition to the native Syrians. The patronage extended to the temple by Stratonike,[105] wife successively of both Seleukos I and his son Antiochos I, also suggests that Hierapolis was being treated very carefully by the Seleukid government.

To summarize, the evidence so far considered goes to suggest that Seleukos' activity took three stages. First he established four great cities and Zeugma, naming them after members of his own family and himself, having simultaneously destroyed Antigoneia. Second, he confirmed the status, or perhaps increased the status, of four of the Greco-Macedonian settlements which he found already in existence. The third stage came later, when he founded two other cities, one to commemorate his defeat of Demetrios and the other to hellenize a native shrine as Hierapolis. This summary hides the somewhat shaky nature of some of the evidence, in particular for the foundation of Beroia, nowhere attested, but certain other aspects will tend to provide support for the pattern which is emerging. These other aspects concern the reasons Seleukos had for all this strenuous activity, and the methods he used to control his creations once they existed. It is, in fact, high time his reasons were considered, and to do that it is necessary to look first at the political situation he faced on entering his Syrian acquisition.

[104] Aelian, *De Natura Animali*, 12. 2.
[105] Lucian, *De Dea Syria*, 17 and 19–21.

These city foundations did not occur as an act of generosity on Seleukos' part, not were they a mere whim. They were, rather, a coolly calculated political device, designed to establish his political authority firmly in his new territory, and to provide a firm foundation for further expansion.

Seleukos faced some major problems. First of all, and certainly best known, was the immediate quarrel with Ptolemy over the possession of Phoenicia and Palestine,[106] but the part of Syria which Seleukos did acquire presented other problems as well, which were similarly intractable. First, the Greeks and Macedonians who already lived in Syria had been planted there by Antigonos and might be expected to continue to be loyal to the old king's son Demetrios. Second, Demetrios was still at large, possessed of a fleet which dominated the eastern Mediterranean from his bases at Tyre and Cyprus (and maybe Arados as well[107]). Third, not only was Ptolemy hostile in the south, but Lysimachos held control of Asia Minor beyond the Taurus to the north, and Pleistarchos, brother of Kassandros, held Kilikia.[108] Amid all this, Seleukos' new possession looked more like a very vulnerable salient than a valued new province (See Map 1).

Seleukos had to move swiftly and delicately to conciliate his various enemies, while at the same time fastening his grip on the new land. He assured Ptolemy that he would not fight for southern Syria, and at the same time, by referring to their old friendship, subtly put Ptolemy in the wrong[109]. Pleistarchos could be ignored for the present, for he had little actual power, and his only real supporter, his brother Kassandros, was far away. Demetrios was a much more important enemy, and Seleukos' major problem was to detach the Greeks and Macedonians of Syria from their allegiance to him. His

---

[106] Diod. 21. 1. 5; Justin 15. 4. 21–2; Plut. *Dem.* 31.

[107] Fleet: Plut. *Dem.* 30–2; Tyre and Sidon: Plut. *Dem.* 33; Arados: Rey-Coquais, *Arados*, p. 155 says that Demetrios abandoned Arados in 301, which is an inference from Plut.'s failure to name it. Demetrios held Cyprus in 298 and until the Ptolemaic conquest (Plut. *Dem.* 33 and 35).

[108] The precise extent of Lysimachos' power in Asia Minor is not certain. The problem is App. *Syr.* 55, who gives Phrygia to Seleukos, whereas in 286 Lysimachos' son chased Demetrios all the way to the Taurus (Plut. *Dem.* 47); cf. *PW* xiv. 1, 'Lysimachos'; Pleistarchos: L. Robert, *Le Sanctuaire de Sinuri près de Mylasa: I, Les Inscriptions grecque* (Paris 1945), 55 ff.

[109] Diod. 21. 1. 5.

solution had two elements: conciliation of Demetrios, and the establishment of the new cities. By 298 diplomatic negotiations had produced a marriage alliance with Demetrios,[110] while within Syria his new cities at once fortified the new province, conciliated the former followers of Antigonos, and attracted new settlers who would dilute the numbers of the Antigoneians and who would owe allegiance only to Seleukos. As part of this process, the city of Antigoneia was destroyed and its people moved to another site or sites. All this, negotiations and foundations, colonization and marriage, took place in the two years 300–298, and a difficult diplomatic feat it must have been to keep all this in action at the same time.

The test of the success of this policy came in 286–285, when Demetrios invaded Syria over the Amanus. His purpose was presumably to seek support among the old soldiers of his father and those citizens of the former Antigoneia whose loyalty, he hoped, was not extinct.[111] But Seleukos was equal to the problem. He refused to fight Demetrios and thereby avoided putting those old soldiers to the test. Then he captured Demetrios. And finally, when he held Demetrios prisoner, he refused, ostentatiously and publicly, to execute him—thereby putting Lysimachos in the wrong by publicly rejecting his bribe. The explanation for this strange conduct— for it is not a normal political habit in a man who has fought his way to the top to spare defeated and dangerous enemies— is that Seleukos had in mind a particular audience which he considered to be important, and who must not be outraged— that is, the old supporters of Antigonos and Demetrios who lived in Syria.[112]

Thus the destruction of the city of Antigoneia can be seen as in part an exorcism of Antigonos. Other factors probably

---

[110] Plut. *Dem.* 32.

[111]. Plut. *Dem.* 48–49. Plut. does not actually say that Demetrios invaded Syria in expectation of support—but why else did he? In effect the rest of the world had had enough of him, and had rejected him: he had been actively rejected in Macedon and Greece, and had received no support in his march through Anatolia. Only Syria was left. While he still had hopes of support, his men stayed with him, but by the end of the winter no-one had joined him, and his last troops melted away.

[112] One other possible factor is the marriage of Seleukos to Demetrios' daughter Stratonike, but that would not have stopped Seleukos from *fighting* Demetrios, though he might have refrained from executing him. It certainly did not stop Demetrios from attacking Seleukos. Anyway, Seleukos and Stratonike were no longer married by 286.

entered into the matter as well: for example, the site of the
older city may not have been as good as that chosen for
Seleukeia or Antioch. Yet Seleukos was very careful to respect
the memory of Antigonos and his defunct city by carrying the
Tyche of Antigoneia, the statue of the eponymous city goddess,
to his new city, and setting it up there.[113] Again, this was
presumably an act designed to conciliate the people of the new
city who had had to shift their homes.

When he founded Antioch, according to the account of the
events which Malalas wrote down in the sixth century AD,[114]
Seleukos went through a long elaborate performance involving open air sacrifices, an eagle stealing the meat, Antiochos
the king's son following the bird as it flew, and the designation
of the bird's landing place as the site of the successor-city to
Antigoneia. Seleukos is then said to have planned out the city
using elephants to simulate the towers he planned to have
built as part of the city wall.

This is one of a series of stories associated with Seleukos I,
designed to convince his subjects that the king was divinely
favoured and guided.[115] The eagle is the bird of the story
because it is Zeus' bird, hence it could be argued that it was
Zeus who chose the site of the new city. Actually, of course,
whatever performance was put on at the time, Seleukos
himself chose the site of the new city, with his advisers. The
performance does, however, raise the question of why
Seleukos should go through with such an elaborate charade. It
is not possible to believe that the king would perform such an
extraordinary sequence of actions if he did not consider them
important. Seleukos was extremely busy at the time with the
negotiations and the foundations, so his participation in the
elaborate ceremonies of city-foundation was something which
he must have regarded as essential.

The audience to which he was directing this performance
can only have been, once again, the Greek and Macedonian
inhabitants of Syria, the former subjects of Antigonos and
Demetrios. His own people, his pre-Ipsos soldiers, would not

[113] Mal. 201.
[114] Mal. 200. H. Seyrig recognized a capital from Bourg es-Sleyb as portraying the
scene: 'Scène historique sur un chapiteau du Musée de Beyrouth', *Revue des études
anciennes* 42 (1940), 340–4.
[115] S. K. Eddy, *The King is Dead* (Lincoln, Neb. 1961), 108–9.

need to be impressed so much, since, being victorious, they would be loyal and rewarded. The new colonists would owe their new lands to him, and so they could be reckoned loyal at least for a time, though no doubt they would be pleased to know that their patron had the favour of the gods. Maybe Seleukos was also aiming at the Aramaic-speaking Syrians; it would do no harm for them to know that their new king had the god's favour, and the promotion of Hierapolis by Seleukos was surely designed, at least in part, to impress these people.

Yet neither of these groups had any effective political and military power, whereas the former followers of king Antigonos did have such power. It may be that they had the advantage of numbers as well. Seleukos' army at Ipsos had been the smallest of the three involved in the battle: 32,000 men plus elephants and chariots as against 80,000 for Antigonos and 50,000 for Lysimachos.[116] A proportion of Antigonos' army will have been domiciled in Syria, in the various places named for Greek and Macedonian towns, and the city of Antigoneia presumably had a fairly sizeable population as well. Some of the men in Seleukos' army already had their homes in Babylonia and Media and further east. It is thus very likely that the majority of the Greeks and Macedonians in Syria were former supporters of Antigonos. The incentive behind Seleukos' actions is therefore clear: he had to conciliate his new subjects in every possible way.

Seleukos' ceremonial foundation of Antioch seems to have been repeated elsewhere, though details are scarce—the eagle story is repeated for Seleukeia, for instance.[117] It is a clear symbol of the control exercised by the king over the choice of site. That control extended much further. As founder Seleukos provided the land on which the cities were to be built, the laws by which they were governed, and the people who were to inhabit them.[118] In return, so to speak, they gave him, as king, greater power and wealth, since it was citizens of such places which formed the backbone of his army, and taxes extracted from such places which helped to fill his treasury.

[116] Diod. 20. 113; Plut. *Dem.* 28. 3 and 38. 3.
[117] Mal. 199.
[118] C. Préaux, *Le Monde hellénistique*, vol. ii (Paris, 1978), part 3, ch. 1. W. W. Tarn, *Hellenistic Civilisation*, 3rd edn., rev. G. T. Griffith (1951), 145–6.

The political context, therefore, provides a compelling set of reasons for Seleukos' action in establishing these cities. In a remarkably short time, their existence greatly increased his political and military power, both offensive and defensive. It was from this Syrian base that he expanded his power in the next twenty years: Kilikia fell to his control within seven years,[119] and his victory at Korupedion gave him control over Asia Minor and Macedon.[120] Had he lived, he would undoubtedly have moved against Ptolemy as well. In this he was using Syria as his strategic base very much in the same way as his vanquished predecessor Antigonos.

It is this strategic imperative, originally but never wholly defensive, which helps to explain the peculiar distribution of the cities. First, there were the two large cities, Seleukeia and Laodikeia, on the coast. Each was provided with a large artificial harbour[121] and a dominating acropolis. Between them, these harbour-cities provided Seleukos with naval bases on the all-important Mediterranean, and established his control over his own stretch of the coast. This thereupon lessened whatever reliance he had placed on the friendship and co-operation of Arados, which, with Demetrios still at large, and Ptolemy's navy close by, might well be a less than trustworthy staff to lean on.

Inland, the other two great cities, Antioch and Apamea, were so situated as to control the main land route from north to south. Apamea was the key to the whole system, far more so even than the coastal cities. It was deliberately placed up on the plateau rather than on the better-watered lowland, with an acropolis which still today clearly betrays its military

[119] Kilikia was taken from Pleistarchos by Demetrios in 298 on his way to Rhosos and the alliance with Seleukos (Plut. *Dem.* 31–2); Seleukos himself was in possession of Kilikia in 286 when Demetrios returned (Plut. *Dem.* 47) and had presumably occupied it in 294 when they had quarrelled (Plut. *Dem.* 32).

[120] These were the formal spoils; Seleukos, of course, did not have time to reach Macedon before he was killed, but between Korupedion and his death, he was technically king of Macedon.

[121] Seyrig, 'Séleucos I', pp. 304–7, was the first to emphasize these harbours and to draw attention to their artificial nature; also K. Lehmann-Hartleben, *Die antiken Hafenanlagen des Mittelmeeres* (Leipzig, 1923), 214–7. The recent BAR volume on *Harbour Archaeology*, ed. A. Rabin, which is the Proceedings of the First International Conference on Ancient Mediterranean Harbours, held at Caesarea Maritima in 1983 (BAR S 257), has no reference to Syrian cities.

origins.[122] The city lay astride the main route from the south which here had to pass along the plateau edge, for to the west were the Ghab marshes, and to the east was the steppeland which, as the archaeological evidence suggests, was inhabited only by nomads. Thrown out in all directions, south, southeast, and north, were Apamea's dependent towns—Larissa, Arethusa, Seleukobelos, Megara, and so on. These were sites on the approach roads to the central fortress-city, but especially on those from the south, from Ptolemy's lands (See Map 3). It is this militarily central position which is recalled in Strabo's account of Apamea, when he refers to the royal stud, the elephants, and the military headquarters being sited at the city.[123]

Yet it is worth emphasizing that Apamea's positioning looks to be notably defensive. It is a long way from the actual boundary of the Ptolemaic kingdom, which was far to the south in the Biqaa valley. Apamea was not established to control the area between it and Ptolemy's lands: it was placed where it was in order to protect the lands to its north, 'behind' it. That is, Seleukos and Ptolemy tacitly laid out the area between their territories as a sort of noman'sland. Seleukos controlled the northern part by means of Apamea's outposts, but only as far as the latitude of Arados. Hama, for example, was not yet occupied, nor was Emesa, though Arethusa was. Ptolemy established his forward posts at Gerrha and Brochi, two forts which were strong enough to block Antiochos III's invasion in 221.[124] Between the Arados–Arethusa line and Ptolemy's forts in the Biqaa, the land was essentially unoccupied. It is only after the conquest of Ptolemaic Palestine that this land ceased to be a frontier area and began to be settled again.

Antioch is at the fourth corner of the fortified quadrilateral of cities, but it is without any particular, specific role. It was

---

[122] Qalat al-Mudiq, the name of the town which now occupies the Apamean tell, was a frontier fortress of the principality of Antioch in the Crusader period from 1106 to 1150 (S. Runciman, *A History of the Crusades*, vol. ii (1953), 52–3 and 328), and even today the approach to the single gate is by way of a narrow, steep road which winds a quarter of the way round the walls, allowing easy surveillance from the town of anyone approaching.

[123] Str. 16. 2. 10.

[124] Pol. 5. 46. 1–4.

neither a military headquarters nor a harbour, though it did have at its disposal a wealthier territory than any of the others (except perhaps Laodikeia, later). Yet Antioch was the lynch-pin of the whole structure, and its very lack of a specialized role was important for its future. Its position made it the main communications centre, with roads radiating to the other three cities, towards Kilikia, and to the east. It was, in fact, the one place which connected all these areas. No doubt this was originally mainly a military consideration, but roads can be used by others besides soldiers. Antioch was thus the point of concentration for resources from the rest of the kingdom, and the reserve position behind the other three great cities. This made it the natural headquarters of the king. It was this role which ensured the city's growth.

These four cities occupied between them about half of Seleukid Syria, and enclosed within them the mountainous territory of the Bargylos. The other half of Seleukid Syria, between Antioch and the Euphrates, contained, in Seleukos' original scheme, four cities as well, but these—Kyrrhos, Chalkis, Beroia, and Zeugma—were smaller, and the scheme was subsequently altered by the addition of Hierapolis and Nikopolis. They were clearly less vital in a military sense, and were perhaps intended partly to establish control over the routes to the eastward, partly to occupy the territory and overawe the native inhabitants. At least three of these new cities would appear to have been pre-Seleukid, to judge by their names (Beroia, Kyrrhos, Chalkis), and there were also Doliche and Europos, which also appear to be pre-Seleukid, but not being selected by Seleukos for expansion, they continued to be of a small size only.

All these cities had to be inhabited. The former subjects of Antigonos and a certain number of Seleukos' own people would provide the initial Greek-speaking population, but immigration from Greece must also have been important. There are traces of these immigrants in the temples known in Antioch, but otherwise the details escape us. Seleukos' main military difficulty until then had always been manpower. He had had the smallest army at Ipsos, and even after that victory he could not afford to challenge Ptolemy. However, the new cities, when established and inhabited, would provide him with a reservoir of military manpower suitable for further military expeditions. The result of this was an army which was large enough in 281, to allow Seleukos to challenge and beat Lysimachos whose army was drawn from both Macedonia and Asia Minor.

It is thus clear that Seleukos was very successful in establishing his power in Syria on firm foundations. The manpower problem was evidently solved, and permitted him to expand his power westwards. But it was equally necessary for him to ensure that his control over these cities did not slip, and that he could pass on a firmly united kingdom to his son. That is, he had to institutionalize the personal authority he had acquired as conqueror, victor, and founder. The evidence suggests that he did this in two ways, one physical and one governmental.

The plans which can be recovered of Seleukos' cities demonstrate the great size and importance of the acropolis. In every case the acropolis is exceptionally large. At Beroia it was perhaps a fifth of the total city area, and at Chalkis maybe even more. In every case, the acropolis dominated the city by its position and size, just as the city dominated the country round about. Indeed, in some cases—Kyrrhos, Apamea, and Seleukeia-in-Pieria in particular—the site seems to have been chosen with the aim of ensuring that the acropolis could exert control over both its city and the country round about. Kyrrhos, for example, is in a very awkward place, so awkward that it has never flourished, but it is a good site for an acropolis with a city at its feet. The city is laid out on a relatively flat site, defended on one side by a steep river bank, and it is overlooked by the steep little hill on which the acropolis is perched.[125] Seleukeia-in-Pieria is placed in a corner of its plain with the purpose, it would seem, of being able to enclose within the one city wall both the artificial harbour and the strong acropolis. It is not a site where a city would naturally grow, and indeed, deprived of support, it has since died. It is difficult to say which is the more important in these cases, the city or its acropolis.

[125] The steepness does not necessarily appear from maps, but it is immediately obvious on the ground; the slope from the main street up to the acropolis is steep enough to be difficult to climb without bending over, and it forms the slope of the *cavea* of the theatre.

Furthermore, every acropolis in the cities of Syria is at the edge of its city; no acropolis is completely enclosed by its city, as is that of Athens, for example. Every acropolis commander had the options of communicating with the outside by passing through the city, or of ignoring it. This preserved the garrison commander's freedom of action if the city was hostile, and suggests that the acropoleis were there to control the cities as much as to be centres of their defence (See plans of cities, 6*a*–f.).

The second instrument of control incorporated in the city was the office of *epistates*. This is often translated as 'governor',[126] but it was a more subtle position than that; perhaps 'resident', the title used by the captains and majors who were posted to the courts of Indian princes during the British Raj, best carries the meaning. This title is known from inscriptions at Laodikeia-in-Media,[127] and at Seleukeia-in-Pieria,[128] both from the beginning of the second century BC, by which time it is clear that the office was well established in those cities. Most likely it originated with the founder himself, if for no other reason than that he had so much to do in the first years that an agent of his in each city would be a necessity.

One of the methods by which the *epistates* and the king maintained control is illustrated by the inscription from Seleukeia-in-Pieria. The city was asked by king Seleukos IV to admit one of his Friends to honorary citizenship. It was not phrased as an instruction, but the city was clearly expected to accede. The king's message went to the *epistates* and the city's magistrates. The city no doubt welcomed the chance to honour the Friend, since this would be a way for the city to gain rapid and direct access to the king in case of need. The Friend would be, in part, the city's representative at court, just as the *epistates* was the king's representative at the city; but the *epistates* was already in post, whereas the Friend was not. That is, the king had already ensured that his man was in place in the city, whereas the city's representative at court was a less important matter.

---

[126] As for example by M. M. Austin, *The Hellenistic World from Alexander to the Roman Conquest* (Cambridge, 1981), no. 176.

[127] L. Robert, *Hellenica* 7 (Paris, 1949), 5–22.

[128] *IGLS* 1183.

The implication of the activities of *epistatai* is that the cities subject to their authority were very limited in their autonomy. In the circumstances of their foundation—by and for a king— this is scarcely surprising. But it is worth emphasizing here, since the problem of the autonomy of these cities is one I shall return to later. After all, these were, in form and presumably in appearance, and largely in population, Greek cities. They were 'colonial', in the sense that they were planted in a foreign land, just as the Greek cities in Sicily or Italy or round the Black Sea were colonies of Greeks. Those earlier colonial cities had assumed from the start the authority and attributes of independent states. This new wave of colonization was also carried into effect through the medium of the city, and each city (so far as we can tell) had the old attributes of independence—magistrates, walls, acropolis, *boule*, assembly and so on.

It is conventional today to call these cities *poleis*, but the precise meaning of that term and its applicability to these particular cities are disputable. The term itself has acquired that particular meaning which implies autonomy, self-govern-ment, even independence,[129] and it was this view of *poleis* led Tarn to his vision of the Seleukid kingdom as an organism which was evolving from a kingdom into a confederation of city-states.[130]

Yet this view of the *polis* is not the one which was held by Greeks at the time. When, in the second century AD, Pausanias gave a definition, he wrote of the buildings he would expect to see—theatre, *agora*, gymnasium, government offices, a fountain[131]—which did not include a place of assembly, though the theatre might be so used, nor does he mention autonomy. Six centuries earlier Xenophon's usage is distinctly vague, and he applies the term indiscriminately to any urban agglomeration which was not a village. For instance he uses it for Myriandros and Thapsakos[132]—to remain in Syria—yet neither has been located on the ground,

[129] e.g. M. Grant, *The Etruscans* (1980), 20.
[130] Tarn and Griffith, (note 118) 155.
[131] Pausanias 10. 4. 1.
[132] Xen. 1. 4 and 7.

which suggests that they were small and were without any notable buildings.

If the strict modern usage of the word *polis* is adhered to, it is necessary to have clear evidence of the status of each city in the form of an inscription or a clear literary reference or coinage minted at the city. In those terms almost all the cities of Syria in the Hellenistic period would be denied the title. At the same time, if Xenophon's usage is adopted the term would become meaningless, to be applied to every settlement larger than a village. Even worse, Pausanias' criteria would eliminate every single city in Syria, since few have any of the buildings he required, and none can be shown to have had them all.[133]

In fact, of course, these are neither the only, nor perhaps the most useful usages of the term in the ancient world; they merely illustrate the range. It would be perverse in the extreme to deny the term *polis* to, say, Antioch, simply because no theatre of Hellenistic date has been found there. At the same time, the applicability of the term to, say, Laodikeia-ad-Libanum or to Europos causes considerable difficulty because of their tiny size.

So the term *polis* is too useful to be ignored. It carries with it certain resonances—of Greekness, of some self-government, of power—which are too valuable to be discarded. It provides a certain standard against which urban agglomerations can be measured, even if, paradoxically, that standard is itself very difficult to define. The term can therefore be used in the general sense of a city with at least some powers of self-government, though in Syria it has been seen that these powers fall well short of independence or even autonomy.

It is the notion of self-government in the *polis* which has dominated the study of the Hellenistic cities. Instinctively beginning with the situation in old Greece, where *polis* continued to mean a self-governing city, historians such as Heuss[134] and Jones[135] looked at the cities of the Hellenistic kingdoms in those terms, and searched for signs of autonomy.

---

[133] See, for instance, the elaborate discussion in Tarn and Griffith (note 118), on pp. 145–50.

[134] A. Heuss, 'Stadt und Herrscher des Hellenismus', *Klio* Beiheft xxxix (1937).

[135] A. H. M. Jones, *The Greek City from Alexander to Justinian* (Oxford, 1940).

This is the theory behind the work of Jones in Syria and Palestine, summed up in his use of the word 'urbanization'.[136] The implication is that an advance in the human condition is registered by the establishment of Greek *poleis* in the eastern lands, whether by the conversion of a local urban settlement or by the founding of a new one.[137]

The twin cultural elements of evolution theory and nineteenth-century imperialism are clearly visible in these theories—and even more so in Tscherikower's detection of the military colony as the basis of Seleukid colonization.[138] Heuss's work was effectively criticized by Bikerman,[139] but it is Jones's work which has dominated the view of cities in the East.

Yet if an approach is made from a different direction, from the point of view of the dynasty, or from that of the inhabitants of the land itself rather than that of Classical Greece, then matters do not look quite so clear cut, and above all the theory of 'urbanization' as one of advance and progress is found wanting. To take one point in particular which will be demonstrated in detail later, it is remarkably difficult to find any Syrian city which *acts* in an independent way. There is one exception, one city which did determinedly work for autonomy and then for independence, eventually with success, but it is not a Greek city but Phoenician—Arados.

There is, of course, no evidence that Seleukos ever intended his new cities to be autonomous, though it was presumably he who, as founder, was ultimately responsible for their constitutions. He had an alternative model to work to, in which autonomy was never an issue. This was the city in which he grew up, Europos in Macedonia, which was presumably typical of Macedonian towns. In the difficult frontier situation in Macedonia, where raiders from over the border might appear at any time, autonomy for cities was a good deal less

---

[136] Jones' work began with articles: 'The Urbanisation of the Ituraean Principality', *JRS* 21 (1931), 265–75, and 'The Urbanisation of Palestine', *JRS* 21 (1931), 78–85, and culminated in *CERP*.

[137] This is Jones' assumption throughout *CERP*; note also Tarn and Griffith (see note 118) pp. 134–8 on the effects of cities on the status of the peasantry.

[138] V. Tscherikower, 'Die Hellenistischer Stadtegrundungen von Alexander der Grossen bis auf die Romerzeit', *Philologus* Supplement xix, 1927.

[139] E. J. Bikerman, *Institutions des Séleukides* (Paris, 1938).

important than their security, which was provided by the king.[140] The new foundations of King Philip followed that pattern, and so did those of his son Alexander, whose city-founding activity extended from Thrace to India. The nomenclature used was largely Greek, as one would expect, though not entirely. The Macedonian term *peliganes* was used for the governing council at Laodikeia-ad-Mare,[141] and this reflects both the Macedonian origin of the royal founder, and the Macedonian origin of many of the original inhabitants.

Seleukos' activity in Syria, therefore, resulted in the establishment of a network of Macedonian-type cities to control and to defend his new province. He had founded them, brought in people to inhabit them, allocated them land, and set up an administrative structure to foster and control them. When he died in 281 BC all this had been done, but the artificiality of the scheme is obvious. Whether and how these cities survived would depend on a variety of factors, geographical, social, dynastic, and political.

[140] N. G. L. Hammond and G. T. Griffith, *A History of Macedonia*, vol. ii, (Oxford, 1979), 648–9; G. Cawkwell, *Philip of Macedon* (1978), 40.

[141] P. Roussel, 'Décret des Péliganes de Laodicée sur Mer', *Syria* 23 (1942–43), 21–32.

3

SELEUKOS' CITIES: SITES AND SITUATIONS

SELEUKOS' Syrian cities were carefully placed geographically so as to ensure the king's control over his conquest. But the king's wishes in this respect could not override geographical factors, and the future history of the land was also out of his control. In the two centuries after his death the pattern he imposed slowly changed. Cities declined and new cities grew, so that when Syria became a Roman province, the urban pattern had distorted from its pristine regularity into a far more natural one.

To emphasize the artificiality of the overall network formed by Seleukos' foundations is not to say that geographical factors were wholly ignored. The desert to the east was inhospitable to large settlements under the prevailing technology. So were the mountains, whose difficult communications and small and divided economic resources inhibited the development of settlements larger than villages. In the fertile lowland areas the constraint was availability of food and, above all, water. Hence the cities required land around them from which to draw their food. This was a lesser constraint along the coast, where it was possible to import food from greater distances because of the relative cheapness of sea transport compared with that by land,[1] but this possibility seems not to have been relied on, at least at the beginning.

The distribution of cities, as they existed at the end of the reign of Seleukos I, clearly reflected these constraints. The four great cities had no close neighbours; in the case of Antioch, its rival Antigoneia had been destroyed to make way for it. Inland, the wide area of fertility stretching eastwards from Antioch to the Euphrates was evenly dotted with cities,

[1] A. Burford, 'Heavy Transport in Classical Antiquity', *Economic History Review* 13 (1960), 1–18.

between 65 and 100 kilometres apart. The exceptions are Beroia and Chalkis, only 35 kilometres apart, but they each had long distances to their other neighbours. This pattern of distribution even holds good for the coastal cities; it is clearly deliberate.

It even seems that the urban settlements which Seleukos found already existing in Syria were accommodated to the pattern he imposed. Arados is about the same distance from Laodikeia as is Seleukeia, and these three cities together controlled the whole coast between Ptolemy's land south of the Eleutheros river and that of Pleistarchos in Kilikia. Hierapolis' promotion to city-status does not seriously distort the eastern part of the network, and the late foundation of Nikopolis is at a regular distance from its neighbours. It would appear that the pattern by which the original cities were distributed was deliberately adhered to later on.

A closer consideration of just where these cities were placed confirms the care with which their sites were selected. There are two aspects here. First the general situation within which the city is planted with respect to communications, natural resources, climate, and so on. The second is the precise site, on a hill, in a valley, by a river, and so on. Some aspects of all this are invisible to us now because of the lack of information. We do not know much about manufactures in any of the cities, for example, though it is fair to assume that there were craftsmen at work amd markets for their products. Another function of any city is exchange of goods, however, and when the situations of Seleukos' cities are considered it is remarkable how often they can be seen to have a specific exchange function.

Ports are good examples, since their very purpose is to exchange the products of the sea and the products which come by sea for those of and from the land. Seleukeia and Laodikeia were established as ports where there had only been minor coastal settlements before, and were provided with large artificial harbours. They supplemented the port of Arados, and these three were supplemented in turn by the development of Alexandria in the north. The four cities were almost equidistant along the coast, and were also, in land terms, situated in productive coastal plains. Their resources were products of agriculture, including vines (Laodikeia became a notable wine exporter in the later Hellenistic period[2]), products of the sea, wood and stone from the mountains. Three of the cities had reasonably good land communications with the interior, though Laodikeia's were difficult. The wealth of the coastal plains is also the basis of the growth of a number of smaller towns later, and the communications with the interior are the basis for the continued wealth of the four large coastal cities.

In the interior the conditions were different: poorer rainfall, more difficult communications; but all the main cities are at communication nodes or became part of the communication network. Antioch and Zeugma were at river-crossings; Kyrrhos, Chalkis and Beroia were on the alternative routes between the coast and the Euphrates. Apamea lay just north of the Orontes crossing at Atcharné: its position was clearly determined by other considerations. Similarly Nikopolis was close to, but did not actually block, a pass over the Amanus. All these places, however, also exhibit particular economic reasons for their existence. Beroia, Chalkis, and Hierapolis are all close to the edge of sedentary occupation as it was in *c.*300 BC. They were, therefore, the obvious places at which nomads and farmers could exchange their respective products. The same was true of Apamea, which was also close to the fish and fowl of the Ghab marshes and Apamea's own lake. At Antioch were the fish of the Amuq lake and the grain of the plainland, and the mountain products of the northern Bargylos. Nikopolis is in a narrow productive valley between mountain ranges; Kyrrhos is high among hills, and was perhaps a market centre, though in both of these instances the economic motive of the settlement is clearly less powerful than in the others.

There were alternatives to these situations. For example Antigoneia had been placed in the middle of the plainland in the Amuq basin but relatively distant from other resources, whereas Antioch, Antigoneia's successor in geographical terms, was placed on the edge of two zones, the plain and the hills. It is possible that the drawbacks of the site of Antigoneia

---

[2] Str. 16. 2. 9.

had become evident when Seleukos arrived, and that this was one of the factors in his decision to abandon the site. There are other areas, the plains north of Aleppo, for instance, or the rich farmland inland from Arados, which were also ignored. It seems clear therefore that the cities founded or developed by Seleukos were all quite deliberately situated at the junctions of economic zones.

When the precise sites are considered, further evidence for the care and deliberation of the choices emerges. Since each site is obviously individual, variations can be expected, but it appears that all of the sites were required to conform to certain criteria.

The two great ports founded by Seleukos I, Laodikeia and Seleukeia, were both provided with large artificial harbours, but the sites chosen differed in many ways. Seleukeia stretched from the shore of the Mediterranean to a hill top four kilometres inland and 320 metres above the level of the sea. The harbour, now silted and dry,[3] was excavated at the foot of the hill, and the walls enclosed it within the city. These walls climbed up the hill on a series of ledges, and the topmost ledge became the acropolis. The hill thus enclosed was split into two parts by a stream, and other streams formed steep valleys on either side of the city, their sides acting as natural ramparts. The buildings of the city seem to have been concentrated near the harbour, on the first of the ledges, and on the acropolis.[4] The lowest area around the harbour is called the *emporion* by Polybios,[5] and the slope up to the first ledge is so steep that the modern track climbs by hairpin bends, and at least one staircase of the ancient city was cut from the rock.[6]

Seleukeia is tucked away in a corner of its coastal plain. It

---

[3] In Chapot's plan (see next note), the harbour is marked as a marsh, but it is now reclaimed and is under intensive cultivation. The artificiality of the harbour—and of that of Laodikeia-ad-Mare—is emphasized by H. Seyrig, 'Séleucos I'.

[4] This is the conclusion to be drawn from the two main accounts of the city: V. Chapot, 'Séleucie de Pierie', *Mémoires de la Societé des Antiquaires de France* 66, (1906), 149–224; *Antioch-on-the-Orontes* III, contains summary accounts of the excavations between 1937 and 1939 at the site.

[5] Pol. 5. 58. 3–11, a description of the city from a military point of view, which is clearly based on a first-hand account. It is not clear whether Pol. himself ever visited the city: F. Walbank, *A Historical Commentary on Polybius*, vol. I. (Cambridge, 1957), 586.

[6] The staircase is still visible: *Antioch-on-the-Orontes*, iii, fig. 4, p. 5.

has its back to the Amanus range, faces the sea, and to its south-east the plain stretches to and beyond the mouth of the Orontes. The plain is certainly fertile and productive, perhaps even sufficiently so for the city to feed itself, but it is small. The harbour's existence means that the city could also import food by sea if the need arose—from Kilikia, for example, or from the fertile Syrian coast around Laodikeia-ad-Mare, though we know of no actual instances of this. Water was similarly no problem: the city enclosed one stream and was flanked by others. Equally the rock of the hills and the trees which still cover the higher slopes provided abundant building materials and firm, well-drained foundations.

Yet the site is strange. The Orontes estuary is a hundred yards wide, and although it has a bar at the entrance, the water is nine feet deep inside the bar, and the river is navigable for a few kilometres inland.[7] It was a harbour which was already familiar to the Greeks who had frequented the trading post at al Mina-Sabouni in the past. Its disadvantage is that it is open to the westerly winds and is thus not a particularly good anchorage,[8] but at least it was already there, whereas the port at Seleukeia had to be excavated anew from the land, and was then, as its modern condition so clearly demonstrates, liable to be silted up by the streams from the mountain.[9] It is noticeable that the town of Samandag, which dominates this small coastal plain today, is centrally placed and close to the river mouth; the site of Seleukeia is now deserted but for a village on the mountainside.

Lattakia, on the other hand, is a vigorous and prosperous city to this day, and is modern Syria's main port. Its site is, however, just as artificial as that of Seleukeia. It is founded on an oblong area bounded on the east by a steep spine of rock running north–south, which still forms a distinct boundary to the built-up area.[10] Beyond this line of rock, to the east, the land falls to the wide flat valley along which the Nahr el-Kebir meanders, and beyond that again are the fertile hills of the Bargylos range and the coastal plain. To the north the land

---

[7] Admiralty, *Turkey*, p. 102; F. D. Chesney, *Narrative of the Euphrates Expedition* (1868), 172
[8] Admiralty, *Turkey*, p. 102.
[9] See note 3.
[10] Sauvaget, 'Plan', fig. 7, p. 97, and personal observation.

continues as a plain but not low-lying. To the west and south
is the sea.[11] The southern edge of the city's site is a rocky cliff-
bound cape; the western edge descends to a sandy shore. The
site was therefore a good one for building on, and provided
good and abundant limestone for building with. But the city
depended on its harbour; without shelter the cape is dangerous,[12] though in turn that cape does provide shelter for the
harbour itself from southerly winds. Before Laodikeia was
founded, the natural harbours at Ras Shamra and Ras el-
Basit were in use. They did not die when the new city was
built, but were gradually deserted during the succeeding
century or so.

A high proportion of the cities founded by Seleukos I have
been abandoned and replaced by developed urban centres on
different sites. Apamea's site consists of a tell, on a natural
hill, which was an Iron Age town and is the present town of
Qalat al-Mudiq.[13] This is the westernmost point of the
limestone plateau of the Jebel Zawiye, overlooking the Ghab
valley to the west and separated from a limestone plateau on
which the city of Apamea was laid out. The tell became the
city's acropolis. A wadi curves round to cover the southern
side and half of the eastern side of the city; the north and
north-east walls of the city face the plateau, which rises quite
gently away to the north. The limestone of the area is good
building stone, and there is water in a small lake below the
city.[14]

The plateau is a natural pastureland, but much less good
for arable crops.[15] The site today is mainly a sheep pasture,
with some arable farming on the western side.[16] The lake held
fish, and other fish could be caught in the Ghab,[17] which until

---

[11] Admiralty, *Syria*, p. 59, and personal observation.

[12] A Chinese ship was aground there at Easter 1983.

[13] See the photograph which is the frontispiece of J. C. Balty, *Guide d'Apamée*
(Brussels, 1981).

[14] J. and J. C. Balty, *Apamée de Syrie, bilan des recherches archéologiques, 1965–1968*
(Brussels, 1969), 62, and personal observation.

[15] Comte de Volney, *Voyages en Egypte et en Syrie* (Paris 1797), describes the area as
an abundant pasturage, as does Str. 16. 2. 10, in referring to the Seleukid royal stud
near the city.

[16] The sheep now wander among the classical ruins, recalling Gibbon's experience
in the Roman Forum.

[17] J. and J. C. Balty, 'Apamée de Syrie', *ANRW* 2, 8 (1977) refer happily to the

recently was an intermittent marsh—dry in late summer and autumn, flooded in winter and spring. Arable crops could be grown to the south of the city, in the area of the modern Sqalbiyé and Atcharné and south of the Orontes.

The city's communications were dictated by the form of the land. The north–south trend of the Bargylos mountains and the Ghab marsh, and the rapid reduction of rainfall as one moves eastwards meant that the main route through the city was along the edge of the plateau, north towards Jisr esh-Shogour, a bridging point over the Orontes, with a branch leading north-east towards Chalkis; to the south the route led across the Orontes at Atcharné and towards the Eleutheros gap and Arados; south-east a route led to Larissa and then along the Orontes towards, in the end, Damascus and Palestine.[18]

Like Seleukeia, and like Antioch until about AD 1800, the site of Apamea is virtually deserted today. Qalat al-Mudiq is a small town; the economic centre of the area are now Sqalbiyé, a long, sprawling market town five kilometres to the south, and off the plateau, and Atcharné, at the bridge over the Orontes, another ten kilometres southwards. This is reasonable, since these are the real route centres and the centres for the interchange of the local products: those of the Ghab, the plateau, the river to the east, and the arable land to the south. This economic situation is not in any essentials different from that in the Hellenistic period, though the population is denser now, and the Ghab has been drained recently and is now settled. That is, Apamea's site was not the best, considered from an economic point of view, and this must have been obvious at the time of foundation. However, the flat landscape below the plateau prevents easy fortification, and fortification

lake as 'très poissoneux', p. 105; fish was one of the city's exports in the Roman period: F. Heichelheim, *Roman Syria*, vol. iv, part II, of T. Frank (ed.), *An Economic Survey of Ancient Rome* (Baltimore, 1938), 154.

[18] The modern main route is to the east of this, heading due north from Hama through Khan Sheikhoun and Marrat en-Noman. This is an easier route than that along the edge of the plateau, but it can only exist once the area is already settled. It would seem that it was only in the Roman period that the route was developed, under military impetus. It continued in use after the decline in the local population in the Middle Ages because it was part of the Hajj route from Anatolia and Mesopotamia to Damascus. In the Hellenistic period, without settled villages and hence without supplies along the route, it would have been easier to stay close to the plateau edge.

would have seemed essential in Seleukos' situation in 300 BC, as it would to any people who intended to live in the city.

Antioch would appear to be a good example of a well-sited city, whose modern name of Antakya suggests a continuity with the past. Yet appearances deceive. It is true that Antakya is on the same site as Antioch, that modern Antakya's streets are in several instances clearly based on those of the Roman period, and that its ancient acropolis is still a military post. But the modern Antakya is in fact a new creation, dating from about AD 1800, at which date the site had been deserted for almost half a millenium.[19] The modern correspondence in streets is due to the survival of ruins; the earliest part of the new town, the old *suq* by the bridge, totally ignores the ancient layout of the city.[20]

The site is now a bridge-town, a local market, and an administrative centre. In the Seleukid state it was, first and foremost, a replacement for Antigoneia. It was established on the bank of the Orontes, at the foot of a steep mountain on top of which the acropolis was placed. The site had a number of awkward features. It is to some extent liable to flooding and the two streams which flow from the mountain are violent and capable of bringing down quantities of debris: they had to be diverted and canalized.[21] The city is in a corner of the plain from which it drew its supplies. (Antigoneia had been more central.) The acropolis is separated from the city proper by a steep slope, and eventually the two had to be attached to one another by long walls.[22] On the other hand, the city was at the junction of the economic zones of the plain and the mountain; it was close to the route along the Orontes valley to the sea and Seleukeia; it receives a strong, refreshing, and invigorating breeze on summer afternoons along that valley;[23] it has good water supplies in the river and the streams.

[19] J. Weulersse, 'Antioche, essai de Géographie urbaine', *Bulletin des études orientales* 4, (1934), 28–9.

[20] Ibid., 28.

[21] The Princeton excavators took notes of the 1938 floods, which were local to Antioch, and in particular they remarked on the destructive power of the streams which flow down from Mount Silpion: *Antioch-on-the-Orontes* iii. 5–6.

[22] The date of these walls is not clear, and they may be Roman; cf. Downey, *Antioch*, plate 11 for the dating and sequence of the city walls.

[23] It has been suggested that the main street was laid out to take advantage of this breeze (Downey, *Antioch*, p. 72) but since the direction of the street is the obvious one from a geographical point of view, meteorology is perhaps not necessarily the reason.

Nevertheless, when he had the first choice of site, Antigonos had chosen differently, and once Antioch ceased to be a political centre, after the Mamluk conquest in AD 1268, it very quickly faded away into ruins.[24] In economic terms, that is, the city is not well sited. Its nineteenth century revival is due to its bridge, and its modern growth to the particular political circumstances which made it the capital of the Hatay.

Seleukeia-Zeugma's function was exemplified in its name. It was founded at the place where Seleukos I built his bridge over the Euphrates to connect his new Syrian lands with the older Mesopotamian territories. It was thus a nodal point in the communication system of the Seleukid state, with routes radiating from it, but principally westwards to the Syrian cities and eastwards to Edessa and beyond. The river itself is not a good medium for communication, being swift and turbulent;[25] nor is its valley really satisfactory as a land route, since its level plain is liable to flood in the spring and early summer, and then to be marshy for shorter or longer periods.

This Seleukeia was built at a point where the river turns through a ninety-degree bend.[26] The erosion of the right bank had brought the river close to a hill, Balkis Tepe, which rose 200 metres over the river in no more than half a kilometre. The left (east) bank, by contrast, was low and flat, rising no more than 30 or 40 metres in the first kilometre.[27] The city was founded so as to include the hill of Balkis Tepe, and the bridge was put across the river at the foot of the hill. On the left bank was built Apamea, which by the time of Strabo, Pliny and Ptolemy was under Parthian rule and so had come to be regarded as a separate city, or at least as a separate settlement.[28] In the time of Seleukos, however, it was surely only a suburb of the main city, joined together by the bridge as the marriage knot joined Seleukos and Apama.

[24] S. Runciman, *History of the Crusades*, vol. iii (1954), 326, n. 2.
[25] D. G. Hogarth, *A Wandering Scholar* (London, 1896), describes (pp. 103–6) a hair-raising crossing somewhat upstream from Birejik and Zeugma, but one which the local people clearly took as a matter of course. It involved using a leaking boat, which was, essentially, cast adrift to cross at the mercy of the current.
[26] Wagner's plan (*Zeugma*, p. 527) shows this layout, based on a field survey, but not on excavation.
[27] Wagner, ibid. 93, fig. 8, cross-sections illustrating the differences between the two sides.
[28] Pliny, *HN* 5. 86. Isidore of Charax, i.

This is a point which needs demonstrating, since the existence of two separate cities has been generally assumed.[29] The bridge was the reason for Seleukeia's existence as a city. If the bridge had been put elsewhere, the city would have been elsewhere as well, for the city guarded the bridge. The acropolis on the Balkis Tepe was the city's acropolis, but it was also the headquarters of the royal garrison whose prime function was to guard the bridge. Possession of that bridge gave the Seleukids constant access to the east, and, later, gave the Parthians easy access to the west. But the eastern bank— that is, Apamea—did not have an acropolis, and its size was only a quarter of that of the western half, Seleukeia proper (see Map 6(*f*)). Yet Apamea was just as clearly designed to guard the bridge as was Seleukeia. No military commander could consider dividing responsibility between the two sides; that is, Apamea must have been under the authority of the military commander whose head-quarters will have been in the acropolis in Seleukeia. And that commander, in order to perform his task efficiently, must have had control over the acropolis, of the walls on both banks, and of the bridge itself. It would obviously be dangerous to insist that one military commander deal with two separate cities. Thus, taking Apamea's small area into account, the obvious conclusion to be drawn is that Apamea was a suburb of Seleukeia. Once the river became the international boundary in the time of the Seleukid collapse, and then again in the time of Pompeius, Apamea *did* become a separate political entity. In Parthian hands it would be garrisoned, just as Seleukeia, on the right bank, had a Roman garrison, and the bridge became the international frontier.

The position of Seleukeia-Zeugma has many resemblances · to that of the present-day main crossing point of the Euphrates at Birejik, but in reverse. At Birejik the high bank is on the east, and the hill is crowned by an astonishing castle, while the west bank is low and thinly peopled. The land is very similar for both cities: on the Syrian side it is moderately well cultivated, watered and productive, while the river will produce fish and the flood plain can be used for quick-growing

---

[29] As by, e.g., Jones, *CERP* 216.

crops after the floods recede.[30] On the Mesopotamian side the land is drier, more stony, and more suitable for pasture than for arable. The ancient bridge thus connected agricultural systems which were to some degree complementary, and the city became a market place for the exchange of products from diverse economic regions: from the two sides of the river, from the valley, from the river itself, and even perhaps from the hills to the north and from the desert-steppe to the south. This market function, however, only developed after the bridge was built and the city founded. The bridge was the reason for the city's existence, and the market simply followed. Further, when the bridge was removed, the city died.

The site chosen for the city of Chalkis was a tell, called Qinnesrin, at the end of a line of small hills about a kilometre from the Qoueiq river to the east and the same distance from the marshes of the Madkh to the south.[31] The hills provided the building stone which still litters the tell surface, and the land north along the river and to east and west is fertile and productive of cereal crops. The city's position between the impassable Madkh and the difficult hills made it a route centre, with roads leading north to Beroia, west to Antioch and south to Apamea. It was well placed to be the mediator between the products of the farmers and the nomads. The name of the city may be connected with the presence in the area of a source of copper, though there were other and better sources near Beroia and further north.[32] Whether, and how intensively, these sources were productive at the time and later is not known. It may be that Chalkis' mine was the only active one at the time of the city's foundations, the others being opened (or reopened) later.[33]

---

[30] The modern practice of agriculture in the valley is described by G. van der Kooij, 'Some Ethnographical Observations of Archaeological Import at the Village of Hodeidi, Syria', *LIEAO* 5 (July 1982), 80–4. The practice was perhaps not so very different in the Hellenistic period, though proof is another matter altogether.

[31] P. Monceau and L. Brossé, 'Chalcis ad Belum; notes sur l'histoire et les ruines de la ville', *Syria* 6, (1925, pp 339–50, especially the map, p. 345.

[32] R. J. Forbes, *Metallurgy in Antiquity*, (Leiden, 1950), 300. J. D. Muhly, 'Copper and Tin: The Distribution of Mineral Resources and the Nature of the Metals Trade in the Bronze Age', *Transactions of the Connecticut Academy of Arts and Sciences* 43 (1973), 208–14, disputes the general conclusion that copper was mined near Aleppo, but the evidence does suggest that some at least was available.

[33] E. Herzfeld, *The Persian Empire* (Wiesbaden, 1968), 88.

The tell is at present deserted, though the lines of streets
and the outlines of buildings are clearly visible, as is the line of
the city wall on the east. The lower part of the city is occupied
by the modern village of Nebi Is, named for a Muslim saint
who is buried on one of the nearby hills. This village is
relatively new, for it consists almost entirely of the character-
istic conical-domed clay huts built in the nineteenth and early
twentieth centuries by the new settlers. These huts were built
without wood, since there was none available, and were often
founded on stones from the ancient sites nearby. That the new
settlers chose not to inhabit the high tell is perhaps a sign of its
awkward size, but the recent re-establishment of the village
emphasizes once more that this ancient site was deserted in
the early nineteenth century, and for a long time previously. It
is another site like Antioch.

Kyrrhos, on the other hand, is more reminiscent of
Seleukeia, being at present totally deserted. It was placed on a
hill, with extensive views all around, and next to a river. The
river, in fact, lies at the foot of the cliff on the top of which is
the city wall. Ancient, probably Byzantine, bridges still exist
in the near neighbourhood,[34] and the city was a notable route
centre, with roads leading off to the south-west and Antioch,
to the south-east and Beroia, east to Zeugma and the
Euphrates crossing, northerly into Kommagene, and west
towards Nikopolis and the Bagche Pass over the Amanus. The
hills around are fertile, multicoloured in the spring with the
red soil, white rock, green crops, under a blue and white sky;
given care, it is a productive land. As a site for a city, however,
it is awkwardly high, needing a climb from whatever direction
it is approached, and there seems to be no real reason to go *to*
the city rather than merely past it. The present road, in fact
little more than a farmer's track, avoids the site by going
round the city's hill to the south, though it does utilize the old
bridge. Food and water and building stone are thus easily
available, and routes converge. Yet there is no city there now,
nor anything more than a village for twenty kilometres all

[34] E. Frézouls, 'Recherches historiques et archélogiques sur la ville de Cyrrhus',
AAS 4 and 5, (1954–5), 121.

around.[35] Economically a city is not needed here and it is difficult to provide economic reasons for it in the past.

All these cities are, or have been, deserted since the end of the Roman period. Like Seleukeia, Zeugma and Kyrrhos are now totally deserted, while Antioch, Chalkis and Apamea have shrunk and have been recently reoccupied after long periods of desertion. In purely economic terms, that is to say, the sites of these cities are less than ideal. Urban centres have developed at different sites at some distance from Kyrrhos, Zeugma, and Apamea, as from Seleukeia. The same site has been reoccupied by nineteenth-century settlers at Antioch and Chalkis, but neither is more than a shadow of its ancient self. The increase in population and economic activity since *c.*AD 1830 has caused the two sites to be reoccupied, but only by a small market town and a village respectively.

The other cities have been occupied constantly since ancient times, on the pattern of Laodikeia-ad-Mare. The most notable is Aleppo, ancient Beroia. The site is close to the Qoueiq river, though a short distance from it to avoid floods. The walls enclosed two tells, one on the rocky hill which became the acropolis, the other occupied by a village.[36] Water was brought into the city by the canalization of a stream which was made to flow through the centre of the new city.[37] The city's food supplies could be produced locally: the river valley was cultivated along most of its length in this period,[38] and the land is capable of supporting vines and olives.[39] It

---

[35] City-growth at present might be inhibited by the proximity of the Turkish-Syrian boundary, just to the north of the site of Kyrrhos, though this has not seriously affected Killis, similarly close on the northern side, nor Azaz on the Syrian side.

[36] Sauvaget, *Alep*, ch. 4. The citadel has been 'sculpted' to a more regular shape since the city grew in importance. The tell is still visible as a hill in the old city, with the city wall cutting through a corner of it. The present wall at that point is the old Hellenistic one, facing the river. The city has expanded in every other direction except this.

[37] Sauvaget, *Alep*, pp. 45–6 demonstrates the close connection, in planning terms, of the street system, the walls and the canalized stream, thus implying that all three are part of the original layout of the Hellenistic city. S. Mazloum, *L'Ancien Canalisation d'Eau d'Alep* (Damascus, n.d.), rather suggests, but does not prove, that the canalization is pre-Hellenistic.

[38] This is the implication of the pottery evidence found by the Qoueiq Valley survey (chapter 1 and Appendix 3).

[39] Sauvaget, *Alep*, plate 49 shows land use in the immediate area of the city, *c.*AD 1940. This shows the land's potential use, not its actual Hellenistic use.

was on a route from Chalkis (and thus ultimately from
Antioch and Apamea) to Zeugma. It could provide, like
Chalkis and Zeugma, a suitable market place for the exchange
of arable and fruit produce for the animal products of the
steppe.

Also still occupied and modestly flourishing is Nikopolis,
now Islahiyé, and called, until fairly recently, Niboli.[40] The
town is on the lower slope of the Amanus, to the eastern side of
the valley of the Kara Su. It is the present economic centre of
a part of that valley. The river flows south-east between the
parallel mountain ranges of the Amanus and the Kurd Dagh,
and its valley is divided into two sections by a sinuous basalt
flow. The southern part of the valley has its centre at the town
of Kirikhan, now somewhat dominated by Antakya. The
northern section is Islahiyé's; further north the route divides
into a road heading west to cross the Bagche Pass, one leading
north–east to Marash, and another easterly road to Gaziantep
and Birejik. This last is the modern version of the route which
originally led through Kyrrhos to Doliche and Zeugma.

Islahiyé is thus some kilometres south of the natural road
junction, just as Nikopolis was.[41] The reason seems to be that
the site is a better market centre for the produce of the area.
This section of the valley is agriculturally productive, especially when irrigated, though it is marshy in parts where
neglected. The Kurd Dagh and the river valley provide
grazing for sheep and goats. The Amanus provides wood, and
there was a mine producing stibnite in the mountains between
Nikopolis and Alexandria.[42] Building stone came from the
mountains, too.

This half-valley formed a natural political unit, with its
market centre as the political capital. In the Iron Age the local
centre had been the city of Samal (the present Zincirli). That
had been wrecked as a city by the Assyrians, though minor
occupation continued into the Byzantine period.[43] Nikopolis
was about ten kilometres south-west, and on a different, less

---

[40] Jones, *CERP* 244; Niboli is still given as the name on the 1913 GSGS map.
[41] The present road junction—four routes—is all but deserted, yet it would seem
to be a natural urban growth point.
[42] Forbes, *Metallurgy in Antiquity*, p. 262.
[43] F. von Luschan *et al.*, *Ausgrabungen in Sendschirli* iv (Berlin, 1911).

exposed site, but it can legitimately be regarded as the political and economic successor to Samal.

The site of Hierapolis is one which is still occupied, as a small market town. It is at the highest point of an area of treeless rolling downland, in a hollow of land in which is a perennial pool of water of some depth.[44] The pool feeds a river which flows away north–eastwards to the Euphrates. The land is fertile, 'through which a plough could be driven for miles without striking a stone',[45] so food and water are both available, although it is close to the zone of transition between the well-watered land and the steppe. In this circumstance, one of the major assets was the perennial spring. There are suggestions that the surrounding land was wooded in the ancient world,[46] and if so this implies a higher rainfall and the possibility of agriculture, but there is no sign that the place was ever large or wealthy. The town lay on a major east–west land route, and Persian period remains show that this route was active in that period.

Certain conclusions emerge from these detailed descriptions. The first is that the ultimate failure rate of these cities is very high. Of the original eight which Seleukos founded, only two, Laodikeia and Beroia, have a record of continuous existence since 300 BC Two have died altogether, Seleukeia and Kyrrhos. The other four have revived in the last two centuries but before 1800 were as deserted as Seleukeia is now. Since in the long term the main functions of cities may change, but the economic basis will be the one constant factor, it is significant that it is the economic factor which most clearly has failed to sustain these cities. That is, they cannot have been planted on their chosen sites for economic reasons. Apamea has been deserted because it is economically more sensible to locate in the Orontes valley. Seleukeia died because there is a more sensible port a few miles away at the mouth of the Orontes. And so on.

[44] D. G. Hogarth, 'Hierapolis Syriae', *Annual of the British School at Athens* 14, (1907–8), an account written before the denser inhabitation which followed the First World War, but after the deliberate Turkish governmental policy of resettlement in the area had begun.

[45] Ibid. 186; G. Goossens, *Hierapolis de Syrie* (Louvain, 1943), 4 n. 2.

[46] M. B. Rowton, 'The Woodlands of Ancient Western Asia', *JNES* (1967), 261–77.

These economic factors were surely obvious to the planners. Their decision to abandon the site of Antigoneia has been confirmed by the fact that the site is still deserted, while their choice of Antioch's site, awkward though it is, is partly confirmed by its recovery since 1800. One aspect of their choice is clearly the deliberate decision to found their cities at economic junction zones, so ignorance of elementary economic geography is not a reason for their choice of uneconomic sites. There must be another reason.

Examination of the remaining plans and layout of the cities suggests—along with the situation in which Seleukos was placed politically and strategically in 300—that the dominating consideration governing the choice of site was military. There is a difficulty here, however, for the Hellenistic cities are all hidden beneath later accretions, either modern or Roman, and where excavation or investigation has taken place it has often concentrated on the abundant Roman remains. It is therefore necessary to begin by investigating the extent to which the Roman remains correspond to those of the preceding Hellenistic. In fact, in several cases it is possible to demonstrate that the elements of the Roman city plan are continuations from the Hellenistic, and in other cases this continuity can be seen to be probable, though proof is lacking; there are sufficient examples of this continuity of plan to make the general assumption that the Roman plan of a Syrian city is also that of the preceding Hellenistic city, at least in general terms, if not in every detail.

First, the question of continuity. Apamea provides the best example. The city was laid out on a sort of peninsula, more or less flat on top, with steep slopes on three sides. To the north the plateau slopes gently upwards away from the city; on that side alone there is no obvious line for the boundary of the city to take. If the city had expanded or contracted, it is here that the evidence will be found, not at any of the other sides, whose lines are fixed by the local geography. Two excavations in the city are relevant here: one was at the north gate, and the other at a site along the main street.[47] The north gate is shown to have Hellenistic foundations, though the visible remains are

---

[47] J. Mertens, 'Sondages dans la Grande Colonnade et sur l'Enceinte', *Colloque Apamée* 1, (Brussels, 1968), 68–71.

actually Roman. This confirms that the line of the north wall was the boundary of the Hellenistic city as well as of the Roman, and it also confirms the line of the main north–south street of the city. The second excavation, in that main street but in the centre of the city, found the Hellenistic surface below the Roman which is visible now, and so showed that the street itself is, in origin, of Hellenistic date. Since the street system is of the rectilinear type, the line of one street confirms the whole system. In these crucial instances, therefore, the two small excavations have shown that the Roman city has preserved the outline form of the preceding Hellenistic city, and that the city retained the same shape from its first planning.[48] The plan of the Roman city, in outline, is thus the plan laid out by the surveyors of Seleukos I at the foundation of the city.

Very much the same conclusions can be drawn from an excavation at Kyrrhos. Again, certain parts of the line of the circuit wall are inevitable, given the site, as is the position of the acropolis. At the foot of the outer wall of the acropolis, Hellenistic masonry has been located directly under the Roman, acting as the foundation of the later wall. The two types of masonry are quite distinct: the Roman is a yellow limestone cut into regular blocks and laid neatly in rows; the Hellenistic stone is white, and irregularly shaped—that is, 'polygonal' masonry.[49] The city is laid out between a hill which became the acropolis, on the west, and the river, whose cliff-like bank forms the city's boundary on the eastern side. The main street lies north–south, passing the foot of the acropolis. The boundaries of the city to north and south are less clear, though the example of Apamea suggests that the present (Roman) walls are also the Hellenistic boundaries. The most doubtful boundary is to the north, where the land is flat and there are ancient remains outside the walls.[50] The

---

[48] Apamea is a clearer case than most because it has since been deserted, except for the acropolis, which is the present town of Qalat al-Mudiq. It is the acropolis, of course, which would be the most informative archaeologically, but only the lower slopes have been investigated—the dense occupation of the modern town precludes much work there now.

[49] Frézouls, 'Recherches historiques' (note 34), p. 121.

[50] These do not seem to have been investigated. They could, of course, constitute a necropolis.

boundary could have been mobile along that side, but only
there; all the other sides and the acropolis were fixed in the
earliest years, and were continuous into the Roman
period.

At Seleukeia-Zeugma, Wagner's survey has located a city
wall through the middle of the area which was inhabited in
the Roman period.[51] To the west of this wall he located the
site of the Roman legionary camp, while the Roman civilian
city is to the east. (The river flows east–west at this point.)
That wall connected the Balkis Tepe, the hill which was
presumably the acropolis, with the bank of the Euphrates; the
bridge-head was thus included within the city walls, as might
have been expected. The wall is thus best interpreted as
marking the line of the Hellenistic city boundary; however,
much of the rest of the circuit on the Syrian side is conjectural.
The eastern head of the bridge was protected by the suburb of
Apamea, laid out on the flat east bank of the river, in the
manner of a barbican. This shows no signs of alteration in size
at any date, despite its small size. Here again, therefore, the
Roman wall was built on the line of that of the Hellenistic
period, in all probability.

Seleukeia-in-Pieria is a huge site, which was clearly
designed to enclose both the port and the acropolis within the
city, even though much of the interior was too steep ever to be
inhabited or built on. Further, the city's early importance did
not survive its capture by Ptolemy III in 246, and so the huge
area enclosed by the walls was an original foundation
decision, for at no later date was the city ever important
enough to warrant such a size. The visible walls are of Roman
period construction, but their line is most likely to be of
Seleukid date, thus preserving the shape given to the city at
the moment of its foundation.[52]

Laodikeia-ad-Mare presents a very similar set of conditions
to those at Seleukeia-in-Pieria. They were contemporaries,
and both had artificial harbours.[53] At Laodikeia the acropolis

[51] Wagner, *Zeugma*, p. 94.

[52] Some 'polygonal' masonry in the eastern wall on the middle terrace is reported
by V. Chapot, 'Séleucie de Pierie', *Memoires de la Societe des Antiquaires de France* LXVI,
1907, pp. 190–1, from Père Bourquenond, *études . . . publiées par les PP. de la Compagnie
de Jésus* (Paris, 1860), 403–26 and 583–612. This report has not been confirmed since,
yet it is not at all unlikely.

[53] Seyrig, 'Séleucos I', pp. 305–7.

was on the highest point of the spine of rock which still more or less marks the eastern edge of the town. Both harbour and acropolis are presumably part of the original foundation, and their positions virtually dictate the lines of the city walls, one leading due south from the acropolis along the continuation of that spine of rock, the other due west from the acropolis to the sea north of the harbour.[54] The coincidence of the Roman and Hellenistic city walls has not been archaeologically demonstrated, but it seems to be very likely.[55]

Of the cities of Seleukos I, therefore, two—Apamea and Kyrrhos—can be shown, on present archaeological evidence, not to have altered their dimensions between their foundations and the Roman period, and three others—Seleukeia-Zeugma, Seleukeia-in-Pieria and Laodikeia-ad-Mare—lack the archaeological evidence of this, but in each case the city layout argues strongly that they remained unaltered. By contrast, it is clear that the size and shape of Antioch did change very significantly during the Hellenistic period, for Strabo reports that it was enlarged twice,[56] and research has identified a whole sequence of walls.[57] Antioch is thus a clear exception to the rule derived from the other five cities.

None of the other city-sites has been investigated as much as Antioch, and none nearly enough to provide further evidence on this problem, but, equally, no other city of Syria can be shown to have expanded in the Hellenistic period. Of the cities for which evidence is available, therefore, Antioch stands out as the exception. In all other cases, the evidence is that the Hellenistic city plans are the same as those of the Roman period.

The continuity does not, however, extend to all the details of the city plan. It has not been possible to find a single example of a Hellenistic theatre in Syria, though there are Roman examples in many cities.[58] The only stadium known in

[54] Sauvaget, 'Plan'.

[55] A series of small discoveries and rescue excavations is reported by G. Saadé, 'Explorations archéologiques de Latta quié', *AAAS* 26 (1976) 9–29. Most of the finds are Roman in date. The find spots are mainly located north of the ancient north wall, and most finds are funerary. Little has been discovered inside the ancient city.

[56] Str. 16. 2. 4; G. L. Downey, 'Strabo on Antioch: Notes on his Method', *TAPA* 72. (1941), 85–95.

[57] Downey, *Antioch*, pp. 616–20, and the map, plate 11.

[58] E. Frézouls, 'Les Théâtres antiques de l'Orient Syrien', *Atti del VIII Congresso Internazionale di Archeologia Classica* (Paris, 1963), 339–51.

Syria is at the Phoenician city of Marathos.[59] In grosser
elements, some continuity does exist. The street system at
Apamea has been unchanged from the city's foundation to the
Byzantine period, and the positions of the gates at Laodikeia-
ad-Mare suggest the same continuity. Yet no clear street
system of any period has been revealed at Seleukeia-in-Pieria,
which is admittedly a difficult site, and no Hellenistic streets
are known at Antioch, though the assumption of a rectilinear
layout has been made by the excavators, with the implication
that it was originally Hellenistic.[60] The main colonnaded
street is Roman in architecture, a gift to the city from Herod
the Great,[61] and the expansions of the city mean that the
street layout may well be Roman too in many respects. At
Kyrrhos a rectilinear layout of Roman date may reflect an
earlier Hellenistic pattern.[62] Sauvaget has argued for a
Hellenistic date of the rectilinear street system he detected at
Beroia,[63] but it has not been demonstrated in an archaeological investigation. Despite these hesitations, the existence
of such street patterns can perhaps be assumed in these new
cities, the more so as evidence from other places—Dura-
Europos, for example,[64] or Damascus[65]—testifies to the
contemporary practice elsewhere.

There are, however, no doubts about two items of the plan
in all cases: the city walls and the acropolis. In particular all
the acropoleis are large and dominating. At Antioch it was on
the mountain which frowns over the whole city; the separation
of the city from its citadel meant—as its siege and capture by
the Crusaders in AD 1097 showed so clearly[66]—that the
capture of the citadel necessarily led to the fall of the city, but
the citadel could hold out alone even if the city had fallen. At

[59] It is one of the most visible remains of the ancient city, close to the (excavated)
temple.

[60] Downey, *Antioch*, plates 7 and 8, for example.

[61] Jos *AJ*, 16. 5. 3; Downey, *Antioch*, pp. 173–4.

[62] Frézouls, 'Recherches historiques' (note 34), plate 1.

[63] Sauvaget, *Alep*, pp. 40–2.

[64] M.I. Rostovtzeff *et al.* (eds.), *The Excavations at Dura-Europus*, Preliminary
Report, Ninth Season, part 1, has a Hellenistic city plan at fig. 12.

[65] J. Sauvaget, 'Le Plan antique de Damas', *Syria* 26 (1947), pp. 314–58;
C. Watzinger and K. Witzinger, *Damaskus: Die antike Stadt* (Berlin, 1921), map 3; and
see F. E. Peters, 'City-Planning in Greco-Roman Syria: Some New Considerations',
Damaszener Mitteilungen 1, (1983), pp. 269–77.

[66] S. Runciman, *A History of the Crusades*, i. 213–64.

Apamea, the acropolis is an outcrop separated from the city by a deep-cut stream bed; it is in fact the tell of the city of the Bronze and Iron Ages, and is now still a fortified town of distinctly antique aspect, very difficult to approach.

At Beroia the acropolis developed into the extraordinary sculptured fortress which is now the citadel of Aleppo; in area it is perhaps a fifth or a sixth of that of the whole Hellenistic city. At Kyrrhos its area is less but its domination is just as total: the city-plan shows that the outline was drawn deliberately to include the steep little hill which is crowned by the acropolis fortress. At Chalkis, the acropolis was the enormous tell of the pre-existing city. At Seleukeia-Zeugma, again, a hill was the acropolis, and the bridge was carefully placed just below that hill.

This pattern is consistent. At every city founded by Seleukos I whose layout can be discerned the acropolis has an overwhelmingly dominating role. There are other similarities as well. In no case is the acropolis entirely enclosed within the city; in every example known the acropolis is at a corner or on a side of the city. That is, it could communicate with the land outside the city independently. The conclusion seems inescapable: the acropolis of every one of Seleukos I's cities was expressly designed to dominate and control the city it overlooked. This says volumes about the expectations of king and citizens.

PART 2

After Seleukos

4

THE CITIES AND THE VILLAGES

THE central event in the urban history of Syria was Seleukos I's decision in 301 or 300 to establish a series of ten cities in the land. Before that, there were a small number of urban centres in Syria; after his reign several other sites developed into cities; but Seleukos' work was crucial.

It was not, however, final. The cities he had founded changed over the next three centuries. It is scarcely possible to write the history of any of these cities (except for Antioch[1]) in any detail, but they can be considered as a group of urban entities, and broad developments can be distinguished. On an individual basis it is just possible to indicate which cities declined and which grew during the long Seleukid period. Refined analyses are out of the question, and the reasons for the changes which are detectable are to a large extent speculative. Nevertheless the exercise is worthwhile, for it reveals a good deal about the effectiveness of Seleukos' work.

Three sizes of urban settlement can be discerned in Syria by the end of the reign of Seleukos I. Two of these are quite straightforward. A comparison of the outline plans of Apamea, Seleukeia-in-Pieria, and Laodikeia-ad-Mare with the suggested outline of the earliest Antioch shows that all four were very much of a size (see Maps 6(a)–(d)). Seleukeia was the largest, about 300 hectares,[2] but it was on a very mountainous site which reduced its effectively usable space. The other three were very similar in size. Antioch was perhaps 150 hectares, plus an uncertain area for Strabo's second quarter,[3] which Downey gives as about 75 hectares[4]—a

---

[1] Antioch has been well treated, notably in Downey, *Antioch*, and his shorter version, *Ancient Antioch*, (Princeton, NJ, 1963). The only other city in Syria with individual treatment is Rey-Coquais, *Arados*. Wagner *Zeugma* is not a history, but an archaeological work.

[2] My own calculation, from the outline map in Seyrig, 'Séleucos I', p. 304, fig. 4.

[3] Str. 16. 2. 4.

[4] Downey, *Antioch*, p. 79.

possible total of about 225 hectares. Apamea was about 205 hectares,[5] and Laodikeia about 220.[6] Making allowance for Seleukeia's steep slopes, therefore, it is clear enough that all four cities were laid out to be very similar in size. These four, then, constitute the group of largest cities.

The second group is of cities which again are all similar in size. It consists of the original four cities planted between Antioch and the Euphrates. A comparison of the outlines of Kyrrhos, Chalkis, Beroia, and Seleukeia-Zeugma (including its trans-Euphratean suburb of Apamea) shows that these four were again much the same size, all of them being between 65 and 80 hectares.[7] (See Maps 6(*e*) and (*f*).)

There was also another city in Syria which can be fitted into this group. This was Arados, the island-city off the coast in the south of Seleukos' new land. In actual area, Arados island is only about half the size of Beroia and its colleagues, but the city is known to have been densely inhabited, with houses of several storeys.[8] Arados' denser population puts it into the second group, despite its lack of physical size (Map 6 (*g*)).

This is just one of the many ways in which Arados provides a contrast with the other cities of Syria. It is time to consider this city, for it is that very contrast which in turn provides a useful tool for understanding those other cities. In just about every possible way it was different from them: in site, in size, in situation, in plan, in geography, in economic function, in history, and in population. This difference continued to manifest itself all through the Hellenistic period.

The city was built on the largest of a string of small islands which lie parallel to the Syrian coast. The island is only 800 metres across at its widest and in the ancient world it was, as it is now, fully built over. Its food supply, therefore, must needs come from the mainland, though its water supply was an even bigger problem. There are wells on the island, and

[5] Ibid. Downey's calculations are suspect. His conversion of hectares to acres is wrong for Apamea, and the hectare figure is misprinted. He also gives a size for Antigoneia, but since the *shape* of that city is not known, no calculations can be made.

[6] Sauvaget, 'Plan', p. 103.

[7] Kyrrhos: E. Frézouls, 'Recherches historiques et Archéologiques sur la Ville de Cyrrhus', *AAS* 4–5, (1954–5), plate 1; Chalkis: R. Monceau and L. Brossé, 'Chalcis ad Belum', *Syria* 6, 1925, 339–50; Beroia: Sauvaget, *Alep*, plates 52 and 53 in vol. ii; Zeugma: Wagner, *Zeugma*, Map 2.

[8] Str. 16. 2. 13.

storage cisterns, but the most renowned source in antiquity—though hardly typical—was a submarine spring between the island and the mainland, which could be tapped in emergencies.[9] The island is low-lying and the inhabited part was protected by an enormous double wall. This was a defence against the sea, rather than against any human enemies. A survey of the walls has shown that they were carefully maintained throughout the Persian and Hellenistic periods, though they dated, probably, from the Iron Age.[10] The port faced eastwards, towards the mainland, so that the island provided shelter from the westerly winds from the sea. This port consists now of a shelving beach, though it was probably supplemented by an artificial mole which partially enclosed the harbour in its ancient state.[11]

The island-city and -port was extended by its mainland suburb, Marathos, which developed a little to the south of Arados, behind the coastal sand dunes, where a stream reached the sea. The combination of the two settlements meant that the whole strait between them acted as a port. Marathos became the terminus of the overland route from the interior, and it was thus the place at which goods were loaded for transfer to Arados, no doubt in small boats or lighters.

Marathos is a larger site than that of Arados, but for most of its existence as an urban settlement it was subordinated to the island-city. Its periods of independence were generally brief and came about not as the result of local initiative by Marathians but by an action of the ruler of the mainland. Even in times of separation, the two cities were in a symbiotic relationship, each essential to the other: Marathos, apart from being the terminus of the overland trade route, was also the nearest source of the mainland products which the island required; Arados was the commercial centre, the best port of the coast, and the possessor of the marine and capital resources needed for trade. The two are therefore best considered as a single urban settlement, separated by a wider-than-usual stretch of water.

---

[9] Ibid.

[10] H. Frost, 'The Arwad Plans, 1964: A Photogrammetric Survey of Marine Installations', *AAAS* 16. (1966), 16–17.

[11] Admiralty, *Syria*, p. 61, and see the photograph in A. Poidebard and J. Lauffray, *Sidon: Aménagements antiques du Port de Saida*, (Beyrouth, 1951), plate 3, 1.

The reef which provided some shelter for the coast was also, of course, a danger to ships. Many were wrecked in the narrow passage between two of the southernmost visible rocks, the pottery which was spilled dating from the fifth century BC to the sixth AD.[12] There are also reefs north and south of Marathos between the main reef and the coast. It was no doubt for this reason that the centre of the mainland activities of the Aradian merchants shifted northwards to Antarados. This is not in its natural state a good harbour, unlike Marathos, but ships could reach it without going through the reef,[13] which was an important consideration when ships became bigger and cargoes therefore more valuable during the Hellenistic and into the Roman periods.[14] The growth of Antarados took place at the expense of Marathos, which was deserted by the first century AD.[15] Thus Antarados, like Marathos, was also a mainland suburb of Arados rather than a separate urban site.

When united, therefore, Arados and Marathos must be regarded as a single city, and in combination, the double city is much larger than those in the second group of Seleukid cities. Arados' own insular area was constant and relatively small, but the addition of the mainland territory of Marathos more than doubled that area,[16] and the density of population was much greater. When united, then, Arados-Marathos must be counted as one of the group of cities of the large size, with Antioch and the rest; when separated, on the other hand, the two cities could only rank with the smaller second group.

The problem of Arados raises a point which strikes anyone who studies cities: to describe the size of a city by reference

[12] Frost (note 10), p. 27.

[13] Today Tartus has an artificial harbour, but small boats still use the jetties of the old town.

[14] J. Rougé, *Ships and Fleets of the Ancient Mediterranean*, trans. S. Freezer (Middletown, Conn., 1981), 74–8.

[15] S. Abdul-Hak, 'Découvertes archéologiques récentes dans les sites greco-romains de Syrie', in *Atti del VII Congreso Internazionale de Archeologia Classica* (Rome, 1961), iii. 32–6, 'Amrith'.

[16] The actual boundaries, or even the general extent of Marathos and Antarados are not known. Antarados is buried under modern Tartus; Marathos' site is open and has been investigated by archaeologists. Dunand in 1954 promised a plan of the site in a future publication, but this has not yet appeared. A sketch plan, but with no indication of boundaries for the city, is in Saliby, 'Essai de restitution du Temple d'Amrit', *AAAS* 21 (1971), 284.

only to the perimeter of its walls is to use a very crude indicator indeed. There is nothing which says that the walls marked the true margins of these cities. A single glance at the site of Seleukeia-in-Pieria is sufficient to show that the city did not spread evenly over the area enclosed by the walls, and, in fact, it would appear that more or less sizeable parts of the interiors of many cities were uninhabited. Sauvaget's plan of Hellenistic Beroia assumed as much.[17] At Antioch the walls which attached the acropolis on top of Mount Silpion to the city down by the river enclosed the steep and inaccessible slopes and crags of the mountain. This situation is less obvious at Apamea and Laodikeia, but the examples of the other two large cities are sufficient to make the point.

A better indication of city-size would be the number of inhabitants each contained, but the size of the population of these Syrian cities and towns is not known with any precision. There are, however, some indications which have been used. Calculations, for example, have been made for Antioch. The basis is the information from Malalas[18] that Antigoneia had a population of 5,300 citizens. These had originally come from Macedon—presumably demobilized soldiers—and Athens. Seleukos is reported to have transferred these colonists to Antioch,[19] and so the argument goes that Antioch began with 5,300 citizens.[20] Two other figures have been used to provide some confirmation for this number. Polybios reports the free population of Seleukeia-in-Pieria as being 6,000 strong in 219.[21] Then, at the same time, a contingent of the Seleukid army which Polybios calls the 'Kyrrhestai', 6,000 in number, rebelled,[22] and these in turn have been equated with the citizen-soldiers of Kyrrhos.[23] So from these three figures the impression develops that the normal population of a Seleukid city in Syria was about 6,000 citizens. This figure in turn is very close to that suggested by Plato as being the ideal

[17] Sauvaget, *Alep*, plate 52.
[18] Mal. 201.
[19] Str. 16. 2. 4.
[20] e.g., Downey, *Antioch*, pp. 81–2, Jones, *CERP* 243.
[21] Pol. 5. 61. 1.
[22] Pol. 5. 50. 7–8.
[23] B. Bar-Kockva, *The Seleukid Army* (Cambridge, 1976), 30–31, implicitly equates the citizenry with the military contingent.

number of citizens for a city.[24] Thus reality appears to reinforce theory, and even, one might hazard, to be based on the theory.

This structure is, in fact, built on very insecure foundations. Not one of the figures (except Plato's, perhaps) stands up to serious examination. In the case of Antigoneia, the figure of 5,300 is from the sixth century AD, and while there is no reason for doubting it, other than its very late date, it is as well to remember that there is a considerable degree of doubt about exactly where these people went when Antigoneia was dismantled by Seleukos. Diodoros Sikulos says they were sent to Seleukeia-in-Pieria,[25] and a connection between Antigoneia and Seleukeia has also been noticed in that the mint of Antigoneia seems to have gone to Seleukeia, while Antioch's mint seems to be more closely connected with Seleukeia-on-the-Tigris than with Antigoneia.[26] It is also hard to believe that all the citizens of Antigoneia tamely did as they were told by the man who had just killed their own king and destroyed their own city; nor is it easy to believe that Seleukos would concentrate a large body of potential rebels in his main fortified coastal city at a time when Demetrios, whom many of them might well regard as their rightful king, was still alive and active and in control of a great fleet. To transfer the figure of 5,300 from Antigoneia to Antioch is thus misleading, and is very likely to be wrong.

In the case of Seleukeia-in-Pieria, Polybios' figure of 6,000 refers not to the citizens but to the 'free population', a much vaguer term. Further, that 6,000 did not include an unknown number of exiles from the city, for he is referring to the situation inside the city at the end of the Ptolemaic occupation. The 6,000 were only those living in the city when it was captured by Antiochos III in 219; the exiles then returned and were restored to 'their civic rights and their property'.[27] Thus the figure of 6,000 has no relevance to the number of

---

[24] Plato, *Laws*, 738 A, suggested 5040 families, which, as G. R. Morrow points out (*Plato's Cretan City* (Princeton, NJ 1960), 128–30) means a male citizen population of 10,000 or 12,000, and a total population, with women, children, slaves, and metics, of about 80,000.

[25] Diod. 20. 47.

[26] Newell, *WSM*, 89.

[27] Pol. 5. 61. 1

actual citizens, which may be either higher or lower than that—though one may assume that it is the minimum and that after 219 the number of citizens was considerably greater than 6,000.

The same number recurs in Polybios' brief notice of the revolt of the Kyrrhestai at Apamea in 220. These are nowhere said to be citizens of Kyrrhos, and the equation depends both on assuming that the Kyrrhestai came from Kyrrhos, which is reasonable enough, *and* that Kyrrhos' army contingent consisted of all its citizens, which is not so reasonable. Some citizens will have stayed at home, on guard in the city, or ill, or reluctant—the revolt demonstrates their disaffection—or too old, or even too young, to fight. Nor is it reasonable to assume that such a contingent consisted only of citizens. The figure is therefore of little use for any purpose other than that given by Polybios: it was the approximate number of troops in the contingent called the Kyrrhestai in 220.[28]

There is a further point about these figures. They are all very similar, and the further step has usually been taken to suggest that 6,000 was the normal citizen population of a Seleukid colony.[29] Yet of the three cities, Antioch and Seleukeia-in-Pieria were physically three times the size of Kyrrhos. There must have been *some* relationship between the size of a city's population and the size of the area its walls enclosed; at the very least one would expect that the population of Antioch and Seleukeia would be a good deal larger, to put it no stronger, than that of Kyrrhos. For all these reasons it must be concluded that the recurrence of the figure 6,000 is not relevant to the size of the population of the Syrian cities.

There is still a further problem to consider, this time one which is apparently peculiar to Antioch. The initial settlement of that city is a good deal more complicated than the mere transfer of the Antigoneians, even if that were certain. Strabo reports[30] that Antioch was divided in his day into four parts,

---

[28] The fact that Pol. wrote in Italy should be a warning; he frequently used such a figure as 6,000, and that was the establishment of a Roman legion. Its very repetition is suspicious: it might be better translated by some such term as 'division' or 'regiment'. F. W. Walbank, *A Historical Commentary on Polybius* (Oxford, 1957–79), does not discuss this matter.

[29] As for example by B. Bar-Kockva, *The Seleukid Army*, pp. 30–1.

[30] Str. 16. 2. 4.

and that the first quarter was founded by Seleukos I for those people he had transferred from Antigoneia. These Antigone-ians were certainly part of the original inhabitants of Antioch, for the statue of the *Tyche* of Antigoneia was transferred to Antioch, and it is known to have been there later.[31] This is not to say that all the Antigoneians went to Antioch, for some credence has to be given to the evidence that Seleukeia was a destination for them as well. The site of Antigoneia was included within the city-territory of Antioch,[32] and so it would be quite logical for the defunct city's goddess to remain with Antioch. So it can be assumed that some thousands of the first people in Antioch came from Antigoneia.

It is the second of Antioch's quarters as defined by Strabo which is the real difficulty. He says that it 'was founded by the multitude of settlers'.[33] These 'settlers' are often thought of as Syrians—that is, native Aramaic-speakers[34]– though they are not distinguished in this way as settling at any of the other Syrian cities, and the same term is used by Strabo to describe the people who had been transferred from Antigoneia.[35] There seems no reason to assume that Strabo meant anything other than that these were more Greeks and Macedonians, extra to those from Antigoneia. It does not really seem likely that Seleukos would found a city named for his own father and populate it only with citizens from the city of his greatest enemy. For safety's sake, also, he will have planted people of his own in the new city, people whose loyalty was first of all to him, and they would preferably be in a majority. It would make good sense, in fact, to divide the Antigoneians into smaller groups; this may be the explanation for the confusion in the sources over where they went, to Antioch or to Seleukeia—the answer is, perhaps, to both, where they were joined by other 'settlers'. So the question of numbers becomes

[31] Mal. 201.
[32] Dio Cassius 40. 29. 1.
[33] Str. 16. 2. 4.
[34] Jones, *CERP* 242–3; Downey, *Antioch*, p. 94.
[35] The word Str. uses, translated as 'settlers', is *oikotoron*. This is a nice vague term, which is not citizens or colonists. Yet it can only mean people who had moved from one place which had been their home, in order to settle in Antioch. These may well have been Syrians, but the context is the settlement of a new Greek city, and the most economical understanding demands that the words be interpreted to mean Greeks other than the former inhabitants of Antigoneia.

more difficult the more it is considered, and the answer more
indefinite the longer the sources are considered. For Antioch
no reliable figure can be seriously suggested.

Little or no reliance can be placed, therefore, on the three
sets of figures which have been used to estimate city-
populations. But perhaps some other information can be
extracted from them. The figure of 6,000 free inhabitants
which Polybios gives for Seleukeia-in-Pieria can be regarded
as a minumum; soon afterwards the exiles returned to increase
that number. But who exactly these 6,000 were is not clear.
Did the figure include women? Non-Greeks? The only group
explicitly excluded are slaves. Beyond that there is the
question of what multiplier should be used to reach a figure
for the total number of inhabitants—if, that is, the number
refers to men alone. It is perhaps more useful to consider the
figure of 5,300 Greeks and Macedonians who are said to be
the citizen-population of Antigoneia. This, with wives,
children, and so on, has been calculated to give a population
of about 25,000.[36] The city had a circumference of seventy
stades,[37] about eight miles, which is a little smaller than the
suggested circuit of the wall of the first Antioch, or that of
Apamea without the citadel.[38] A population of only 25,000 for
such a large city-area is credible only as a starting figure, and
does not seem reasonable for Antioch in, say, 280 BC, at the
end of Seleukos' reign, when it had been established for
twenty years. Still less is it credible for Antioch when that city
had become the effective capital of the whole kingdom in, say,
170 BC The uncertainty of these figures and calculations
defeats any attempt to deduce the size of any particular city in
Syria from them. The one indication of relative size is thus
their physical size, as shown by their walled outlines. This
means that it is necessary to ignore the possible variations in
density of occupation at each city. Since the unit of measurement is so crude, it is just as well to restrict the classification of

[36] Downey, *Antioch*, p. 82.
[37] Diod. 20. 47. 5.
[38] The figure for the circumference of the wall is no help for working out the area
enclosed by that wall, since we do not know the actual shape of the city. If it was
triangular, as seems to be implied by the suggested confluence-site, then 70 stades
would mean an enclosed area of over 3.5 sq. km. But there seems little profit in
comparisons without knowledge of the basic plan.

size to the very simple measures of 'large', 'medium', and 'small', at least for the moment.

Seleukos I had undertaken an enormous task, and it is worth realizing the sheer scale of the project. The four large cities, named for Seleukos' family, were all—taking the areas within the outline of the walls—approaching the size of contemporary Alexandria-by-Egypt, and Seleukeia-in-Pieria was just about the same size as Rome of the Servian walls. The second ranked cities—Beroia, Chalkis, and so on—are all bigger than contemporary Miletos. In a sense, Seleukos I might be said to have founded four Romes and six Miletoi, in a very few years. That is, of course, misleading, for none of these Syrian cities was ever, it seems, full of inhabitants, with the exception of Antioch, which had to be enlarged. But it does make the question of the number of inhabitants even more difficult. Even assuming a city-population of 6,000 Greeks, just for the sake of argument, and therefore, a total population of about 25,000 settlers for each of these cities, the total of new inhabitants is a quarter of a million. But the figure of 6,000 is a minimum, and quite inadequate even as a minimum for the large cities. Assuming 6,000 to be the typical citizen population of only the middle-sized cities, and allowing the larger cities a population commensurate with their physical size, then the four great cities must be thought of as having well over 50,000 free inhabitants each, and now the number of new inhabitants moving into Syria in the reign of Seleukos I approaches half a million. Moving and settling these quantities of people was an enormous undertaking.

These 'large' and 'medium' cities, founded or not by Seleukos, can be discussed in some detail, because their very size generated records, even if the information reaching us is meagre and distorted. Yet there was also a further size of city, which can be classified as 'small'. For a change, it will be convenient to begin with older-established settlements.

Besides Marathos, Arados also controlled, at various times, a number of other mainland ports,[39] three of which developed into towns or cities during the Hellenistic period. Their common characteristics are small harbours and access to a

---

[39] That these were small ports is an inference from ancient accounts, especially Str. 16. 2. 12, but also from the present position.

fertile hinterland.⁴⁰ Moving north from Arados, Balanaia is
the first anchorage reached, past a stretch of cliff coast. There
a small river reaches the sea, there is a shingle beach, and it is
at the southern end of a fertile and well watered plain. At the
next change of coast is Paltos, situated where the cliffs begin
again at the northern end of the beach which stretches north
from Balanaia. Paltos also provides access to another section
of Balanaia's fertile plain. The cliff coast then stretches for
another twenty kilometres northwards. At the only break in
the cliffs is Gabala, where the sea has eroded out a semi-
circular harbour with a shelving sandy beach. It is the only
good harbour between Balanaia and Laodikeia—for Paltos is
only a river-mouth—and it is at the centre of another fertile
plain which is up to four miles wide, and which is watered by
rivers and springs and wells, a northern extension of that
which stretches fom Balanaia to Paltos.⁴¹

These three places will have come into existence as ports of
supply for Arados. Their function was as collecting and
exporting points for the agricultural products of the fertile
plains behind them. These plains are small and the ports
were, and are, also small. They define, by their location and
their access to the hinterlands, the Aradian *peraia* as the
ancient sources know it.⁴²

In 300 BC they seem to have been no more than villages, but
they were growing even at that time. By the 220s three of
them—Gabala, Balanaia, and Marathos—were sizeable
enough to be set up as separate cities by king Seleukos III.⁴³
This was not a status they kept for very long, but the event
demonstrates that they were not mere villages any more.

These 'small' cities appear briefly in the sources and then
vanish again, perhaps for centuries. They also tend to grow.
Most of them remained small, but seem to be larger than
villages. The conditionals I am using are tiring but necessary:
much of this is thoroughly uncertain.

⁴⁰ See Admiralty, *Syria*, p. 61, for a concise description of all this coast and its
immediate hinterland. Str. 16. 2. 13 calls the coast 'surfy and harbourless'.

⁴¹ Admiralty, *Syria*, p. 61, and personal observation.

⁴² Defined by Strabo as including all from Paltos to Marathos and Simyra (16.
2. 12), but his definition is by these towns, not by particular bounds; Arr. I2. 13. 7
reports wider bounds.

⁴³ H. Seyrig, 'Monnaies hellénistiques: XVIII Séleukos III et Simyra', *Rev. Num.*
11, (1971), pp. 7–11.

For only two of the cities which fall in this group can outline plans can be drawn: Europos and Arethusa (Map 6(*g*)). At Europos, which had been Carchemish in the Iron Age and Assyrian periods, Woolley found Greek remains only on the old acropolis, except for a single pipe in the lower town. Most indicative of all, the town walls and gates showed both Iron Age and Roman construction, but no Hellenistic work. Much of the Hellenistic deposit on the top of the acropolis was destroyed by the building of a huge temple of Kommagenean type;[44] despite this it is reasonable to conclude that Seleukid Europos consisted only of a small settlement which was confined to the old Iron Age acropolis. At Arethusa no excavations have taken place, but there exists an outline plan which indicates a town area of about a quarter of that of the middle-sized cities such as Beroia.[45] This is of the Roman city, most likely, but it is possible that it marks also the outline of the preceding Hellenistic town as well.

Two more cities, foundations of Seleukos, cannot be planned in outline, but would seem to fall into the smallest category. They are the two cities, Hierapolis and Nikopolis, which were added to Seleukos' original scheme. Bambyke was made over into Hierapolis, and the presumption must be that other changes were made to the place at the same time. Settlement by colonists is to be expected, and a garrison is surely likely given the previous history of the place. These developments would enforce an enlargement of the city, but there is no sign at any time in the Hellenistic period that the place was ever large. The temple dominated it in Lucian's time,[46] and no doubt had done so before. It was only in the later Roman period, when the city became the site of a great fair, that it grew to a notable size.[47] In the Hellenistic period it seems reasonable to assume that it was smaller than its neighbours at Beroia and Zeugma and Kyrrhos. In the first century BC, Strabo called it a 'small town' (*polichne*)[48] but since

[44] C .L. Woolley, *Carchemish*, vol. ii, (1954).

[45] The outline is reproduced in Sauvaget, *Alep*, p. 43, fig. 14, redrawn from an aerial photograph.

[46] Lucian, *De Dea Syria*.

[47] G. Goossens, *Hierapolis de Syrie* (Louvain, 1943), ch. 9, part 3, pp. 151–4, and the texts there cited.

[48] Str. 16. 2. 8.

he uses the term also for Beroia and for the unknown Herakleia it cannot be pressed for much precision. We thus know something of Hierapolis, but of the history and size of Nikopolis' we have no information at all. All that can be said is that the pre-Greek and post-Roman settlements in the area have always been small, for the valley of the Kara Su in that stretch, though well watered and fertile, is not really very extensive. These factors suggest that the city was small at the start and remained small.

Other settlements of this small size can be discerned, though it is not always easy, or even possible, to be certain that a Hellenistic settlement actually existed, since the visible remains—as at Europos—and the ancient sources are generally Roman. Names can help. Arethusa and Europos are places whose names imply that they were founded, or perhaps only occupied, by Greeks and Macedonians before Seleukos' conquest. The retention of those Macedonian names is also a clear sign that they were continually occupied by Greek speakers. The same must follow from other early names. Larissa, with its Alexandrian soldier settlers, and Doliche, strategically placed halfway along the road from Zeugma to Kyrrhos, were others.

Communications within Syria are another major clue to the development of the cities. Like the cities, however, the Hellenistic system of roads was swamped and hidden by the Roman, which is well known, and of which substantial physical remains still exist.[49] In the circumstances the Roman system is not a reliable guide to the earlier roads. It has been established in chapter 1 that the frontier of settlement moved eastwards in the Hellenistic period, and it continued to do so in the Roman. Thus the roads which were laid out along the newly colonized lands must be of Roman origin, not Hellenistic. Therefore it is only by considering the evidence for the actual use of roads in the Seleukid period that the Hellenistic road system can be sorted out. As it happens, there is just enough of such evidence to establish a clear network.

Certain physical constraints did not change. The mountain ranges were crossed by relatively few passes: the Bagche and

[49] The Roman network is clear from R. Mouterde and A. Poidebard, *Le Limes de Chalcis* (Paris, 1945), which also records the existence of physical remains.

Beilan over the Amanus, though there were also several lesser known routes in use over both the Amanus[50] and the Bargylos.[51] Nevertheless the river routes through the mountains—the Orontes and the Eleutheros—were obviously the more favoured by traffic than any of those over the mountains.

Inland the rivers and marshes were and are not navigable. The Orontes in particular is a major obstacle to east–west movement, and crossing places are relatively few. An even greater obstacle was the Euphrates, though here the actual crossing used in the Hellenistic period is known, at Zeugma, replacing the earlier crossing at Thapsakos.

Within these constraints a broad network of routes can be discerned from evidence which survives, which is principally records of the movements of armies. It will be convenient to list the incidents:

1. Alexander crossed the Amanus by the Beilan pass, and marched to Marathos. From there he marched south, undoubtedly along the coast, against Tyre, sending Parmenio through the Eleutheros gap to attack Damascus. That the gap was a route-in-use is also shown by the fact that Mariamme, at the eastern end of the pass, was part of the Aradian *peraia*. On his return Alexander crossed the Euphrates at Thapsakos.[52]

2. Seleukos I shifted the Euphrates crossing to Zeugma.

3. Antiochos III in 221 marched south from Apamea into the Biqaa valley, pausing at Laodikeia-ad-Libanum on the way.[53] This means he was west of the Orontes, and so will have crossed the river at Atcharné or Larissa.

4. Antiochos III marched from Apamea to Seleukeia-in-Pieria in 219.[54] The obvious route is north along the Orontes, past Antioch and through the Orontes gap.

5. In 164/163 the regent Philip brought an army back from the east, crossing by the bridge at Zeugma and reaching Antioch.[55] Of the two routes which he could have used after Zeugma, one, through Beroia, was in the hands of his rival

[50] U. Bahadur Alkim, 'The Road from Samal to Asitawandawa', *Anadolu Arastirmalari* 2 (1965), 1–45.

[51] P. J. Riis, 'The North-east Sanctuary and the First Settling of Greeks in Syria and Palestine', *Sukas* I (Copenhagen, 1970).

[52] Arr. 2. 13. 8; 15. 1; 15. 6.   [53] Pol. 5. 45. 7.

[54] Pol. 5. 59. 1.   [55] Jos. *AJ* 12. 9. 6.

Lysias,[56] so the route through Kyrrhos—which in fact is the shorter—will have been used.

6. Diodotos-Tryphon marched from Apamea to Antioch in 145.[57]

7. Tryphon fled from Orthosia to Apamea in 138.[58] He will have used the Eleutheros gap to Mariamme and so north.

8. Between 96 and 69 Beroia was the centre of a principality which included Hierapolis,[59] and which was assisted by a Parthian army from Mesopotamia,[60] and this confirms the use of the route connecting the two towns with Zeugma. Beroia had been attacked from Antioch,[61] which implies a useable route along which the army could march.

9. The route from Zeugma to Antioch through Kyrrhos was dangerous in the first century BC, when Kyrrhos—or Gindaros, both on the route—had a reputation for brigandage.[62]

All this establishes the existence of a major spine-route connecting Antioch and Apamea, used repeatedly, and crossing the Orontes at, perhaps, Jisr esh-Shoghour. From Apamea two routes led southwards, one into the Biqaa valley and the other east through the Eleutheros gap to Marathos on the coast. From Antioch other routes radiated: west to Seleukeia-in-Pieria through the Orontes gap, north to Alexandria-by-Issos through the Beilan Pass, presumably with a branch northwards to Nikopolis along the Kara valley, east to Zeugma by way of Gindaros, the Afrin valley, and Kyrrhos, and to Zeugma by way of Chalkis, Beroia and Hierapolis; in addition there will also have been a route connecting Antioch with Laodikeia-ad-Mare, across the northern part of the Bargylos. Further, it seems reasonable to presume the existence of a route along the coast, connecting the several towns of the coastal plains around Laodikeia and Arados. However, there is no reason to assume that this was an important route, since the sea was so much more convenient. Its course was no doubt that followed by the later Roman road.[63]

---

[56] Jos. *AJ* 12. 9. 7.
[57] Jos. *AJ* 13. 5. 3.
[58] 1 Mac. 15. 37; Jos. *AJ* 13. 7. 2.
[59] Str. 16. 2. 7.
[60] Jos. *AJ* 13. 14. 3.
[61] Ibid.
[62] Str. 16. 2. 8.
[63] R. G. Goodchild, 'The Coast Road of Phoenicia and its Roman Milestones', *Berytus* 9 (1948), 91–128.

This is as far as the evidence or reasonable presumption can take us. The most obvious difference from the Roman routes is that there is no evidence for the steppe route from Hama north to Chalkis. This is a road the Romans built; eventually it became the Hajj route from the north to Damascus. The pattern of the road network in the Hellenistic period emphasizes all the more the vital importance of Antioch and Apamea for control of Syria, and above all the central role of Antioch, which was the nodal point of routes from all directions, and was the one city which gave access to all parts of Syria.

The pattern of routes also provides the major clue to understanding the establishment and growth of 'small' urban settlements in various parts of the country. These small cities lay along the major routes in distinct patterns. Once recognized, these help in turn to understand many of the events of Syrian history.

To take first the area south of Apamea (Map 3). The city itself effectively blocks the route north from the no man's land between Seleukid and Ptolemaic Syria. It was established at a bottleneck between the Ghab marshes and the steppe and desert. Yet south of it Seleukos maintained already established towns at Larissa and Arethusa, which controlled the route along the Orontes. Both of them were and still are castle-towns, built on high rocky promontories and clearly military in purpose. These two became supplemented by other settlements along the same route, at Epiphaneia-Hamath, which was occupied from about 200 BC, at Laodi-keia-ad-Libanum, which was named as such by 221, and at Emesa. All these three are established on high tells, close to the river. All five of the places are strung along the river at regular intervals of 25 or 30 kilometres, say, a day's march for a military force.

A second line can also be discerned, but this is much less well authenticated. South from Apamea a road crosses the Orontes at the modern town of Atcharné, and then runs along the foot of the mountains as far as the Eleutheros gap. Along this road are two places, Masyaf and Mariamme, which grew to be of urban size by the Roman period. Also on that road is

Salukiyé, which was identified by Jones and Honigmann[64] as the site of Seleukobelos, and Raphanaia, which later became the site of the camp of a Roman legion. Just north of the bridge is Mesta Blouné, identified tentatively by Mouterde as Apollonia,[65] which was said by Strabo to be a dependent of Apamea.[66] These identifications are all horribly tentative, but it is noticeable that these places are, once again, placed along the road at roughly regular intervals, this time of ten to fifteen kilometres.

Some at least of these places were deliberately planted. Larissa and Arethusa are pre-Seleukid, Epiphaneia, Seleukobelos and Laodikeia have dynastic names, and this demonstrates clear Seleukid interest. So also, perhaps, was Apollonia. Other names are of Semitic origin, and this implies that they had grown without dynastic intervention. But the route along the river was strung with dynastically named places on powerfully fortified sites, along a route which was one of the most obvious of invasion routes, the river. This line of fortifications also incidentally blocked the possibility of cross-river raiding by nomads from the eastern steppe. The resulting increase in security is shown by the evidence of Hellenistic settlement on the desert side of the river, to the east. It will also have had an effect on the west of the river, and was no doubt one of the reasons for the revival of settlement there, in the great bend of the river, a revival which by Roman times had resulted in the development of numerous villages and towns in that area.[67]

Within the main network of cities established in 300 there was little room for major urban developments. But a small place such as Doliche could exist, and there are fragments of evidence for other small urban sites. One of these was the town which has been located by Syrian archaeologists at Ayin

---

[64] Jones, *CERP*, 452 n. 24; E. Honigmann, 'Notes de géographie syriennes', in *Mélanges syriens offerts à René Dussaud* (Paris, 1939), 129–33.

[65] R. Mouterde, 'A travers l'Apamène: II, Mesta Blouné, Apollonia?', *MUSJ* (1949–50), 16–21.

[66] Str. 26. 2. 10.

[67] See the list in J. and J.–C. Balty, 'L'Apamène antique et les limites de la Syria Secunda', in *La Géographie administrative et politique d'Alexandre à Mahomet* (Strasbourg, n.d.), 41–75.

Dara, between Antioch and Kyrrhos. This may have been
Gindaros, and if not, Gindaros was its successor in the valley.
The site was just south of the boundary of Antioch's territory;
it may be significant that the distance between Antioch and
Kyrrhos was greater than that between any other two of
Seleukos' cities—a good 100 kilometres. This is clearly too
long for a single day's travel, so travellers would need to break
their journeys, and Gindaros/Ayin Dara is about two-thirds of
the way from Antioch to Kyrrhos.

A second of these towns may have been at Tell Rifaat,
where there was certainly a Hellenistic temple.[68] It too is sited
at a halfway point, this time between Beroia and Kyrrhos. A
third example might be Magarataricha, if that is the site of the
Megara which was one of Apamea's dependent forts;[69] again
it is towards the edge of Apamea's territory as indicated by the
dated inscriptions studied and plotted by Seyrig.[70]

These urban settlements grew up in the interstices of the
network set up by Seleukos I, and they are all small, and all of
them were distant from the main cities. Above all, there are
very few of them; that is, the cities established by Seleukos
occupied the land fully, monopolized its resources, and left
little or no space or surplus for other settlements to grow.
Outside the network, however, there were many more towns
and cities. One group developed in the south, beyond the
network, as already mentioned; another group grew along the
coast.

Along the whole length of the coast the two cities
established by Seleukos I were supplemented by others which
grew during the Hellenistic period. There were three in the
small plain of Iskenderun: Alexandria-by-Issos, Rhosos, and
the town-site at Ada Tepe located by an archaeological
survey.[71]

Alexandria-by-Issos is the only city which developed into a

---

[68] M. V. Seton Williams, 'Preliminary Report on the Excavations at Tell Rifaat',
Iraq 23 (1961), 68–87, and 'Excavations at Tell Rifaat 1964: Second Preliminary
Report', *AAAS* 17 (1967), 69–84.

[69] Capt. Piquet-Pellorce and R. Mouterde, 'Magarataricha', *Syria* 9 (1928), 207–
15.

[70] H. Seyrig, Appendix II, in G. Tchalenko, *Villages antiques de la Syrie du Nord*, vol.
iii (Paris, 1958), 2–62.

[71] Williams, 'Cicilian Survey', *Anatolian Studies* 4 (1954), 147.

major centre without benefit of royal foundation. It is on the
coast at a good (but not perfect) harbour,[72] and on the coastal
route from Kilikia towards Antioch and north Syria generally.
A claimed foundation by Alexander is incorrect, and there is
even less evidence for it having been one of Seleukos' cities. It
may well, however, owe its origin to events in Seleukos' reign.
From 301 to 294, the boundary of Seleukos' kingdom was just
north of the site of the future Alexandria, for during that time
Kilikia belonged to Pleistarchos and then to Demetrios.[73]
There will have been a guard-post and a customs-post at the
site during those years, but the existence of a full city is much
less likely. Seleukos never planted cities on his boundaries;
always he left a frontier-space between them and his actual
boundary. Apamea and Nikopolis are other examples. For the
small coastal plain of Iskenderun, Rhosos would be more
Seleukos' type of site and in 298 he used it as the rendezvous
for a meeting with Demetrios.[74] It may be that this is a sign
that he was intending to develop Rhosos itself; if so, his
annexation of Kilikia in 294 made it an unnecessary development by shifting the boundary to the line of the Taurus. It is
possible that Alexandria was founded between the annexation
of Kilikia and the end of Seleukos' reign, that is, between 294
and 281; we do not know; there is no evidence. The first
certain evidence that the city existed is in the reign of
Antiochos IV Epiphanes (175–164) when the city became the
site of a mint, issuing its own coins;[75] that is, it had become a
city. Considered objectively, this all suggests that the city had
developed without the benefit of royal interference or encouragement. Rhosos meanwhile had slumbered on, a small
place in 298 and still a small place in 30 BC when it was
honoured by Augustus for being the home town of his
admiral.

The small plain at the mouth of the Orontes had room for
one city, Seleukeia, but the rich coastal plain to the north of
Laodikeia-ad-Mare saw the growth of a whole group of towns.
One is unlocated, Herakleia-ad-Mare, known from the
geographers Claudius Ptolemy and Strabo,[76] and two are

[72] Admiralty, *Turkey*, p. 101.
[73] Plut. *Dem.* 31–2.
[74] Plut. *Dem.* 31. 2.
[75] Head, *HN*, 716.
[76] Ptol. 16. 15. 3; Str. 16. 2. 12.

known, at Ras el-Basit and Ras Ibn Hani. None of these were large, but all of them were active centres by the later second century BC Similarly none of them was close to any of the great cities, but this is a denser concentration of urban centres than in inland Syria. It reflects, no doubt, the more benevolent climate and the greater agricultural potential of the coastal strip.

The dating of all these minor settlements is extremely uncertain. Many of them are only attested in the Roman period, though their growth obviously began in the preceding Hellenistic. Occasional items of data do help out. For example, Herakleia-ad-Mare, whose site is not known, is located somewhere north of Laodikeia in Ptolemy's geographical listing; it happens that a market weight has been found, dating to 108 BC, thus confirming that it was a settlement large enough to have an organized market supervised by an *agoranomos* at that date.[77] By extension it is reasonable to assume that other places known later and in Ptolemy had grown from Hellenistic beginnings.

At the same time it is clear that many of them did not exist at the beginning of the Hellenistic. One or two can be traced back, but the relative thinness of the Syrian rural population precludes many towns in the early period. In addition, the hostility of that population to Macedonian rule, impotent though it was, would require the settlers to live in their fortifications. Nevertheless there is a clear development between, say, 300 and 100 BC, so that by the latter date there are many more small civic settlements than at the earlier. Where archaeology has produced evidence, as at Tell Rifaat, Ayin Dara, and other places, it shows that the foundation and expansion of these places happened during the Hellenistic. And in turn this focuses our attention on the smallest of the settlements in Syria, the villages.

When the new cities were established, their effect upon the rural inhabitants was diverse. In some cases, villages were incorporated into the city; in others, villages were depopulated; any village with a new city close to it had a new market for its produce; but equally it had a new landlord, fully capable of extracting rents and taxes. These varied effects

[77] *IGLS 1252.*

were felt throughout Syria, for there is one certainty in this matter which is beyond dispute—and it is pleasant to have at least one—that is, that the cities were founded in land which was already occupied and farmed.

This, when one thinks of it, is natural and inevitable. Cities do not get founded in deserts; they require food supplies, and so they are established in or very near fertile land; and that is invariably already cultivated. And this in turn meant villages.[78] Some direct effects are known.

At Laodikeia-ad-Mare, the city was built on the sites of two villages, Ramitha and Mazabda;[79] Seleukeia-in-Pieria probably took into itself the people of the Greco-Syrian settlement at al Mina-Sabouni close to the mouth of the Orontes;[80] at Aleppo the tell of the village which was incorporated into Beroia still forces the modern inhabitant and visitor into a steep climb just inside the western walls of the medieval city;[81] Apamea's acropolis was the tell of the old Iron Age town of Niya,[82] though here the continuity of occupation is not clear.

In these cases, however, the actual process seems to be that the village was simply incorporated in the city; at Beroia, this is certain, and the old village has left its mark on the modern street system. In a sense, this is surprising, since the usual concept of colonization involves the newcomers expelling the previous inhabitants. This had certainly happened in the previous period of Greek colonization, and it is just as certain that Greek and Macedonian legality would have permitted expulsion. Seyrig, for example, proposed that all of Syria was royal land even in the Persian period, though the evidence is poor;[83] he also suggested that in the Hellenistic period it could

---

[78] G. M. Cohen, 'The Seleukid Colonies: Studies in Founding, Administration and Organisation', *Historia* Einzelschriften 30, (Wiesbaden, 1978), pp. 21–5 goes to considerable lengths to demonstrate that cities were founded on or near villages throughout the Seleukid state; he does not consider their mutual need for local supplies.

[79] Ramitha in Stephanos of Byzantium, s.v. Laodikeia; Mazabda in Mal. 203; the site is big enough to have included two villages.

[80] This is, of course, presumption, but al Mina does cease to exist at the same time as Seleukeia was founded: C. L. Woolley, *A Forgotten Kingdom* (1953), 180.

[81] Sauvaget, *Alep*, pp. 50–1, and fig. 13, p. 41.

[82] J. C. Balty, 'Le problème de Niya', *Apamée de Syrie, bilan des recherches archéologiques*, 1969–71 (Brussells, 1972), 53–63.

[83] Seyrig, 'Séleucos I', p. 301; but the evidence is based only on a comment by

be regarded as 'spear-won' by any Seleukid king who chose to
enforce the implications of that term. Further, in 301–299
Seleukos I had no time to argue the legal niceties of
landownership.

Yet this theory ignores the practical situation which
Seleukos had to face. Even if the land belonged to the king in a
formal, legal sense, the Seleukid government had to exercise a
certain amount of care and tact and diplomacy in its initial
dealings with the king's new subjects. The presence of old
Antigoneians has been seen to have exercised a serious
influence on Seleukos' actions. The presence of the far more
numerous Aramaic-speaking Syrians surely also acted as a
constraint upon him. It would be politically stupid to
antagonize these people unnecessarily. And all Seleukos'
actions at this time demonstrate a marked political intelligence at work. Further, it would not take much to conciliate
the Syrians; a few gestures (like the religious charade at the
founding of Antioch) would do. So there is conciliation of
Bambyke and its conversion into a *polis*, and patronage of the
temple by Stratonike, the king's wife; there is also the
continued existence of the Aradian monarchy. Neither of these
is necessary, unless they are regarded as political gestures to
reassure the Syrians.

In these circumstances it seems unlikely that the original
inhabitants were displaced from their homes in large numbers, though some undoubtedly will have suffered. The
introduction of large numbers of Greeks and Macedonians
into the land cannot have helped but be disturbing. But the
basic problem was land. The colonists who were introduced or
transplanted or confirmed in place by Seleukos I were given
land. This was the main inducement for colonization. G. M.
Cohen has shown that there were usually three distinct
elements in this grant: a home site, usually in the city, grain
land, and orchard- or vine-land. This was the *kleros*,[84] and the
three elements, needing as they did different soils and different
conditions for growth, would most likely be distinct and

Xen. that in one particular area the land was allocated to the Persian king's wife
(Xen. 1. 4. 9). It is difficult to accept a generalisation from this. On the other hand,
Seleukos Nikator *was* the conqueror; he had almost a free hand, at least in theory.

[84] Cohen (note 78), pp. 47–51.

geographically separate. The size of the grant varied with the rank and importance of the colonist, according to the productivity and state of development of the land, the availability of the land, its location near or far from the city, and so on. The permutations of these considerations rule out any prospect of certainty as to numbers and sizes. But the *kleros* would obviously have to be sufficiently large to persuade a man to settle down, if he was a soldier, or to move from his home to the new land, if he was a civilian colonist. It must be sufficient, that is, to provide him with a good living, which in turn must mean that he was to be better off than the majority of the local peasants, and indeed better off than the peasantry of old Greece. These factors might dictate a different size of *kleros* for almost every new city: one would expect there to be smaller *kleroi* in the fertile well-watered hinterland of Laodikeia-ad-Mare, for example, and larger ones in the dry lands of Beroia or the hills above Kyrrhos, or in the cultivable but nomad-overrun lands north and east of Apamea.

P. Briant has proposed as a model for the distribution of *kleroi* that settlers' land was concentrated in a band around the city, with undistributed land further out, that is, a concentric arrangement.[85] This model is not based on extant evidence, of which there is none. It is attractive as a theory, and logical, but it pays no attention to the geographical constraints, and when it is applied in particular cases, it proves to be wanting. Take, as an example, Seleukeia-in- Pieria. The city had only a small territory, since it was boxed in by mountains beyond which was the territory of Antioch. Seleukeia's land is fertile, certainly, but it was in very short supply. Furthermore some of that land was already occupied, and occupied by Greeks at that, who lived in the old trading town at al Mina. This settlement died at the moment Seleukeia was founded,[86] and the assumption is that the inhabitants were shifted, or shifted themselves, to Seleukeia. Since they were predominantly merchants, they may not have needed much persuasion to move to the new and bigger city with its new, larger and safer

---

[85] P. Briant, 'Colonisation hellénistiques et populations Indigènes: I, la phase d'installation', *Klio* 60 (1978), 57–92, and 'II, renforts grecs dans les cités Hellénistiques d'Orient', *Klio* 64, (1982), 83–94.

[86] See note 79.

harbour, which would replace the open roadstead or river estuary they had used before. But some of these men would be landowners as well.[87] Did they keep their land? Did they receive *kleroi* as well? It would seem likely that they would have to be induced—bribed, perhaps—to move from their homes into the city, even if it was to their advantage: an augmentation of land would surely ensure that. As argued earlier, the city contained something over 6,000 colonists: its small land area would mean that its *kleroi* would also be small. There is no room, literally, for a concentric theory here.

At Apamea there were different geographical factors operating, but with a similar effect. To the west of the city was the periodic marsh of the Ghab, which may or may not have been inhabited, but which required a very specialized form of exploitation by fowlers and fishermen;[88] to the east was the steppeland, and here again the exploitation of the economic resources was very specialized, this time towards pastoral farming, at least until reclamation and resettlement had taken place. Apamea's territory spread north and south,[89] between these constraints. To the south a new factor apparently operated; this is an area with very few Hellenistic remains, and those which can be found date from the latter half of the period, after *c*.200 BC. There are, on the other hand, indications that resettlement of the steppeland to the north and north-east of Apamea began in this period,[90] though again the evidence is thin. This would, of course, be the safest area in which to place *kleroi*, well away from the threat of damage

[87] This is, of course, an assumption. Al Mina, however, had a long and continuous history. One would expect businesses to pass by inheritance, and since the merchants were wealthy and thus settled, their purchase of land locally is, perhaps, a reasonable assumption.

[88] H. Athanassiou, 'Rasm et-Tanjera: A Recently Discovered Syrian Tell in the Ghab', Ph.D. thesis, University of Mississippi, Columbia 1977, ch. 1.

[89] The city had a large population in the Roman period (117,000 according to *Corpus Inscriptiones Latinae* 6687). It contained Larissa within its territory according to Str. 16. 2. 10. It seems likely that the city's territory was the basis of the new Roman province of Syria Secunda (J. and J.C. Balty, 'L'Apamène antique et les Limites de la Syria Secunda', pp. 41–75), which stretched well into the desert, but north and south as well. The Apamene had a common border with the land of Antioch in the north (H. Seyrig, (note 70), pp. 2–62, esp. fig. 7, p. 57). Without the steppe, the city's territory would be long and very narrow.

[90] Comparing the results of the two surveys of de Maigret and Ridolfini (Chapter 1 and Appendix 3).

which would result from a Ptolemaic invasion from the south. The most important factor in determining land use and settlement in the land near Apamea in the Hellenistic period, however, must have been the need for huge areas of pasture, which follows from Strabo's information that the Seleukid royal stud and the elephant park were both situated here.[91] The steppeland would be ideal for the raising of horses, and the land around would presumably be the source of whatever food the elephants were given. This government requirement will have seriously affected the distribution of *kleroi*, and the resettlement of land by farmers: that is to say, government requirements will have *prevented* the establishment of new settlements in large areas of Apamean territory.

The implantation of ten cities in Syria must have had a major effect upon the overwhelmingly rural population already living there. Since they were all planted in the cultivated land, archaeological traces of that effect are few nearby. But the disturbance was far-reaching, and will have affected every person and every village. The expansion of demand for food, and the increase in wealth, will have encouraged more intensive cultivation, as would also the requirements of rents and taxes. There will also have been Syrians who so resented the new order of things that they may have moved as far from the cities as they could. All this suggests that there should be traces of new settlement along the sensitive desert margins.

Those traces are indeed detectable in the two sections of the marginal land. East of the Madkh marsh a limited reoccupation of deserted land took place in the Hellenistic period. In the Qoueiq valley there is evidence of new occupation in the Hellenistic period at five sites south of Beroia. Further east a group of sites between Beroia and the Jabboul Lake were newly occupied, and a scatter of sites between the lake and the Euphrates have produced Hellenistic pottery, according to survey evidence. In the Euphrates valley, four excavated sites have produced Hellenistic material, three of them at the northern end of the survey area, suggesting a movement of settlement southwards. In the Membij survey area there were

[91] Str. 16. 2. 10.

more sites with Hellenistic than for the whole Iron Age (see also Appendix 3 and Map 5 (*b*)).

These reoccupations do suggest that the Hellenistic period saw an advance of settlement south and east. At the same time it was a strictly limited movement. Of the nineteen sites which show this occupation, ten were in the triangular area between the Jabboul Lake, Beroia, and Bab, others were in the Qoueiq valley near Chalkis, three were at the northern edge of the Euphrates survey area. The geographical relationship of this new rural occupation to the new cities is clear enough, and the most economical explanation of it is as a response to the building and colonization of those cities.

Further north, away from the desert, there is also evidence of an expansion of rural occupation near Zeugma. Whereas only one Persian period site is known in the Sajur valley, there are a string of Hellenistic sites, located by a very superficial survey. There must be more in the area, but the actual discoveries suggest a development of rural settlement along the routes from Zeugma towards Antioch, both by way of Beroia and by the Kyrrhos route.

In the desert margin south of the Madkh marsh the surveys are much less informative (Map 5 (*c*)). Near the marsh there is just one Hellenistic site, Tell Tuqun, which had also been occupied before. Hama was reoccupied from *c*.200, and occupation also began at the new city site of Apamea and nearby at Huarté and Tell Qarqur. Further south, limited reoccupation has been noted at Tell Nebi Mend (Laodikeia-ad-Libanum) and Arjouné at the southern end of the Lake of Homs, at el-Mishrifé in the second century BC, and at Homs. The 'Greco-Phoenician' layer at Tell et-Tin, in the lake, may well be Hellenistic as well. This group of excavations, in a relatively small area, suggests reoccupation in the second half of the Hellenistic period, say, taking the date from Hama, after 200 BC. But this resettlement is not due to the establishment of cities, since there were no cities in this far southern sector. The reason must be the increased security provided by the Seleukid garrisons along the river.

In the coastal plains more excavation has been done than elsewhere, though there are no surveys, except in the Iskenderun plain (Map 5 (*a*)). There the survey provides firm indications of settlement in the Hellenistic period at six sites, including the 'town site' of Ada Tepe.[92] All of those sites seem to be newly occupied in the Hellenistic period; they include the city of Alexandria; no doubt there is a connection. In the Orontes estuary area the long-established site at al Mina-Sabouni was replaced by the new city of Seleukeia-in-Pieria.

In the larger coastal plains further south occupation increased (Map 5 (c)). In the Laodikeian area Ras Shamra was deserted early in the Hellenistic period, but its neighbour Ras Ibn Hani was now occupied. So were Ras el-Basit and Paltos, and occupation continued at Tell Durak and Tell Sukas. No doubt all this is connected with the presence of the new city at Laodikeia. On the mainland near Arados, however, the reverse effect seems to occur. The settlements at Marathos and Simyra died out during the Hellenistic period, though Tabbat el-Hammam continued to be inhabited. It is known that Antarados had replaced Marathos by the Roman period, and in this case it seems clear that the settlement migrated gradually to its new site. On balance there was no overall change in the intensity of occupation, and there was no new city founded here, either.

There were, in summary, rather more settlements along the coastal plains after 300 BC than before. In addition to the archaeological evidence there are a number of places whose existence is recorded in literary sources, such as Gabala and Balanaia, as well as new cities at Laodikeia and Seleukeia, and later at Alexandria. The evidence is, therefore, that here the rural population in the Hellenistic period was more numerous than before.

In between these areas, in the long occupied central area, the evidence is both thin and ambiguous. The one part where a serious effort to combine excavations with a survey has been made, the Amuq basin, does not provide any decisive sign (Map 5 (a)). The periodization of the survey is so vague as to prevent clear conclusions. An increase in apparent settlement from the 'Syro-Hittite' to the 'Hellenistic-Roman' periods may only be the result of the easier recognition of the remains

[92] M. V. Seton Williams, 'Cilician Survey', *Anatolian Studies*, 4, (1954), no. 1 (Ada Tepe) on fig. 6, p. 139.

of the latter. Of the six excavations which have been reported, three sites became deserted in or before the Iron Age, two were occupied all through from the Bronze Age to the Byzantine, and at one, Antioch, occupation began in the Hellenistic period. Little real information about the intensity of occupation can be extracted from such brevity.

The archaeology of the Amuq plain does suggest another development, however. The Hellenistic period at Catal Huyuk, south-east of the lake, is marked by the building of a large house.[93] The remains are fragmentary, but unmistakable. There is a suggestion that king Demetrios I Soter (162–150) was in the habit of living outside the city, in a large house.[94] There are no other archaeological remains of this type until the Roman period;[95] on the other hand, the continuity between Hellenistic and Roman periods is strong, and if the wealthy classes of Antioch lived in country houses in the Roman period, they are likely to have done so earlier. Here is another possible modification of the rural settlement pattern.

The accumulation of all this evidence, even if its details are dubious, compels a clear conclusion. In the Iskenderun plain, near Laodikeia, in the Amuq plain, along the roads of the north, in all these areas there is evidence of an intensification of rural settlement. Taken together with the much clearer evidence of the expansion of settlement into the desert fringes, which comes from much of the desert margin from the Euphrates to the Lake of Homs, it is clear that the Hellenistic period saw an increase in the number of settlements, and probably therefore a rise in total rural population. And, since a larger area was under occupation, a rise in total production of food can also be presumed.

That these interconnected increases occurred at the same time as the establishment of a series of new cities is not, obviously, a mere coincidence. The new cities required food and the expansion of settlement is partly the result of that new

---

93 R. C. Haines, *Excavations in the Plain of Antioch: II, The Structural Remains of the Later Phases* (Chicago, 1971), pp. 9–10 and plate 27.

94 Jos. *AJ* 13. 2. 1.

95 Several villas near the city were located by the city's excavators: *Antioch-on-the-Orontes* ii. 3 and 95–147; iii. pp. 7 and 19–25.

demand. But the mechanism is not necessarily one of free-market choice, for the peasantry were not wholly free agents. Many would be on land assigned to the new cities, and many of these would be on *kleros* land, assigned to a new landlord. The rest were on royal land. All were taxed, and those on city land probably more heavily than those on royal land. The Aramaic-speaking peasantry were thus forced to increase their production of food, rather than being bribed to do so. Two results followed. One was an increase and expansion of settlement; the other was the continued alienation of the colonists and the peasantry, shown by the city walls, the great acropoleis, and later by the attempted self-emancipation of the peasantry.

5

THE EVOLUTION OF THE
URBAN HIERARCHY

THE three sizes of city which were apparent in Syria by 280 BC have been called large, medium, and small. Neither the constituents of those groups nor the classification itself remained unaltered for long. Nor did the actual number of cities remain constant. Seleukos himself had founded two more, Nikopolis and Hierapolis, to add to his original eight, and there were always Arados and Marathos and the rest of the Aradian *peraia*. Change and development continued all through the Hellenistic period—and, of course, after.

The three sizes of cities constituted, in geographical terminology, a hierarchy of urban sites. The term 'hierarchy' is used in Urban Geography,[1] although modern geographers would be unhappy at the use of size alone as the criterion for ranking the cities. Other aspects of the geography of the cities and towns are involved, in particular by identifying the different functions which operate in a particular urban area—manufacturing, marketing, communications, administration, and so on. The sheer lack of evidence inhibits such a diagnostic approach to the cities of Hellenistic Syria, though some of the functions of individual cities can be detected, such as Apamea's role as a military centre, or Antioch's as the kingdom's capital; others will be identified further as appropriate. Since, however, this can only be done in a few instances, it is not an approach which can be used systematically; it will be better to rely merely on size to sort out the apparent hierarchy, though the fragmentary sources can be used where possible. It is only size which provides a systematic basis of comparison.

[1] The theory is orginally that of W. Christaller, *Die Zentralen Orte in Suddeutschland* (Jena, 1933), based on work in Bavaria. It has been applied in many areas since. A useful summary is in K .S. O. Brown, *Central Place Theory* (1977), though every book on Urban Geography discusses it.

When the hierarchy revealed by this crude measure of physical size is compared with that expected by the theory of Central Places, which is based on the identification of functions, one thing becomes very obvious: Seleukid Syria in 280, on the death of Seleukos I, does not fit the theory. The theory, originated by the German geographer Christaller, has a Central Place with a multitude of functions surrounded by subordinate towns with fewer functions, which are in turn surrounded by lesser centres.[2] The original theory has been extensively modified by more recent criticism and research, largely based on more detailed research into functions. The basic problem with the theory is that Christaller began not with a real situation (though his original basis was Bavaria) but by constructing a model. As such and as usual it has failed when applied to a real situation, hence the modifications. Interestingly enough it is in colonial and ex-colonial situations where the theory fits best, or least unhappily—the United States, or South Africa, for example. Thus Seleukid Syria seems a likely enough scene in which Christaller's theory can be tested.

Seleukos I did not have the advantage of acquaintance with the theory, and he concentrated his four large cities in a relatively small section of the country, rather than having them distributed throughout the whole, and so with lesser sites intervening between them. Thus, apparently, the theory fails in the face of reality. However, the theory assumes development over a long period of time, and the situation in Syria in 280 was certainly not that. When the historical circumstances are taken into account, the hierarchy was all too obviously an artifical system imposed by the Seleukid government. It was only after the cities were founded that geographical, economic and historical processes could work upon them. What happened to the artificial system which existed in 280 can be investigated here. It turns out that two basic alterations took place: changes within certain of the cities, and the growth of new cities.

The size of the cities, as originally laid out, was sufficient, in every case but one, to accommodate any increase in population. The exception was Antioch, and so the expansion of

---

[2] Frequently illustrated in geographical textbooks, e.g. Brown, *Central Place Theory* pp. 18–32.

that city makes it unique among Seleukos' cities. It began having the smallest area of any of the four great cities, though only marginally. The acropolis on the summit of Mount Silpion was close and dominating, but was not actually connected with the city at first. The city itself was laid out along the riverside, with the long and steepening slope of Mount Silpion between the city and the fortress. The reasons for the city's expansion are not connected, however, with its site, but with political developments in the kingdom. In the later Seleukid period, Antioch became regarded as the Seleukid capital, but this development was not definitive until the expulsion of the Seleukids from Asia Minor after 188. Until then the Seleukid kings had tended to reside at many other places: Ephesos was a favourite in the third century,[3] Antiochos III was married at Zeugma,[4] Apamea was his campaign and administrative headquarters soon after.[5] The kings were thus peripatetic in the first century or so of the kingdom's life. Seleukeia-in-Pieria has been nominated as an alternative candidate for capital,[6] and it has rather better credentials than Antioch: it had the graves of the kings of the dynasty,[7] the name of the founder, some at least of the citizens of Antigonos' former city;[8] in 219 one of its citizens-in-exile, the doctor Apollophanes, described it as the hearth of the kingdom.[9] If there ever was an intended capital, Seleukeia has a better claim than Antioch.[10]

[3] Antiochos II was settled there at the time of his death in 246 (Eusebius, *Chronicon*, ed. A. Schone (Leipzig, 1866), part 1, p. 251).

[4] Pol. 5. 43. 1–4.

[5] Pol. 5. 58. 1. It had been the home of his minister Hermeias until his fall (5. 56. 15).

[6] Newell, *WSM*, 89; it is the term used (*archegetin*) by Pol. in his paraphrase of the argument of Apollophanes for the capture of the city before undertaking another invasion of Coele Syria (5. 58. 4).

[7] Pol. 5. 58.

[8] Diod. 20. 47. 6.

[9] Pol. 5. 58. 4.

[10] There is, however, no reason to believe that such a concept as a 'capital' of the kingdom was ever in the minds of any of the Seleukid kings, until the loss of Asia Minor. At that point Antioch became the base of the kings, and hence the kingdom's capital, because it was in the best position to act as guard for the rest of the kingdom: the dangers were now from the west and the north. When the danger was from the south, that is, from Egypt, then often Apamea was the nearest approximation to a capital. In 219, it seems that the whole of the Seleukid administration was based there (Pol. 5. 58. 1). The whole subject is exhaustively treated by E. Marinoni, 'La Capitale del regno di Seleuco I', *Rendiconti Istituto Lombardo* 106 (1972), 579–631.

If such was the intention, Ptolemy III's capture of Seleukeia in 246 thwarted its realization. He captured Antioch as well, and probably other cities,[11] but he held on only to Seleukeia. The mountains backing the city provided a convenient barrier against Seleukid reconquest for the next quarter century. The Ptolemaic occupation involved the presence of a Ptolemaic garrison, but seems to have been accepted relatively peacefully by the inhabitants, though there were a significant number of exiles from the city by the time of Antiochos III,[12] and its overall effect on the future of the city was drastic. The city's capture had occurred at a moment of weakness and confusion in the Seleukid state, and once lost it was very difficult to recover. Economically its inclusion within the Ptolemaic sphere meant a certain isolation from its natural hinterland, and a city so large and with such a small immediate territory clearly needed access to a much wider area than its own small plain.

Antioch, however, benefited from Seleukeia's misfortune. It is in this very period of Ptolemaic control of Seleukeia that Antioch is first known to expand. Of course, given the sites of the two cities, Antioch had a certain advantage in that it was easier to expand over the relatively level plain than it was up Seleukeia's mountainside, and supplies were somewhat easier to acquire from the large and productive Amuq basin— indeed, Seleukeia may well have imported at least some of its food supplies from Antioch's plain.[13] So the restriction of the growth of Seleukeia will have brought benefits to Antioch by reinforcing the expansion of the inland city.

The first expansion of Antioch is linked with Seleukos II

---

[11] The capture of Seleukeia and Antioch is well known from P. Gurob. The capture of other cities is less clear, though Ptolemy III did claim to have become king over all the Seleukid lands as far as Media: *OGIS* 54.

[12] Pol. 5. 61. 2. The absence of purges and risings is an inference from the complaints of Apollophanes, Antiochos III's doctor and a member of his council, who was an exile from Seleukeia, and was the leading campaigner for the reconquest. Had there been much violence in the Ptolemaic occupation Apollophanes would not have failed to mention it.

[13] Imports were also possible by sea. The ease of sea communications compared with the difficulty of crossing the mountains *and* paying city dues may have been enough to make imports by sea economic. The garrison may well have been fed from Egypt, or, perhaps more likely, from the Ptolemaic possessions in Asia Minor. The Ptolemaic government would not want the garrison to be dependent on supplies from a hinterland under enemy control.

Kallinikos (246–226) by Strabo.[14] The date can be pinned down to the second half of his reign, since from 246 Antioch was first occupied by Ptolemy III for a year or so, then Seleukos was either to the west in Asia Minor or to the south fighting the war with Ptolemy, or in the east vainly trying to recover control over Baktria. In 235 Antioch was the scene of an attempted *coup d'état* by Stratonike, the king's aunt; Seleukos eventually returned from the east and executed her.[15] It seems unlikely, therefore, that he had much opportunity to consider Antioch's needs before about 235. Then in the 220s he was deeply involved in the attempted recovery of Asia Minor from his rebellious nephew Antiochos Hierax. So the late 230s is the most likely period for the king to have time to consider the future of Antioch. By then it had become clear that Seleukeia was lost to the Seleukids for the foreseeable future, and that Antioch was growing.

For what Seleukos actually did for the city was to sanction the incorporation of an adjacent area into the bounds of the city. This particular area is presumed to be the island between the two branches of the Orontes.[16] Its incorporation increased the city's area by perhaps half (see Map 6 (*a*)). It must be presumed, of course, that this was the incorporation of an area which was already partly built over; it is most unlikely that a hard-pressed Seleukid king would anticipate the expansion of the city. It is possible, though, that there were also military reasons for this expansion. Antioch was now in the front line with respect to the Ptolemies all during Seleukos II's reign. It was the obvious base of operations with respect to Asia Minor and Seleukeia, so an increased garrison in the city is to be expected. Another coup might thereby be avoided, either from within the royal family (as by Stratonike) or by the Ptolemaic garrison at Seleukeia. These troops would be accompanied by all the usual military train of pedlars, shopkeepers and others who batten on the well-paid groups in society, as well as their own families. These alone whould account for a substantial expansion of the population.

There is also a further possibility. In the Roman period, the

---

[14] Str. 16. 2. 4.
[15] Justin 28. 1; Jos. *Contra Apionem*, 1. 206 f., quoting Agatharchides.
[16] Lib. Or. 11. 203, distinguishing the 'new city' on the island from the 'old city'.

island was the site of the imperial palace,[17] and it is possible that this was the traditional site of the palace, established there in the Seleukid period. A royal palace, in the sense of an administrative centre, was something that might be expected at such a place by the latter part of the reign of Seleukos II. Palace and garrison, and the hangers-on of both of these, are thus all to be expected in Antioch, given the historical context, and are good explanations for the city's development at this time.

The growth of the city continued over the next three reigns. Antiochos III settled Cretans, Euboeans and Aetolians in the city after his defeat by Rome.[18] Not all of them necessarily stayed in Antioch, but fifteen years or so later his son Antiochos IV extended the city again, by sanctioning the incorporation of the sloping land between the original city and the steeps of Mount Silpion. The area was called Epiphaneia after him,[19] and the laying out of a new main street decisively changed the whole geography of the city. Another sign of the city's expansion is the construction of a new aqueduct, dated to this period by *graffiti* giving the name of Cossutius, known to have been the architect for Antiochos IV elsewhere.[20] This was the last formal expansion of the city in the Hellenistic period and even in the Roman period the city did not expand much beyond the area designated as Antioch by Antiochos IV.[21]

From the time of Antiochos IV onwards Antioch dominates all Syria in a way which had not been evident fifty years before. It was by then clearly the unique city of Syria, a rival for the Egyptian Alexandria. Later, in the civil wars of the 140s and after, it was the possession of Antioch which marked out a particular man as having the best claim to be reckoned the legitimate Seleukid king. The city had, therefore, by the

[17] Ibid. 205–7.
[18] Ibid. 119.
[19] Str. 16. 2. 4.
[20] G. Downey, 'The Water Supply of Antioch on the Orontes in Antiquity', *AAS* (1951), 171–187. J. M. C. Toynbee, 'Some Notes on Artists in the Roman World', Collection *Latomus* 4, (Brussels, 1951), 9 (on Cossutius).
[21] Two new walls were added in the Roman period (see map in Downey, *Antioch*), but neither much expanded the enclosed area of the city. At the same time, the city could obviously expand beyond its walls, a process which would not be documented, unless archaeologically.

second half of the second century, outgrown every other city in the area, whereas none of the other cities had grown. None of them had had any need to expand. None of them had needed to build new walls to incorporate extra-mural suburbs.

Antioch's major rival, once Seleukeia had been shown to be so vulnerable, had been Apamea. Strabo says that it was the arsenal of the monarchy.[22] Its position was certainly strategic, as the military base from which to defend north Syria against any Ptolemaic attack. In this it was so successful that Ptolemaic land attacks were not even attempted.[23] By extension, Apamea also became the base from which Seleukid invasions of Ptolemaic territory were launched. Antiochos III twice used it in this way. The city therefore repeatedly functioned as the military and administrative centre for the whole kingdom. This position, however, lasted only so long as the situation which gave rise to it. After 198, when Antiochos III had conquered Phoenicia and Palestine, Apamea ceased to fulfil that central function. It may have continued as the centre of the royal stud, and as the stables for the royal elephants,[24] but after 198 it was too remote from the frontiers, either to the north or to the south, for its military function to continue as at first had been intended. The city therefore became, so to say, becalmed. Its source of expansion—its military function—was removed, at the very time that

---

[22] Str. 16. 2. 10.

[23] The successful Ptolemaic invasions were both by sea: in 246 to Seleukeia and Antioch, and in 145 to Antioch. The barren nature of the northern Biqaa valley and of the area north of Damascus to the east of the Anti-Lebanon range would also deter invasions, though Antiochos III tried that route in 221 from north to south—but he failed (Pol. 5. 45. 5–46. 3). His route south was blocked by Ptolemaic fortresses. In failing to capture them he condemned his army to a siege in a barren countryside, which was unendurable. Next time, in 218, he marched along the coast (Pol. 5. 61. 8–62. 3). The problem for the Ptolemaic kingdom was exactly the same, in reverse, for the fortress of Apamea was bounded to the south by a poorly cultivated area in the Orontes bend.

[24] Both the stud and the elephant stables would be too large to be easily moved, and there was no obvious alternative site. The terms of the Treaty of Apamea in 188 made the Seleukid king surrender his elephants (Pol. 21. 24 and 42–3), but either he did not do so or new animals were acquired later, for Antiochos IV certainly had some (Pol. 30. 24. 11; 1 Macc. 3: 34), though he may have got them from Egypt in his campaign there. How long the Seleukids continued to hold elephants is not clear, but communications with India had become difficult if not impossible by the 150s. The elephant corps does not ever seem to have been large enough to perpetuate itself by breeding (H. Scullard, *The Elephant in the Greek and Roman World* (London, 1974), 185–190).

Antioch had acquired a new source of expansion and so was growing. So both Seleukeia and Apamea failed to grow and quite possibly declined in population, though both clearly remained large in size.

The fourth of the great cities, Laodikeia-ad-Mare, is much less easy to characterize. Geographically it had even more awkward communications with the Syrian interior than had Seleukeia, and very much more difficult than those of Arados. Its growth was thus to some degree limited, though its immediate hinterland was productive enough. It may be, as well, that the Ptolemaic presence at Seleukeia extended beyond the immediate environs of that city. Just to the north of Laodikeia, at Ras Ibn Hani, an inscription has been found which consists of a list of names and home-cities. It is interpreted as a list of Ptolemaic mercenaries.[25] If this is correct then it implies that the area to the north of Laodikeia to within a few miles of the city was under Ptolemaic control, or at least under its military influence. The date of the inscription is unclear, but the third quarter of the third century BC is historically the most likely. Thus it is quite possible that Laodikeia's growth was restricted in a similar way to that of Seleukeia, by Ptolemaic pressure.

The four great cities which had been founded in 300 as equals had thus become differentiated during the first century of their existence. Antioch, after a time, expanded to become the unchallenged major city of the whole of Syria. Apamea possibly grew somewhat during its military heyday, but that source of growth was removed after 200. Seleukeia, there seems to be no doubt, shrank from the time of its Ptolemaic capture, and possibly Laodikeia declined about the same time and from the same cause. However, it is not possible to differentiate between those three as one can between all of them and Antioch, and the three must be regarded more or less as equals in 200, just as they had been at their foundation.

At that date, therefore, after a hundred years, the hierarchy of those large urban sites had altered. The growth of Antioch puts that city in a new classification, separate from its erstwhile colleagues. Now, therefore, the formal language of

[25] J.–P. Rey-Coquais, 'Inscription grecque découverte à Ras Ibn Hani', *AAAS* 26 (1976), 51–61.

the Urban Geographer can be utilized to replace the vague terms employed so far. Antioch is a metropolitan centre, a First Order site, exerting influence over a huge area. Seleukeia, Apamea and Laodikeia are Second Order centres, with influence over their region, but not of a world-city dimension. To this group can be added Arados. In 218 the island-city had regained control over its *peraia*, by agreement with Antiochos III.[26] This immediately enhanced both the importance and the physical size of the city, since Marathos once more became a suburb, ceasing to have any independence. Arados-plus-Marathos was politically united from 218 to 167, and the joint city is to be regarded as about the size of the three cities by about 200.

In the next century or so, from the time of Antiochos III to the death-throes of the Seleukid monarchy this city-ranking does not seem to have changed much. Antioch continued to expand at least until the middle of the second century, into the area incorporated as Epiphaneia by Antiochos IV, but perhaps not afterwards, since political troubles afflicted the city repeatedly from 150 onwards. Arados' final union with Marathos in 129[27] ensured that city's continued economic predominance in the south. Laodikeia, if it really had been restricted in its growth in the third century, certainly grew in importance and prosperity during the second. It was very little affected by political problems, though it was not immune from them, and by the first century BC it was a thriving manufacturing and exporting city,[28] on a standing of equality with Arados. Apamea suffered by the loss of its military role, and it is probable that this meant a decline in its size as it also meant a decline in its importance. Even so, it still remained the most important urban centre in the whole interior between Antioch and Damascus, with a ring of dependent towns around it.[29] Seleukeia suffered from the proximity of Antioch, now that Antioch was so dominant, and it tended to go a different political way from Antioch, except for one odd episode in the 140s. At the top, therefore, the urban hierarchy of Syria thus remained more or less the same about 100 BC as it had been in 200.

Below this Second Order level, however, it is always

[26] Pol. 5. 68. 7.
[28] Str. 16. 2. 9.
[27] Str. 16. 2. 12.
[29] Str. 16. 2. 10.

difficult to detect change and development. The former 'medium' rank, Beroia, Zeugma, Kyrrhos and Chalkis, can now be termed the Third Order. The old 'small' cities are therefore now in the Fourth Order, and the villages are the Fifth Order sites. The further one goes down the scale the more difficult it becomes to detect either growth or decline. Nevertheless the attempt is worth making, even though the results are unsatisfactory and indecisive. In some cases, however, more or less clear conclusions can be reached.

Alexandria-by-Issos did not exist in Seleukos' time but by the reign of Antiochos IV it was sufficiently important to be the site of a mint.[30] Its original position on the very border of the kingdom, while Kilikia was controlled by other rulers, implies that it began as a military post, but its natural advantages as a port and on the land route were sufficient, once the border was shifted north to the Taurus, to provide the stimulus for growth. During the Ptolemaic occupation of Seleukeia, Alexandria was the nearest port to Antioch which was still in Seleukid possession, and this will have been a further factor in its development. It must be reckoned as one of the third order centres by about 200 BC, and it seems to have maintained that position thereafter.

Further south, Gabala also grew but more slowly, never reaching prominence, but achieving some independent growth. It was separated from the Aradian sphere and had reached a modest size by the end of the second century, being important or enterprising enough to produce coins of its own in the early first century BC.[31] North of Laodikeia, the town Herakleia-ad-Mare and the settlements at Ras Ibn Hani and Ras el-Basit all grew to an appreciable size in the later Hellenistic period. (It may be that the ancient name refers to one of these two archaeological sites, though Ras el-Basit is probably Poseidonia.[32]) However, none of these places was sufficiently large or wealthy to compete with Alexandria-by-Issos, still less with Arados or Laodikeia, so they must all be counted as being in the fourth, rather than the third order.

---

[30] Head, *HN* 716, 763.

[31] Head, *HN* 716, 763; H. Seyrig, 'Gabala' in 'Questions Aradiennes', *Rev. Num.* 4 (1964), 9–28.

[32] P. Courbin, 'Bassit', *AAAS* 33, part 2 (1983), pp. 119–27; this is the latest assertion; there have been several earlier; it is not yet proved.

This development fits well enough with the hierarchy theory, for one would expect to find smaller centres developing in the intervals between the larger. A similar pattern worked out across the north, with towns such as Ayin Dara or Gindaros, Tell Rifaat and Doliche, growing at about the halfway points between the greater cities. South of Apamea, however, the absence of competing cities, combined with the security provided after 200 by the Seleukid conquest of Palestine and Phoenicia, permitted the development of both villages and town settlements.

Larissa would seem to have grown from its original fourth order size. It had been a dependent town of Apamea until it rebelled.[33] This event caused a good deal of amusement to Poseidonios, who remarked sarcastically on the manner of the Apameans going to war. We do not actually know the result of the war, or its date, but the fact that Larissa was capable of mounting such a challenge to Apamea implies that the difference in size between the two was by then considerably less than it had been at their foundations. Apamea had perhaps declined somewhat with the end of its central role in Seleukid military affairs, but Larissa will also have grown.

Further south, Hamath was reoccupied in the late third century, according to the pottery evidence, and a generation later it was big enough to be awarded the name Epiphaneia, presumably by Antiochos IV.[34]. Laodikeia-ad-Libanum seems to have had a certain life about it in the second century, though its use as a camp by Antiochos III's army in 219 does not imply that it was a town then.[35] Between these two places, also in the second century, the site of Emesa became the base of one of the Arab tribal dynasties from the desert. The vigour of the dynasty and its accumulated loot will have stimulated the growth of the place.

Here then there is an area where urban development took

---

[33] Athenaeus 4. 176 b—c, quoting Poseidonios (*FGH* iii. 253). The date is not known. It could have been in the 80s (as Jones, *CERP* 254, says), or as early as the 140s. Poseidonios included the incident in his third book, and, since his history began where that of Pol. left off, then the third book should be early. The date of the war, however, is not relevant to the point being made here.

[34] A. P. Christensen and C. F. Johansen, 'Les Poteries hellénistiques et les terres sigillées orientales', *Hama* 3/2, (Copenhagen, 1971), 1; Morkholm, *Antiochus IV*, pp. 117–18.

[35] Pol 5. 68. 7.

place with little interference by the central government. Little *direct* interference, that is. There was some, for instance the implied encouragement of Epiphaneia and Laodikeia by their acquisition of dynastic names, and more important the royal success and conquest which first established the conditions which permitted the growth. But other places were clearly left to develop as they could, and this is evidenced by the widespread use of Semitic names for the villages and towns. These places were settled and developed by the enterprise of the Aramaic-speaking peasantry, who resolutely gave their homes Aramaic names.[36] Out of them all, however, perhaps only Emesa reached true urban size in the Hellenistic period, stimulated, ironically, by its role as the local capital of an Arab dynasty. A number of places which are known to be towns and cities in the Roman period began their growth at this time—Mariamme,[37] Raphania,[38] and Seleukobelos,[39] all in the triangular area between the Orontes and the line of the mountains.

In the southern area, as in the coastal region, the evidence suggests overall growth. The expansion of rural settlement which is detectable in the archaeological evidence is repeated in this investigation of the specifically urban centres. All along the coast from Alexandria to Balanaia, and all across the southern area south of Apamea, there is clear evidence of the growth of settlements. Villages become towns, as at Alexandria and Gabala, at Ras el-Basit, at Mariamme and Emesa. What were towns in 300 grow, as at Larissa and Arados-Marathos. This growth occurred particularly in areas which had not been the scenes of Seleukos' city-foundations. Within the net of cities from Antioch to Zeugma, on the other hand, the evidence fails to suggest growth, except in odd cases, and a

---

[36] J. and J.-C. Balty, 'L'Apamène antique et les limites de la Syria Secunda', *La Géographie administrative et politique d'Alexandre à Mahomet* (Strasbourg, n.d.), 41 –75.

[37] A *polis* in the Roman period: *IGLS* 2106, 2114.

[38] Raphanea's growth was presumably due to the siting there for a time of the legions III Gallica and VI Ferrata in the first century AD (Jos. *Bellum Judaicum* 7. 1. 3), but it may have begun its preliminary growth earlier.

[39] The name demands foundation, or at least naming in the Seleukid period. It does not ever seem to have been called a *polis*, but it still existed as a settlement in the later Roman period, when it became the site of a plantation of barbarians (*Suda*, s.v. Seleukobelos).

hard look tends to suggest the opposite for some cities, that is, decline, even oblivion.

The great difficulty is that decline means that a city fails to appear in the sources, and such negative evidence is generally unreliable. As an example, take the contrasting histories of two neighbours, Beroia and Chalkis. Beroia appears intermittently in the sources throughout the Hellenistic period, always in a minor role, only once as a major participant in events. It was founded by Seleukos I, was the scene of the imprisonment of a high priest from Jerusalem in 163,[40] and in the disturbed times of the early first century BC it was the seat of a 'tyranny',[41] and stood a siege by the Seleukid king Philip I until rescued by a Parthian army and Arab allies.[42] In the later first century Strabo referred to it as a 'small town'.[43] And yet this does not tell us very much. The most that can be assumed is that the city had a continuous existence from its foundation into the first century BC, and that at that time it was a notable military post. Signs of growth are nil, however, and it seems likely that it was about the same size in 100 BC as it had been at its foundation.

Its neighbour Chalkis was founded at the same time, as a satrapal centre. It appears in the record for the first time in 145, when it was captured by Diodotos-Tryphon at the beginning of his revolt.[44] He was allied in this enterprise with a local Arab ruler, who was the foster-father of the child-king Antiochos V, in whose name Diodotos was challenging Demetrios II. So far Chalkis and Beroia have parallel histories. Thereafter, however, Chalkis disappears again from the record until it is listed by Pliny[45] in the first century AD, basing himself perhaps on Augustan material.[46] Little beyond the existence of the place can be discerned, however, since it is merely one name in the list. Then in AD 92 a new era was begun for the city, and this has been plausibly interpreted as showing that the city was freed from a dynast in that year.[47]

---

[40] 2 Macc. 13: 4.
[41] Str. 16. 2. 7.
[42] Jos. *AJ* 13. 14. 3.
[46] Jones, *CERP*, 260–1.

[43] Str. 16. 2. 7.
[44] Diod. 23. 4ᵃ. 1
[45] Pliny, *NH* 5. 80.

[47] Head, *HN* 778; the interpretation is that of Jones, *CERP* 262, though it is not necessary to accept his identification of the king as Aristobulos, son of Herod.

Who this presumed dynast was is not known, but it is possible that he was the descendant of the Arab king who had helped Diodotos seize the city in 145.[48] Chalkis occupied an important strategic situation for the relations between the desert and the settled lands. It overlooked a crossing point of the Qoueiq river, and so it dominated the route round the northern end of the salt-marsh of the Madkh. In the hands of a Seleukid garrison it provided protection for the settled lands to its north and east—which may well be why it had been a satrapal seat; in the hands of an Arab tribe, on the other hand, it was a gateway from the desert into the wealth of the settled lands. In terms of the city's history one would suppose that its frontier position, subject to raids whoever possessed it, would mean a likely decline from its position of early importance— no satraps are known, for instance, after the putative satrap of Seleukos I's time—and this would mean a concomitant decline of population and of strength in the third and second centuries. If it was in the hands of the Arabs after 145, it will have benefited from their heightened political activity during the first century BC, just as Emesa clearly did. There seems no doubt, however, that the city which had begun its existence as a satrapal seat, was a good deal less important than its contemporary and neighbour Beroia by the late Hellenistic period. Thus one may postulate decline.

Seleukeia-Zeugma had even more physical advantages than Chalkis. Its situation at the single major crossing point of the Euphrates gave it the advantage of being the obvious resort of merchants and armies and mobile kings. In 221 Antiochos III was married in the city,[49] which implies a standard of comfort fit for such a ceremony, and it will have been the scene of the Seleukid army's marches to the east in c.240, 222–221, 212, 187, 164, 162, 140 and 129, and of its rather less frequent returns.[50] How far the loss of control over Mesopotamia by

[48] It is more than likely that such a dynasty, if it existed, was established in the Hellenistic period. Few if any of the cities of Syria became dynastic seats in the Roman period, though they were disposed of in a fairly cavalier fashion during the Roman civil wars. Nevertheless, if a dynasty based at Chalkis did exist, its origin is more likely than not to be pre-Roman (see also Chapter 6).

[49] Pol. 5. 43. 1.

[50] C.240, Seleukos II marched to recover Baktria and Parthia (Justin 41. 4. 8–10); 222–221, Antiochos III did the same (Pol. 10. 27–31 and 49, and 11. 34); 187,

the Seleukids affected the city is difficult to judge. On the one
hand, it might be argued that traffic would decrease, yet in its
new role as a frontier post the importance of the city would
obviously increase, and so the city's garrison probably also
increased.⁵¹ Perhaps the various changes cancelled each other
out, leaving the city about the same size, but owing its
importance to rather different causes.

Nikopolis still existed in the Roman period, but no more
can be said than that.⁵² It can be assumed to have maintained
a minimum size; its function in economic terms was as a local
market centre, and this would ensure its continued existence
at a modest level. Hierapolis similarly continued: it was the
scene of one of Antiochos IV's performances, when he ritually
married the goddess.⁵³ The event suggests the continuing
political importance of the temple. This would ensure the
city's continued attraction for tourists and pilgrims; but
growth is not very likely.

Kyrrhos is as badly recorded as the rest. From its
foundation by Seleukos I it is recorded only obliquely as the
presumed source of the troops who rebelled against Antiochos
III in 220 and were mainly killed in punishment.⁵⁴ If it was
the source of these men, their destruction will presumably
have restricted the growth of the city. It became a mint under
Alexander I Balas (150–145),⁵⁵ a generation later than many
other towns, which had usually been minting since the time of
Antiochos IV (175–164), and this may imply that the city was
by then of only minor importance. This is to some degree

Antiochos III headed east to his death in Elam (Justin 32. 2. 1 and others); 164,
Antiochos IV did the same (1 Macc. 3: 37); 162, Demetrios I marched against the
challenger Timarchos (Diod. 36. 27ᵃ); 140, Demetrios II marched to recover
Babylonia (Justin, 36. 1; App. *Syr.* 67); 129, Antiochos VII did the same (App. *Syr.*
68; Justin 3.8. 10). Armies are known to have returned in *c.*235 (Justin 41. 4), in 220
(Pol. 5. 57. 1), in 205 (at Pol. 13. 9. 5, Antiochos III has survived his eastern
adventure and is on his way back to Syria), in 163 (under the Regent Philip (Jos. *AJ*
12. 9. 2 and 7)), and in 161 or 160 (after Demetrios I's victory over Timarchos (App.
Syr. 47). The armies of Demetrios II and Antiochos VII did not return, and then
there were no more Seleukid armies available to march east.

⁵¹ Philostratos, *Life of Apollonios* 1. 20 has a scene at a customs post at the bridge.
⁵² It was in the Roman province of Kilikia, not in Syria: App. *Syr.* 57.
⁵³ Granius Licinianus (ed. M. Flemisch, Leipzig, 1904), 28.
⁵⁴ Pol. 5. 50. 7.
⁵⁵ Head, *HN* 777.

surprising, since Kyrrhos was built on a major route connecting Antioch with Zeugma, and thus on the most important trade route between the Mediterranean and the East. The city should have gained some benefit from this. It does not, however, appear in the records again. In Strabo's account, a garbled passage implies that Gindaros was more important than Kyrrhos in his time,[56] and it is possible that Kyrrhos declined so much that it ceased to be reckoned as a city at all. It certainly declined if the absence of records can be any guide. Its revival in the Roman period occurred because it was the site of a legionary base;[57] the site is a poor one for urban development. On the whole, such evidence as there is seems to suggest that the city had declined so far that it had ceased to be more than a village—as a city, it had, in effect, died.

These six cities therefore, which all seem to have begun about the same size, developed differently. Beroia and Zeugma seem to have maintained their importance and their size. Kyrrhos, on the other hand, had probably died by the end of the Seleukid period. Chalkis had likely enough declined in size while Nikopolis and Hierapolis seem likely to have been smaller than the others from the start and had stayed about the same size. By 100 BC, then, we can call Beroia and Zeugma third order centres, Nikopolis, Hierapolis and Chalkis fourth order, and Kyrrhos dead.

The whole urban hierarchy at the end of the Seleukid period is, despite these uncertainties, now fairly clear. Antioch was the metropolis, comparable, as Strabo said, with Seleukeia-on-the-Tigris, and Alexandria-by-Egypt.[58] Below it were four cities now of the second rank—Seleukeia-in-Pieria, Laodikeia-ad-Mare, Arados-Marathos, and Apamea. Only one of these was inland, and in all cases major changes had taken place in the functions or political situations of the individual urban centres. The third order centres consisted of cities which were mainly in the north, between the sea and the Euphrates. Alexandria-by-Issos had developed more or less spontaneously. Beroia and Zeugma had maintained their

[56] Str. 16. 2. 8.
[57] Tacitus, *Annals*, 2. 57. 2 (*Legio* X *Fretensis*).
[58] Str. 16. 2. 5

positions. Beneath this level, fourth order centres, as one would expect were fairly numerous, scattered between the larger cities and composed partly of new towns and partly of declining old ones. The villages were everywhere, and had extended into the desert margin.

By this time, however, 100 BC, conditions for all of these settlements, of whatever 'order', had radically changed. This was due to the failure of the dynasty of the founder to maintain the vigour and purpose with which Seleukos had begun its history. The effect of this breakdown on the cities varied, of course, and in part it was the origin of many of the changes which have been investigated in this chapter. It is necessary, therefore, now to take up the thread of the relationship of the kings and their cities.

6

THE KINGS AND THE CITIES

THE evolution of the Syrian cities in terms of size and the gradual development of their hierarchy was not simply a matter of geographical factors working themselves out to an inevitable conclusion. There was nothing definitive about the process. After all, the artificiality of the urban system in Syria during Seleukos' reign was such that the 'natural' evolution of the system would need to contend with the determination of Seleukos' heirs and successors to maintain the system unaltered. The foundation of the cities—most of them—had been a royal act, and the royal will was one of the factors which geography could not take account of.

This royal will was manifested in three ways. First, and in a sense negatively, was that very determination to maintain the original system. Second was the foundation of supplementary cities, a process which had begun with Seleukos himself in his foundations of Hierapolis and Nikopolis. And third was the attitude of the cities themselves towards the monarchy and its civic system. It will be convenient to deal with new cities first, then consider the relationship to king and cities through the two centuries following the murder of Seleukos I.

In those two centuries other cities were founded, but there was nothing on Seleukos' scale. These later foundations are a good deal more obscure than the earlier ones, partly because many of them were, and remained, small. The result is that it is not always possible to be certain that those places were really royal in origin. Alexandria-by-Issos is an example of a place whose name convinces some that it was founded by Alexander, though no evidence other than the name exists. Nevertheless a dynastic name is one clue to a royal city.

These names could only have been used by permission of the current king, but later it seems that such names were awarded by the king as a mark of favour or as a sign of their foundation or re-foundation by royal authority.¹ At some point it seems that Arados had the dynastic name of Antioch,² but this clearly does not mean a re-foundation, but only an honorific, and a very temporary one at that.

Some of the places with dynastic names are so obscure that even their locations are uncertain. An Antioch-on-Euphrates existed to the north of Zeugma. It has generally been accepted that its original Semitic name was Urima, which is also used in the Roman period, and that it was at the present Horum Huyuk,³ although Rum Kale, further to the north, has also been suggested. The place was never of any real size, and it was placed opposite the equally small Epiphaneia-on-Euphrates across the river. If they were twins, the founder-king will have been Antiochos IV Epiphanes.

Seleukobelos is just as difficult to locate. In Ptolemy's list it would seem to be somewhere in the area of Apamea, but not all of the places on that list can be located.⁴ Jones' suggestion that the name is preserved in Salukiyé⁵ is perhaps slightly better than that of Dussaud who placed it at Jisr esh-Shogour,⁶ which seems rather too far north for Ptolemy. But neither suggestion can be said to be conclusive.

The site of the old city of Hamath, on the Orontes, received the new name of Epiphaneia from Antiochos IV Epiphanes.⁷ Archaeologically the earliest Hellenistic settlement on the site

---

¹ Jones *CERP*, 246, for example, remarks that 'we may presume that the new cities with dynastic names . . . had autonomy from their foundation, and that the grant of dynastic names to old towns . . . implies the grant of autonomy'.

² Stephanos, Byzantium, s.v. Antiocheia ⁷.

³ This is again a matter of linking disjointed fragments of information. Pliny, *NH* 5. 86 mentions Antioch, and Ptol. 5. 14. 10 mentions Urima, each in about the same position, where Horum Huyuk now stands. It is most economical to equate the three, though actual proof is lacking. Neither Antioch nor Epiphaneia can be shown to have produced coins until the second century AD (Head, *HN* 776).

⁴ Ptol. 5. 14. 14.

⁵ Jones *CERP* 452, n. 24 (end).

⁶ Dussaud, *Top. hist.*, pp. 155–6. Another placing of this site is at Sqalbiyé, a few kilometers south of Apamea, by Honigmann, 'Hist. Top.' no. 412, and in *PW*, s.v. Seleukeia ³, IIA, cols. 1200–3. This is accepted by J.-C. Balty in the 'Discussion' after a paper by J.-C. Courtois on the Ghab, in *Apamée de Syrie, Colloque 1972* (Brussels, 1972), 82, even though Honigmann himself later accepted Jones's Salukiyé (E. Honigmann, 'Notes de géographie syrienne', in *Mélanges syriennes offerts à René Dussaud* (Paris, 1939), i. 129–133).

⁷ The king's chosen surname was Epiphanes, and this is the basis for the attribution. It receives some support from the archaeological evidence: the coins detailed from 'Niveau D' were minted between 167 and 64 (H. Ingholt, *Rapport préliminaire sur sept campagnes de fouilles à Hama en Syrie* (Copenhagen, 1940), 123) and

is *c.*200 BC,[8] so it was a place which was already settled when it was granted its dynastic name. Settlement did not, however, ever extend beyond the top of the old Iron Age tell during the Hellenistic period, and not even the whole tell-top was built over. The large houses which have been revealed in excavation make it clear that the inhabitants were prosperous, that the whole 'city' was carefully planned from the start and that the population living on the tell was only ever a few hundred, perhaps no more than 250.[9] It did not expand out of the restricted space on the tell until the Roman period.[10] The place is so small that the title of city seems wholly inappropriate. This is a situation similar to that at Europos-Carchemish, for instance, and at Laodikeia-ad-Libanum, and perhaps at the barely visible Antioch-on-Euphrates as well.

Laodikeia-ad-Libanum, the ancient Qadesh, had been deserted since the Persian period, if not earlier.[11] The dynastic name first occurs in 219, when Antiochos III's army camped there on its march south.[12] The nature of the Hellenistic settlement at the site is unclear, though at least three sets of excavations have taken place there.[13] As at Hama, however, it does appear that there was no Hellenistic occupation off the tell; that is, once more, the place was small.[14] Whether it was one of the 'five Laodikeias' which Appian said were all founded by Seleukos I[15] seems very unlikely.

There may have been other places with dynastic names, since our sources are so relatively poor, though no more are

this is consistent with the pottery evidence (in A. P. Christensen and C. F. Johansen, 'Les Poteries hellénistiques et les terres sigillées orientales', *Hama* 3/2. (Copenhagen, 1971), p. 1). O Morkholm, *Antiochus IV*, does not, however, include it in his list of the king's foundations on pp. 117–18.

[8] Christensen and Johansen (see previous note).

[9] *Hama* 3. 1.

[10] This becomes clear when the small excavations in the modern city are plotted and dated. None of those in that part have any Hellenistic remains at all, but all or almost all have Roman remains. These excavations are all small but they are well and fairly evenly scattered over the city. For details see Ingholt (note 7).

[11] M. Pezard, *Qadesh* (Paris 1931), 4–11.

[12] Pol. 5. 68. 7.

[13] S. A(bdul-Hak), 'Chronique des fouilles en Syrie: III, Les Fouilles . . . dans la Nécropole de Tell Nebi Mind', *AAS* 1. (1951), 121–6; P. J. Parr, 'Tell Nebi Mend-Qadesh', *Archiv für Orientforschung* 26, (1978) 60–2.

[14] The only plan of this site which is of any use is that published by Parr in *AAAS* (1983), 117.

[15] App. *Syr.* 57.

recorded in the lists compiled by the geographer Claudius
Ptolemy in the second century AD. The four which can be
identified are seen to be very small, and three of them are no
more than reoccupied tells.

Once more, as in the slightly different case with Alexandria,
it is the existence of a dynastic name which provides the only
evidence that these places were 'cities'. Thus they must be
doubted. The sheer smallness of a place like Laodikeia-ad-
Libanum, or the tiny area of the tell at Epiphaneia-Hamath,
casts the strongest possible doubt on the presumed civic rank
of the Hellenistic settlements. As a contrast there is the tell at
Tell Qarqur. Like Laodikeia-ad- Libanum it was the site of a
famous pre-Assyrian city, and again it was the scene of a
famous battle (in 753 BC, when the confederated kings of the
Aramaean states defeated the Assyrian invasion[16]). Also it is
the scene now of archaeological investigations. Hellenistic
remains have been found in all four of the soundings in the
tell, which straddle the whole surface.[17] The implication is
that the Hellenistic occupation covered the whole tell. And
this is an area of 23 hectares, four times the area of Tell Nebi
Mend. Yet no suggestion has been made that Qarqur was a
Hellenistic city. Thus the civic rank of Laodikeia-ad-Libanum
(and of those other small dynastically named sites as well)
needs more evidence behind it .than the name alone. Hence
also the usefulness of the more neutral geographical jargon of
'fourth order' sites used in the previous chapter.

This then is the sum of dynastically named cities. Seleukos I
had founded ten cities in two decades; the rest of the dynasty
founded three in two centuries, and none of them are
convincing as 'cities' in any way. There are, however, also a
number of places which have divine names—Apollonia,
Herakleia (twice)—and it is possible that these were royal
foundations. Both of these gods appear with great frequency
on Seleukid coins. Yet we have absolutely no evidence—apart
from Appian's summary[18]—of royal activity in these cases. It

---

[16] D. Winton Thomas (edn.), *Documents from Old Testament Times*, (1953), 47 and
49, quoting the Kurkh stele (BM 118884).
[17] J. M. Lundquist, 'Tell Qarqur, the 1983 Season', *AAAS* 32, part 2 (1983), 273–
88.
[18] App. *Syr.* 57.

is best to be cautious. After all, there are plenty of places named for Greek or Macedonian towns which would appear to originate before Seleukos' conquest. These divine names may do so as well. Or they may be of 'spontaneous' growth, like Alexandria. It was a superstitious age, and, for a city, the name of a god may have been as potent as any king's name.

The evidence for later royal foundations is thus very poor, and is concentrated (if such a word can be used in so uncertain an area) in the person of Antiochos IV Epiphanes, who, it will be recalled, was also responsible for sanctioning the second expansion of Antioch, giving his cognomen to the new suburb of Epiphaneia. This episode is symbolic of the whole civic-monarchic relationship. Consider Antioch's history, as an example, since it is the one we know best. It was founded by Seleukos I. When it expanded, first in the reign of Seleukos II, then in that of Antiochos IV, it was the kings who were credited with organizing the matter.[19] Similarly it was Antiochos III who was reported to have settled Cretans, Euboeans, and Aetolians in Syria after his defeat by Rome at Magnesia in 189.[20] During the reign of Antiochos IV, again, the king gave his name to at least two 'new' settlements (Epiphaneia-Hamath and Antioch-on-Euphrates), as well as his new suburb of Antioch. In all cases it was the king who took the initiative.

It is, of course, quite possible that this is the result of the way in which the information is presented in our sources, and it may in fact have been part of the original bias of historical writing about the Seleukid kingdom. Yet it is consistent with other evidence. None of the Seleukid cities, even in the second quarter of the second century of their existence, are credited at any time in any source with taking the initiative in such basic civic matters as expanding their size, building a city-wall, or, perhaps most startling of all, building a new *bouleuterion*.[21]

[19] Str. 16. 2. 5.
[20] Lib. Or. 11. 119.
[21] Antiochos IV also gave a *bouleuterion* to Miletos (T. Wiegand, *Milet* i, 2 (Berlin, 1906), nos. 1 and 2) and other gifts to many cities in old Greece (Morkholm, *Antiochus IV*, 55–63). These are clearly diplomatic in purpose. His gifts to his own cities are meagre in comparison, and Antioch is the only one in Syria known to have benefited by his generosity. His gift to Antioch is thus different, and it may well be that the city did not have a *bouleuterion* already (Downey, *Antioch*, pp. 105–6).

There had been occasions when the cities acted without the king or even against him, but these are very few, and can be reviewed briefly. When Seleukos I died, 'the cities of the Seleukis', which appears to mean the cities of Syria,[22] had broken into revolt.[23] A generation later, in 246, during the confusion following the death of Antiochos II, Seleukeia and Antioch had elaborately welcomed Ptolemy III,[24] and probably the other cities did so too. In c.235 Antioch had been persuaded to revolt against Seleukos II by his aunt Stratonike.[25] There is, thus, no real sign of loyalty in these cities to the dynasty of Seleukos.[26] Yet it is also clear that the cities were not acting independently in any real sense: on the first two occasions they simply exchanged one king for another, and Antioch's revolt in 235 collapsed, apparently without any fighting, as soon as the king returned from the east.

There is also just as little sign of any demand for civic freedom or autonomy as there is of loyalty to the dynasty. The city rebellions all occurred at moments of dynastic weakness. In 281 the murder of Seleukos I at Lysimacheia was followed

---

[22] See the comment by Str. 16. 2. 4.

[23] *OGIS* 219.

[24] P. Gurob.

[25] Jos., *Contra Apionem* 1. 206, quoting Agatharkides (*FGH* iii. 196, frag. 19.)

[26] The sprawling, heterogeneous nature of the Seleukid kingdom has provoked historians to search for a reason for its existence and longevity, and the one institution which appeared to make sense of it was the dynasty itself. So loyalty to the Seleukids was said to be the cement which held the kingdom together. F. W. Walbank, in the modern mode, says that: 'Any unity that . . . realm might possess the king had to impose on it with the aid of the bureaucracy and the army' (*The Hellenistic World* (1981), 214), which is saying in one way what Bevan repeatedly says in explaining the failure of rebellions by ingrained dynastic loyalty, as in the collapse of those of Molon and Timarchos. Bevan's main explanation for the collapse of Tryphon's rebellion is to say: 'Antiochus was in Seleuceia', and then add an exclamation mark (*House*, i. 308 (Molon), ii. pp. 194–5 (Timarchos), 237–238 (Tryphon)). In fact, of course, the kingdom did not hold together. Scarcely a decade went by without some province breaking away, successfully or not. Loyalty to the dynasty is a historian's myth. The kings themselves made no pretence at relying on such loyalty, though no doubt for their own *amour propre* they claimed it. The system of control was detailed and all-pervasive, involving provinces and cities, and occasionally super-governorships, in the east or in Asia Minor. These, of course, were the most likely to produce rebellions—Achaios in Asia Minor, Molon and the others in the east. The collapse of these rebellions, particularly those in the east, must be due to the appreciation by the Greco-Macedonians in the cities that their interests were bound up with the success of the Seleukid rather than that of the rebel. Even so, in Asia Minor, this conspicuously did not operate between 242 and 212, nor did it operate in Baktria in 247, nor in Persis at any time after c.280.

by the momentary seizure of power by Ptolemy Keraunos.²⁷ It *should* have been followed by the proclamation of Antiochos I who had been joint-king with his father for some years. In Syria Antiochos was ignored, though Babylonia was loyal to him. But he was already present in Babylonia, and in full control, to such effect that he was able to squeeze the last ounce of taxes from that province in order to recover his inheritance.²⁸ Clearly, it was the absence of both king and army from Syria which allowed the rebellion to occur in 280. The fact that it did occur, however, is evidence, not of an intention of the cities to be seizing freedom, but that Seleukos' power had not yet been fully institutionalized. Obviously he had relied on his own presence and on his garrisons.²⁹

In 246 this dynastic weakness recurred in a disputed succession after the death of Antiochos II, when the senior dynastic representative, Seleukos II, was absent in Asia Minor. It was this absence which allowed Ptolemaic authority to be accepted in the cities. Yet in neither 280 nor in 246 did the cities give any sign that they contemplated making themselves independent. There is no sign in the sources that autonomy was a civic aim, nor are there any coins proclaiming it. Instead in all cases the Seleukid king gradually recovered control. The rebellion in 280, at a guess, was *against* something—probably taxes, garrisons, and so on—rather than *for* something, and certainly not for independence. In 246

---

²⁷ App. *Syr.* 62–3; Memnon, *FGH* 434, F8, 1–7.
²⁸ S. Smith, *Babylonian Historical Texts* (1924), 150–9.
²⁹ Seleukos will have taken his full levy of troops to fight Lysimachos. Since he was on his way to take over Macedon when he was killed (App. *Syr.* 62), he had probably not sent many of these soldiers home yet. The garrisons in the Syrian cities will therefore have been small, though, since Lysimachos had a marriage alliance with Ptolemy (Plut. *Dem.* 31), they will not have disappeared altogether. After the assassination, Ptolemy Keraunos, the assassin, took over Seleukos' army for a time—not just the army of Lysimachos, which was scarcely intact after seven months under Seleukos (Memnon, *FGH* 434, F8, 1–7)—though the exact period is not clear. Thus from 281 into 279 the forces available in Syria (and elsewhere) were small. From 279 onwards, however, the troops will have begun to return home. And next year, probably, war began with Ptolemy II (Will, *Hist. pol.* i. 139–42), which will have ensured a concentration of troops in Syria. These troops were Antiochos', so, when they returned home, the city thereupon became his. There seems to be no real reason to imagine an active campaign of conquest by Antiochos in Syria. His propaganda, no doubt, talked of 'recovery' and 'rescue' rather than conquest and control; the whole episode is so badly known that little is firm knowledge, other than some sort of 'rebellion'.

the apparent relief with which Ptolemy III was received in
Seleukeia and Antioch, when the Seleukid dynasty seemed to
have collapsed, does suggest that these cities felt that a king
was a necessary part of their political system.

Antioch thus provides a pattern of civic behaviour in the
third century, in which there is at first a certain resentment at
the royal power, as in 280, but from then on, in 246, in 235, in
the successive extensions of the city's boundary, the king is
seen as an essential part of the political landscape. To this
pattern the other cities founded by Seleukos I conform, in so
far as we can discern their history.

Contrast the history of Arados. In 333 Alexander had
stopped at Marathos, on the mainland, and it is possible that
a Macedonian garrison and governor were left at the city
when he moved on.[30] The kingship of Arados does not appear
to have been disturbed, and probably still existed well into the
third century.[31] When it fell into Seleukos' share of the spoils
after Ipsos, therefore, it was not essentially different from the
other Phoenician cities to the south, some of which Ptolemy
had seized, and others which were still held by Demetrios.[32]
During this time, Arados, or perhaps Marathos, had been the
site of a royal mint, producing the continuing coinage of
Alexander the Great.[33]

It is from coins that much of Arados' Hellenistic history has
been reconstructed. The city began a new era in 259,
according to coins produced in 243/242 and inscribed 'Year
17'.[34] The new era has been interpreted as marking the

---

[30] This is asserted by Rey-Coquais, *Arados*, pp. 151–3, on the basis of some later
Marathian coins depicting a Macedonian shield. It is a flimsy basis for the theory,
but, given that the Phoenician cities were locally the most powerful political units,
and that Marathos was Arados' weak point, it seems a strong possibility.

[31] Alexander's arrangements were made with the king's son, and there is no sign of
either the son or the father being deposed (Arr. 2. 13. 7). In 318 Antigonos summoned
the local kings to a meeting (Diod. 29. 58. 1) and it seems reasonable to believe that
one of those kings was from Arados, though the origins of the kings are not specified.

[32] Demetrios continued to hold Tyre and Sidon until 288–287, when Ptolemy
conquered them (Will, *Hist. pol.*, i. 94, and notes on p. 96). It may be that he also held
Arados island, but if so he gave it up to Seleukos in 298 when their marriage alliance
was made. This may well have been the background to Seleukos' later demand for
Tyre (Plut. *Dem.* 32).

[33] Newell, *WSM* 194 ff.

[34] Seyrig, 'Aradus', pp. 206–220; J. G. Milne, 'The Coinage of Aradus', *Iraq* 5.
(1938), 12–22.

abolition of the monarchy,[35] which had certainly gone by 218.[36] The coins of 'Year 17' (243/242) are in the name of the city, and they are interpreted as showing that, as a result of an agreement with Seleukos II, Arados gained the right to mint its own coins, and perhaps other privileges as well. The date is significant, for Seleukos II was at the time in need of all the local support he could get in his attempts to recover his inheritance from Ptolemy III, who had seized Syria in the crisis of 246.[37]

The contrast between Arados and the other Syrian cities is marked, for none of the others gained a mint at the time, though the example of Arados makes it clear that such a privilege was available, and that it was a price which Seleukos was prepared to pay for support.[38] Furthermore, every town in the Aradian *peraia* (Gabala, Paltos, Balanaia, and others), subsequently used the era of 259. Thus the whole of the *peraia* was a single unit at that time. The change which the new era marked affected all of those smaller communities.[39] It is evidence, that is, that in 243/242 Arados was in control of its *peraia*.

Arados was able to extract concessions from Seleukos II because, after the king's own fleet from Asia Minor was wrecked in 244,[40] Arados controlled the most important fleet in the Syrian area.[41] Strabo records that the Aradians also

[35] Seyrig, 'Aradus', p. 209; Rey-Coquais, *Arados*, pp. 153-4; Jones, *CERP*, 238.

[36] Antiochos III made an agreement with 'the Aradians' in that year (Pol. 5. 68. 7), which implies that there was no king at the time.

[37] Seyrig, 'Aradus', pp. 217-218.

[38] A few early coins of Seleukeia-in-Pieria and Antioch, all in bronze, were in the names of the cities or of the citizens (Newell, *WSM* 87-92 and 94). These issues soon faded away. The Aradian coins on the other hand were in silver.

[39] It does not show, as Rey-Coquais, *Arados*, p. 157, claims, that the whole *peraia* became a series of autonomous states at the time. He is here the victim of his theory that the *peraia* was a 'community' of states, with the central shrine at Baitokaike an amphictyony perhaps. The evidence is simply not strong enough to support the theory. The more economical theory for the use of 259 all through the *peraia* is that it was all Aradian territory at the time.

[40] Justin 27. 2.

[41] In 332 kings Gerostratos of Arados and Enylos of Byblos and the city of Sidon between them contributed 80 ships to Alexander at Tyre (Arr. 2. 20. 1). A maximum of, say, 40 would be Aradian, but these are unlikely to be the total fleet, for some were probably left at home. Tyre had 80 ships (Diod. 17. 41. 1) but it was a bigger city; it seems unlikely that Arados had less than 50 ships: it does not seem unreasonable to assume that a fleet of a similar size was maintained during the Seleukid period.

gained the right to receive political refugees from the mainland.[42] No doubt this was useful to the king in that his opponents were able to flee there (perhaps, in the context of the time, men who had sided with the Ptolemaic occupation), and not fight on to the death. But it must have been uncomfortable to know that the city harboured his enemies, even though Arados charged the refugees highly for the asylum they got.[43] Seleukos II, once his control over most of the mainland was established and the war with Ptolemy had been brought to an end, took his revenge. In the 220s several of the mainland communities of the *peraia* minted their own coins; this implies that they were then politically separate from Arados.[44] Thus Seleukos' *riposte* was to break up Arados' control over the *peraia* by recognizing the political separation of Marathos, Simyra and Gabala.

The autonomy of these small towns was brief, for the coins cease from *c.*218, and it seems that Arados recovered control of the *peraia* in that year. This can only have come about as a result of a new agreement with the next king, Antiochos III. Presumably there was a connection, once again, between the need of the king for a fleet in order to continue his campaign against Ptolemy—the Fourth Syrian war had broken out three years before[45]—and this change in Arados' political fortunes. Or, it may also be that, with the recapture of Seleukeia-in-Pieria in 219, there was less need for dependence on Arados, and so the city could be treated with some generosity. This in turn would be quickly noted among the other Phoenician cities further south, which were the major prizes in the subsequent campaign. Beyond all that, it may also be that, except for Marathos, the 'autonomous' cities of the *peraia* were really too small to be convincing as independent political entities.[46] So a reconstitution of Arados' *peraia*, by which Arados would exercise some political authority over

---

[42] Str. 16. 2. 14.

[43] The city was paid by the refugees with estates on the mainland (Str. 16. 2. 14).

[44] Seyrig, 'Aradus', and 'Monnaies hellénistiques: XVIII, Séleucos III et Simyra', *Rev. Num.* 13. (1971), pp. 7–11.

[45] Pol. 5. 68. 7.

[46] Excavation of Simyra has suggested that the 'city' was in full decline by the late third century, and that it scarcely survived the next (M. Dunand and N. Saliby, 'A la recherche de Simyra', *AAAS* 7 (1957), 3–16, and M. Dunand, A. Bounni, and N. Saliby, 'Fouilles de Tell Kazel, rapport préliminaire', *AAAS* 14 (1964), 3–14.

the mainland communities, will have seemed a satisfactory political manœuvre. No doubt also this was Arados' price for its wholehearted co-operation in the war.

The vigour displayed by Arados in pursuance of the recovery of its autonomy and of its mainland territory, and its persistence in exploiting Seleukid difficulties for its own local advantage, puts the city in stark contrast to the supineness of the other Syrian cities in this respect. The reasons for Arados' attempts at expanding its area of autonomy are, no doubt, various; geographically, its island position gave the city a certain advantage in dealings with the kings of the mainland; commercially, the city's rulers, a merchant oligarchy,[47] were accustomed to decisiveness and appreciated the advantages of semi-independence; ethnically, it was a self-consciously Phoenician city (where the Phoenician language continued in use into the Roman period [48]) in a Greco-Macedonian state; historically, alone of the Syrian cities, Arados had a tradition of autonomy which reached back for several centuries.

Reversing these reasons gives some indication of why the other Syrian cities displayed such a lack of vigour in pursuing autonomy for themselves. Geographically, they were on land, and so they were militarily vulnerable; their source of wealth was agriculture, in the main, though some commerce certainly developed[49]; ethnically, they were Greek and Macedonian communities, quite possibly feeling threatened by the Aramaic-speaking villagers in their country districts; historically they were all new communities, without any traditions of

[47] There seems to be no clear evidence of the type of government which succeeded the monarchy. Antiochos III treated with 'the Aradians' in 218 (Pol. 5. 68. 7), which might suggest a formally democratic constitution, if one stretches the phrase to the limits of what it will yield. In the second half of the second century BC the action of the city in parcelling out the *peraia* among its citizens might suggest a pre-emptive move to prevent a democratic rising (see p. 167). The city lived by commerce, as did all the Phoenician cities, and a merchant oligarchy, probably open and willing to accept new recruits, is the most likely form of constitution.

[48] *IGLS* 4001, a bilingual inscription.

[49] The commerce of these cities is a subject which is little known, due as usual to a dearth of sources, but which has engendered fairly high assumptions. It is probable that long distance commerce scarcely existed at all in the Persian period, and that its development in the Hellenistic period was fairly minor. Such commerce as there was in the Syrian cities would mainly be local, unless the city was on the coast. Apart from Antioch, the cities which grew most in size were all coastal. Inland cities were distinctly backward in their growth, and even in the Roman period they were relatively unimportant.

independent action, and founded in imitation of Macedonian cities where autonomy was strictly limited.

Other reasons could be adduced, but they will all be reasons for *not* seeking autonomy, and would be based on the assumption that these cities, given the chance, *should* seek autonomy. This has been the general assumption behind most studies of Hellenistic 'urbanization'.[50] But the evidence of the Seleukid cities of Syria is that they did *not* seek autonomy. This is the significance of the conduct of Arados, which did actively seek it. Reverse the assumption, look at the evidence in that light, and it makes more sense to say that the cities felt more need for royal supervision and support than they did for autonomy. Their 'loyalty' to the dynasty was based partly on *force majeure*, dominated as they were by those large citadels, but mainly on the recognition of their helplessness alone. Even when they rebelled, the cities tended to rebel together, as in 280 and in 246.

The reason for this need for mutual support can only be that they recognized that they could not survive individually in independence. The need for support from the king or from other cities means that the Greek cities were conscious of a threat to their well-being, or even perhaps to their very existence, and that this threat affected them all. Yet this threat was one which Arados did not fear. It cannot be the threat from Ptolemaic Egypt. This was a threat to the dynasty, but not, as several Ptolemaic invasions showed, to any of the cities. Seleukeia-in-Pieria in the Ptolemaic kingdom was still a city, trading, being taxed, well garrisoned certainly, but a city still. The only enemy which threatened all the Greek cities but did not pose any threat to Arados was the local Aramaic-speaking population.

Under normal circumstances, then, when a king reigned, the cities were loyal not because of affection for the dynasty, but because together the king and the cities made up an overwhelming potential for force, and the cities then need have no fear of the surrounding peasantry. At the same time the king extended his support to the cities, partly because they were Greek and Macedonian, partly because the Seleukid

---

[50] This is the basic assumption, for instance, behind the various studies by A. H. M. Jones on the subject, especially *The Greek City from Alexander to Justinian* (Oxford, 1940), ch. 6.

king was the direct heir of the founder, but mainly because it was through the cities that the king exercised his power over those who paid taxes—the Aramaic peasantry. As in all enduring partnerships, the cities and the kings both needed each other, and gained mutual benefits from their association.

However, the partnership could only continue if both parties maintained their potency. In this respect it was the kingship which was the more vulnerable. It was more liable to wear and tear than were the cities, for it was a personal office, and depended on the physical existence of a single man. Crises in the relationship therefore occurred when a king died. These crises were especially serious when the king's heir was absent or powerless, or when the inheritance was disputed. Thus, in 280, the filching of Seleukos I's army by Ptolemy Keraunos,[51] combined with the absence of the Seleukid heir Antiochos I, meant that the cities felt threatened, hence their 'rebellion', whatever it actually amounted to. Antiochos' reappearance on the scene, and the recovery of the Seleukid army from Keraunos[52] produced a revival of confidence and a re-subjection of the cities. The apparent intervention of Ptolemy II in this crisis may well be the result of the power vacuum caused by the absence of the Seleukid ruler from Syria. Ptolemy's intervention is most obscure, indeed it is not even clear whether it really took place, though in the end the problem resolved itself into a war of the usual dynastic type, Ptolemy against Antiochos, the 'First Syrian War'.[53] The Ptolemaic incursion was thus not necessarily originally one of conquest; it may have been protective, or even by invitation, in which the cities called for Ptolemy to come and protect them from their own subjects.[54]

[51] Pausanias 1. 16. 2; Memnon, *FGH* 8. 1–7.

[52] Keraunos bought off any threat from Pyrrhos of Epirus by giving him an army (Justin 17. 2), but it is difficult to believe that these men were ex-Seleukids. Nor is it easy to accept that the army he used to beat Antigonos Gonatas was anything other than Macedonian (Justin 24. 1). One must assume that the army Seleukos had brought from the east in 282 had returned to the east at some time after Seleukos' murder, that is, probably during 279.

[53] These events are very obscure, but their resolution into a straight Seleukid-Ptolemaic war by 276 is clear: S. Smith, *Babylonian Historical Texts*, (1924), 150–9; Will, *Hist. pol.*, i. 146–50.

[54] There were, it appears, *two* wars: one following the murder of Seleukos I, dated c.281–279, and a second, called by historians the 'First Syrian War', c.276–274. The Babylonian text printed by Smith (see previous note) carries the clear implication that this war was new in 276. Nevertheless the whole conflict from 281 to

In 246, the Seleukid inheritance was disputed between a baby and an absent adult, both sons of Antiochos II.[55] Ptolemy III's intervention is generally seen in dynastic terms, in which he acted to support the claims of his daughter's child,[56] but from the point of view of the cities, this was not especially relevant. The extraordinary welcome which Seleukeia and Antioch laid on for him needs explaining [57]. After all, there was no real need for any demonstration of joy, and self-interest might have suggested that resistance in the name of the absent Seleukos II would be an intelligent response. Seleukos, after all, was adult, capable, and on his way.[58] Better still, indifference to both claimants until the winner emerged might have brought dividends. This may well be what Arados did. After all, Ptolemy did not arrive with any real force,[59] and both Seleukeia and Antioch were powerfully fortified cities which were quite capable of resisting the small Egyptian army.

The account of the event which we have is, or purports to be, a personal account by Ptolemy himself,[60] and of course he sees the welcome as a personal one. But Ptolemy was quite unknown to the citizens—he had only succeeded to the Ptolemaic throne that year—and so it cannot have been a sincere welcome in the personal sense, though in a political and diplomatic sense it clearly *was* sincere. Thus it is a political welcome: he was being welcomed for what he was and what he represented. His presence and the presence of his soldiers in the cities guaranteed to the cities that the royal-urban alliance would continue in operation, if in a slightly

274 and later is clearly a unity. The rebellion of 'the cities of the Seleukis', attested only by *OGIS* 219, cannot be separated from the international conflict, and it clearly came first in the whole sequence.

55 Will, *Hist. pol.*, i. 246–250.

56 This was, of course, Ptolemy's pretext for intervention. The manœuvres which took place in Antioch once it was clear to Ptolemy that his daughter and her son were dead were clearly based upon this dynastic pretext.

57 P. Gurob.

58 He prepared a fleet in Asia Minor, but it was caught in a storm and wrecked (Justin 27. 2).

59 He had 'as many ships as the harbour of Seleuceia would admit', which in turn means that his *land* force was not large (P. Gurob).

60 Bevan thought it was the account of a Seleukid officer, but Holleaux's interpretation has carried the day (M. Holleaux, *études d'epigraphie et d'histoire grecques*, vol. ii (Paris, 1942), 281–310).

different guise. And it was only a temporary situation. When Seleukos II arrived in Syria once more, with his own army, the cities could revert to their Seleukid allegiance, and Ptolemy's power in Syria simply evaporated, except at Seleukeia, which he held on to by imposing a strong garrison.[61]

The contrast, once again, with the treatment of Arados is strong. Arados extracted privileges from Seleukos II in *c*.242, and Seleukos came back later to punish the city by removing the *peraia* from its control. Compare Apamea, which, like Arados, had a large territory with several dependent towns; and it had certainly 'rebelled'. But it made no attempt to gain privileges from the king. The evidence, it must be admitted, is essentially numismatic, with the assumption that the acquisition of the right to coin in silver is a clear indication of autonomy. By this measure, Apamea, whose coinage is very poor in both quality and quantity,[62] was conspicuously different from Arados, which regularly produced a good coinage of its own. Ten or fifteen years later Arados was punished when its *peraia* towns were granted the same privilege of coining as Arados itself, but Apamea was not, so far as we know, punished at all; that is to say, the punishment meted out by Seleukos II was not for rebelling, but for extracting privileges.

The contrast between Arados on the one hand, and, on the other, all the cities of Seleukos I in their relations with the Seleukid monarchy continued through the third and the second centuries. Arados moved into autonomy and then back into royal control several times; the other cities remained securely attached to the monarchy all through by such devices as *epistatai*, citizen-Friends, garrisons, and acropoleis, but above all by their own wish, for they needed royal support and protection to survive.

The fact that these cities cannot be described as autonomous, still less independent, does not mean that they did not

---

[61] There is no sign of physical attacks on north Syrian cities in this war, though we do know of an attack by Seleukos II on Damascus, and a siege of Orthosia in Phoenicia by him in 242–241 (Eusebius, *Chron.*, ed. Schone, i. 251). These do suggest that it was only after recovering the Seleukis that Seleukos encountered serious resistance.

[62] Newell, *WSM* 163–5.

possess the standard political and administrative equipment of the Greek *polis*. Ptolemy III's account of his welcome at Seleukeia-in-Pieria and at Antioch in 246 provides a clear illustration of this. He was greeted by 'the priests, the (magistrates, the) other citizens, the officers and the soldiers' at Seleukeia, and 'the . . . satraps, and the other officers (and soldiers), the priests, the boards of magistrates and (all the) young men from the gymnasium, and the rest of the (crowd)' at Antioch.[63] Sixty years later Seleukos IV's 'request' to Seleukeia-in-Pieria that the city confer its citizenship on his Friend Archilochos is known to us in the form of a decree proposed by the *epistates* and the magistrates, and the inscription attests the existence of magistrates, a magistrates' office, a deme Olympios, and a tribe Laodike.[64] Antioch had a *bouleuterion* from *c.*170,[65] even if the king gave it to the city, and hence it had a *boule*. The magistrates at Laodikeia-ad-Mare were called *peliganes*, apparently a Macedonian term.[66] These cities, and by a reasonable presumption, the other cities in Syria as well, had all the usual apparatus of a Greek city: demes and tribes, magistrates and priests, people called citizens, and people who were not citizens.

The actual constitutions of the cities were probably democratic, in a formal sense, but the evidence is, as always, tenuous in the extreme. Antigonos recruited Athenians to populate Antigoneia,[67] and it seems unlikely that such people would accept any other type of constitution than a democracy. These became inhabitants of Antioch and/or Seleukeia after 300. In the reign of Antiochos III the city of Teos in Asia Minor recorded that it had concluded *isopoliteia* agreements with Laodikeia-ad-Mare, Seleukeia-in-Pieria, and Antioch-by-Daphne, and each agreement was said to be with the *demos* of the respective cities.[68] In the confusion of the 140s Antioch

---

[63] P. Gurob.

[64] *IGLS* 1183.

[65] Mal. 205.

[66] P. Roussel, 'Décret des Péliganes de Laodicée sur Mer', *Syria* 23 1942–3, 21–32, especially pp. 28–31.

[67] Mal. 201; Lib. Or. 11. 92.

[68] P. Herrmann, 'Antiochos der Grosse und Teos', *Anadolu* 9 (1965), 29–160. The relevant section of the long inscription is on fragment II, block D, lines 100–4.

and Seleukeia issued coins recording that they were 'brother peoples' (*adelphoi demoi*).[69]

On the other hand, democratic constitutions do not necessarily imply that actual power lay with the *demos*. Given the enormous power and influence wielded by the king—the founder or descended from the founder, he appointed the *epistates*, he was the fount of favours[70]—the power of any city-government was automatically weakened. It is likely that the effective local power was oligarchic, though it must be said that this is little more than an assumption[71]. The king would prefer to deal with a small group of councillors—the *peliganes* at Laodikeia or Seleukeia-on-the-Tigris, for example.[72]

The close connection between the city-rulers and the king, marked by the institutions of citizen-Friends and *epistatai*, was perhaps reinforced by a joint ideology of Macedonian-ness. C. F. Edson has pointed out that certain elements of the Seleukid royal ideology emphasize the family's Macedonian origins;[73] the same can be said of certain elements of the cities. The term *peliganes* used at Laodikeia-ad-Mare and perhaps at Seleukeia-on-the-Tigris seems to have been originally Macedonian.[74] At Larissa the Thessalian origins of the founders were remembered all through the Hellenistic period.[75] These details are few and they are no more than straws to build with, though the scarcity of facts on the whole period enhances their importance and significance; it may be that the monarchy and the cities shared an ideology as well as a mutual dependence.

This is the political system by which Syria was controlled

---

[69] W. Wroth, *Catalogue of the Greek Coins of Galatia, Cappadocia and Syria* (1878), 151–2.

[70] The *isopoliteia* agreements of Teos and the Syrian cities (cf. Herrmann, note 8) were clearly sponsored by the king, presumably as a means of tying Teos in with the rest of his kingdom.

[71] A. H. M. Jones *The Greek City from Alexander to Justinian* (Oxford 1940), ch. 10, pp. 157–69.

[72] Roussel (note 66).

[73] C. Edson, 'Imperium Macedonicum: The Seleucid Empire and the Literary Evidence', *Cl. Ph.* 53 (1958), 153–70.

[74] Cf. Roussel, note 66: the term *adeiganes*, in connection with Seleukeia-on-the-Tigris, was the one transmitted in the text of Pol. (5.54. 10), and this is now thought to be a mistake for *peliganes*.

[75] Diod. 38. 4ᵃ, 1, written in the first century BC, of events in the previous century and referring back to Seleukos I.

by the Seleukid monarchy. It was devised, so it would seem, by Seleukos Nikator at the time he was founding his cities. It would take time to settle, and routine is not to be expected right away. The rebellion of the cities at the time of Seleukos' death suggests that the system was not yet in full operation. Perhaps Antiochos I was instrumental in developing and refining his father's scheme. This may be hinted at in the ending of the municipal coinages of Antioch and Seleukeia.[76] The crisis of 246–242 shows the system to be fully operational, requiring only a king, any king, for it to work effectively. That crisis also shows just how little the Aradians liked the system. Yet it operated successfully, with little or no strain, well into the second century BC, which was also the second Seleukid century.

The test of any political system comes when things go wrong and the conditions change from those in which the system originated. For Syria this change began with the death of Antiochos IV in 164. Previous apparent failures of the system, when the succession was disputed or unclear, had occurred in 280 and 246 and again in 175, when Antiochos IV himself had seized the throne from his nephew. But these crises had been very brief, and the recovery of the royal authority had been rapid in each case. From the 160s onwards, however, breakdowns became more frequent, and they lasted much longer.

The weak point in the Seleukid system, as in all monarchies, was the person, character, age, and inheritance of the king. In 164 the unexpected death of Antiochos IV left the succession to be disputed between a child and an absent adult. This had been the situation also in 246 and in 175, but on this occasion, both claimants were in distant lands, and the position was complicated by another dispute between rival vizirs for the custody of the child king. So there was first a dispute between the regents Lysias and Philip, then a successful attempt by the child king's uncle Demetrios to seize the throne.. To do this he had to escape from Roman custody and to insist on the killing of the child. This was followed by

[76] Newell, *WSM*, under the respective cities.

an attempt to detach the East as a separate kingdom under Timarchos.[77]

The crisis had lasted for three years, whereas earlier disputes had been resolved within a year. The winner, Demetrios I Soter, was left in a weakened political position, and then he was in turn challenged by a pretender, Alexander Balas, less than ten years after his seizure of power. Balas eventually defeated and killed Demetrios, but he was much less convincing as a king than he had been as a rebel, and soon he was himself beset, not only by the teenage son of Demetrios, Demetrios II, but also by his erstwhile patron, Ptolemy VI. Fighting followed in which both Alexander and Ptolemy died, and then Demetrios II ruled in Syria. However, he in turn had created antagonisms on his way to the kingship and he had to face a rebellion almost at once. This was not extinguished until Demetrios himself was a prisoner in Parthia, the rebel leader Tryphon was dead and the second son of Demetrios I, Antiochos VII Sidetes, had become king.[78]

Between the death of Antiochos IV in 164, and the death of Tryphon in 138, therefore, Syria had only eight years of peace, out of twenty-six.[79] Furthermore, the fighting itself had been mainly civil warfare, though it was also complicated and aggravated by foreign invasion and interference, during which the whole East was lost permanently. There was also the first successful rebellion from below, by the Jews of Palestine. This was the test which the political system of Seleukos I had to face, in which the cities, being the main strongholds, were inevitably the major prizes. And, given the size and importance of Antioch by the 160s, it was that city which became the main target for all contenders.

Events in Antioch from the 150s to 138 are central to the history of the dynasty and the kingdom. In the 150s the population of the city, for the only time, acted as an

[77] Bevan, *House*, ii 178–87.
[78] Bevan, *House*, ii 208–38.
[79] This tends to be obscured by the practice of breaking the account of events at 146 BC, which comes from regarding the battle of Pydna as decisive, which is not the case for the East (e.g. Will, *Hist. pol.*, vol. ii, ch. 2). Bevan breaks up his account into smaller sections, but the continuity is still lost (Bevan, *House*, vol. ii, ch. 27–30).

independent political force. It is likely that it was the behaviour of Antiochos IV which had been the start of the process of politicization in the city. He had stimulated the electoral process by standing as a candidate in elections,[80] he had built a *bouleuterion*,[81] and he had generally emphasised the importance of the city.[82] The near civil war between the two regents Lysias and Philip in 163[83] may have further forwarded the politicization of the citizenry: it is exactly the situation in which one side might appeal to the people for support. Whatever the immediate origins, by the 150s the Antiochenes were in the habit of rioting and demonstrating to emphasize their wishes. One riot was staged in favour of Andriskos, a pretender to the throne of Macedon.[84] Demetrios I was not intimidated, for he had a closer knowledge of the power of Rome which Andriskos was challenging than had the rioters. Instead he simply removed himself from the city.[85] But this evacuation would aggravate the situation in the city, both by the reduction in prestige which the king's physical absence would entail, and because the royal court was probably one of the main sources of economic activity in the city.

The challenge of Alexander Balas, therefore, came at a time when Demetrios I had peculiar difficulties. Antioch, as a corporate community, failed to support Demetrios in the war with Balas, who was welcomed to the city after his victory.[86] Yet Balas was politically dependent on Egypt and appears to have lived at Ptolemais-Ake more than at Antioch,[87] which

---

[80] Pol. 26. 1. Pol. regards this electioneering as evidence of Antiochos' madness, yet all other aspects of the king's policies are capable of rational interpretation, and show an active political intelligence at work—in Egypt, in Judaea, in relations with Rome (cf. E. S. Gruen, *The Hellenistic Monarchies and the Coming of Rome* (Berkeley and Los Angeles 1984), 662–3), at Arados in financial affairs (Morkholm, *Antiochus IV*, pp. 31–32). Pol.'s interpretation of the king's behaviour as evidencing madness is evidence rather of his own prejudice against the man, perhaps as a result of his friendship with Demetrios, who was a rival of Antiochos' for the throne.

[81] Lib. Or. 11. 125.

[82] For example by staging his grand procession at nearby Daphne in 167 (Pol. 30. 25–216.)

[83] This civil war seems to have been mainly marches, without any real fighting. 1 Macc. 6: 63 claims that Antioch was attacked and taken, but this seems to be wishful thinking.

[84] Diod. 31. 40ᵃ.

[85] Jos. *AJ* 13. 2. 1.　　　　　　　　　　[86] Diod. 31. 32ᵃ.

[87] Ptolemais was Balas' first conquest (Jos *AJ* 13. 2. 1) and where he was married to Ptolemy's daughter (1 Macc. 10: 57–58).

was governed in his name by two men, whose position may have been as joint *epistatai*, though this term is never used of them. One, Hierax, said to have been an actor, was an appointee of the Egyptian court; the other was a Seleukid army officer, Diodotos of Kasiana.[88] It was under their auspices that the strange coins inscribed 'of the brother peoples' were produced at Antioch and Seleukeia.[89] This is clearly a political slogan, though its meaning is obscure. The use of the word *demoi* might suggest an appeal to a political authority other than that of the king; the absence of any previous or subsequent indication of feelings of brotherhood between the two cities also suggests a political change.

Demetrios II, the eldest son of Demetrios I, returned to Syria with an army in 147, and much of the subsequent fighting took place around Antioch. It ended with the deaths of both Alexander Balas and Ptolemy VI,[90] and the subsequent accession to power of Demetrios II. During the war the Antiochenes are said to have offered the Seleukid kingdom to Ptolemy VI.[91] This was presumably an official act of the corporate body of the city, and it must have involved Hierax and Diodotos, therefore. For them its purpose was clearly to avoid their having to submit to Demetrios II. Hierax returned to Egypt after Ptolemy's death,[92] but Diodotos went off into the interior of Syria, where he championed the cause of the infant son of Alexander Balas, known as Antiochos VI, who was being fostered by an Arab chief called Iamblichos.[93]

This series of events demonstrated the limits of the power of

---

[88] Diod. 32. 9ᶜ.

[89] W. Wroth, *Catalogue of Greek Coins in the British Museum: Galatia, Cappadocia and Syria*, (1878), 151 ff. These coins were originally thought to refer to the *four* great cities, and to be a reminiscence of their founding, but Seyrig pointed out that examples of the coins were only found at Antioch and Seleukeia (H. Seyrig, quoted by Bellinger 'End', p. 60, n. 6 apparently a private communication), and, in the absence of more information they would seem to have been confined to, and to refer to, the two northern cities only.

[90] Diod. 32. 9ᵈ; Str. 16. 2. 8; 1 Macc. 11: 17–18.

[91] Diod. 32. 9ᶜ; Jos. *AJ* 13. 4. 7. Whether Ptolemy accepted the offer and should be reckoned as a king in the Seleukid line is a difficult matter. The appearance of his name in a list of deified Seleukids at Teos would seem to settle the matter (F. Piejeko, 'Ptolemies in a list of Deified Seleukids from Teos', *Zeitschrift für Papyrologie und Epigrafik* 49 (1982), were it not for the fact that Teos is a strange place to produce reliable information about Seleukids in 146 BC

[92] Diod. 33. 22. 1   [93] Diod. 33. 4ᵃ.

the Antiochenes. There is no attempt—except perhaps in the
case of the 'brother-peoples' coins—to assert any sort of
independence. The citizens were trying to influence the royal
government, and it seems that Hierax and Diodotos were able
to lead them effectively enough to exert some pressure. In the
event their choice of king, Ptolemy VI, rapidly turned the post
over to Demetrios II,[94] apparently without consulting the
citizens or encountering any opposition from them. There was
no attempt to detach the city from the kingdom and no
demand for autonomy, though this was just the sort of
situation which would allow an auction of privileges to
develop.

It was in fact at this very time that two such auctions did
develop in other parts of the kingdom. In Palestine by 142, the
Maccabaean rulers in Judaea had become effectively independent, after receiving successive bids for their support from
Alexander Balas, Demetrios II, and Tryphon (Diodotos'
throne name after 142).[95] In the same way Arados managed
to enlarge its privileges once again at this very time.[96] It is
thus not for lack of examples nor lack of opportunity that the
Syrian cities failed to develop their area of political com-
petence: it was lack of will. The factors which had operated in
the past to prevent the development of an effectively autonomous government in the cities were even more potent with
the semi-collapse of the royal government. The virulent
enmity of the Judaean state towards the Greek cities of
Palestine[97] gave a clear warning of what might be expected if
similar powers got loose in Syria—and at the same time that
enmity is explained, for the cities were the Seleukid king's
automatic allies in holding down the local Semitic populations.

The prolonged crisis in the Seleukid monarchy which began
with the invasion of Alexander Balas in 153 had thus had
major effects on Antioch by the early 140s. Elsewhere, with
one exception, the crisis, so far as can be seen, had had

---

[94] Jos. *AJ* 13. 4. 7.

[95] 1 Macc. 13: 41–2.

[96] This follows from the story of the attempt on Marathos (Diod. 33. 4. 1–6).

[97] For example, by the year-long siege and eventual destruction of the Greek city of
Samaria (Jos. *AJ* 13. 10. 2).

remarkably few repercussions. The coastal cities had been occupied by Ptolemy's forces in 145, but this had not lasted long.[98] The exception is, as ever, Arados. That city offered a bribe to Ammonios, the minister of Alexander Balas, and thus at some time in the period 150 to 145, to be allowed to take over Marathos again.[99] The figure of 300 talents is mentioned. But when a troop of royal soldiers approached to start the process by occupying Marathos, the Marathians shut their gates and defied Ammonios. Thus Marathos had some local initiative, as did Arados, though there is a clear difference in intent between the defensiveness of Marathos and the aggression and initiative of Arados. The whole episode is an epitome of the Aradian history in the Seleukid period, in which the royal government is regarded only as an element to be utilized for the benefit of Arados. The great crisis of the monarchy might not exist.

In Antioch the troops which Demetrios II had recruited to reconquer his patrimony from Balas were, in 145, loosed on the riotous Antiochenes.[100] Casualties were heavy,[101] but the main effect was to disperse refugees to all the Syrian cities within reach.[102] The discontent which the Antiochenes felt was thus spread. The refugee officer, Diodotos, acting in the name of Balas' son, Antiochos VI, linked up with the Arab chieftain Iamblichos and together they seized control of the city of Chalkis.[103] Larissa, Apamea and Antioch joined him.[104] Seleukeia-in-Pieria was kept loyal to Demetrios by the presence there of his wife, Kleopatra Thea;[105] Laodikeia-ad-Mare was held by the presence of the king himself: Demetrios is recorded to have perpetrated 'random outrages' on the citizens.[106] Josephus at this point is clearly basing himself on a

---

[98] This is an assumption from the fact that Ptolemy campaigned in the north with the intention of extracting as his price the return of southern Syria (Diod. 32. 9ᶜ).

[99] Diod. 33. 5.

[100] 1 Macc. 11: 44–51; Diod. 33. 4.

[101] But not so heavy as the sources allege. 1 Macc. 11: 44–51 has an account in which Jewish soldiers played a large part, but Diod. 33. 4. 14 has Demetrios' Cretan troops taking the main part; cf. Bevan, *House*, vol. ii, ch. 24.

[102] They certainly reached Apamea (Diod. 33. 4 and 4ᵃ) and so other cities which were nearer could have been their destinations as well. The relative ease with which Chalkis was captured by Diodotos suggests that discontent existed there.

[103] Diod. 33. 4ᵃ.   [105] Diod. 33. 28.

[104] Diod. 33. 4ᵃ; 1 Macc. 11: 56.   [106] Jos. *AJ* 13. 7. 1.

source hostile to the Seleukids, of which the use of the term 'random outrages' is a sign. On the other hand, something obviously did happen which allowed the interpretation of irrational oppression to be made. Demetrios' position was certainly close to desperation. Laodikeia-ad-Mare was almost the last stronghold left to him. All the other cities had demonstrated their disaffection, and Laodikeia will have been no exception. But the king was actually present in Laodikeia, and he could therefore take measures to prevent the discontent rising to full rebellion, by selectively eliminating the most vociferous of his opponents. His enemies would be happy to call these 'random outrages'. The local effect was more important: Demetrios held on to Laodikeia, and Diodotos' victorious advance was stopped.

The significance of the civil war of Demetrios II and Diodotos is that each city was individually made to decide which side to join. The process seems to be illustrated by Demetrios' problems at Laodikeia, where, because the king was present, decisive action could be taken which prevented the city's defection. Thus the second phase of this long crisis (i.e. 145–138) now directly involved the individual cities, dividing them one from another and also dividing them internally. Seleukeia and Antioch, having been 'brother-peoples' in 148–147, were on opposite sides five years later. Larissa independently joined Diodotos while the city on which it depended, Apamea, did so only later.[107] And yet the royal authority, even when it was divided between contending kings, was still the more powerful element of the royal-civic partnership. There is no sign of a move on the part of any city to go its own way into actual independence. At Laodikeia the 'random outrages' of Demetrios kept the city loyal to him, but the only possible alternative was to join Diodotos. It may be that some cities chose a particular side in reaction against the choice of a neighbour. Larissa's decision to join Diodotos independently of Apamea may be such a move, though there is no proof, other than the fact that later Larissa did enforce its separation from Apamea, and even at some time fought a war against Apamea.[108] It might be argued that Antioch and

---

[107] Diod. 33. 9.

[108] This is presumably the occasion of the war between Larissa and Apamea which so excited Poseidonios' derision (Athenaeus IV, 176 B—C; L. Edelstein and I. G.

Seleukeia were on opposite sides through neighbourly enmity, but it is more likely that Kleopatra's garrison in Seleukeia was what swayed the balance there. Antioch had had a different experience, particularly in the ferocity of the Cretan garrison of Demetrios II; there, the decision to join Diodotos was not so much one in his favour as one which was against Demetrios. In 138, when Demetrios was out of the way, Antioch joined his brother Antiochos VII Sidetes readily enough, against Diodotos.[109] Similarly the speed with which Diodotos' support dwindled away in the face of the arrival of Antiochos VII suggests that this may have been the general feeling in Syria.[110] Diodotos (who had made himself king under the name Tryphon when his ward died in 142[111]) was eventually reduced to refugee status in the land about Apamea, which was his homeland.[112]

In all this, no cities in Syria were actually destroyed, as happened in Phoenicia,[113] but the fate of two cities may not have been very far from destruction. Laodikeia-ad-Libanum was in a highly exposed position, exposed to raids from Judaea in 145,[114] and its small size meant that its survival is most unlikely. The other possible non-survivor is Chalkis. This was the first city to be captured by Diodotos, with the aid of Iamblichos, the Arab chief who had fostered the child Antiochos VI.[115] After its capture, in 145, Chalkis is not mentioned again until the first century AD. Then it is

---

Kidd, *Posidonius: The Fragments* 1972, no. 54). It was described in the third book of Poseidonios' *Histories*, which began where Pol. stopped, in 145. Thus the date could be as early as 145, or maybe five or even ten years later. The disturbances of the 140s would be a better context than later, however.

[109] 1 Macc. 15: 10; Jos. *AJ* 13. 7. 2.

[110] Antiochos reached Seleukeia-in-Pieria during 138 and had eliminated Tryphon within less than a year; the dating is essentially numismatic: no coins of Tryphon are later than 138; he may have held out somewhat longer in the land around Apamea where he was finally captured (App. *Syr.* 68; 1 Macc. 15: 10–40; Jos. *AJ* 13. 7. 2; H. Seyrig, 'The Khan el-Abde Find and the Coinage of Tryphon', *Numismatic Notes and Monographs* 119 (1950), 1–23).

[111] Diodotos has been the victim, more perhaps than any other Seleukid (if he can be called that), of a campaign of denigration which is transmitted faithfully by the sources. Behind that it is possible that he had a distinctive policy, but it is difficult to discern it. All that can be said here is that it does not seem to have affected the cities, except in so far as they were victims of one or another of the kings.

[112] Jos. *AJ* 13. 7. 2; Str. 16. 2. 10.

[113] Berytos was destroyed by Tryphon *c.*140 (Str. 13. 2. 19).

[114] Jos. *AJ* 13. 5. 6, where it is called Qadesh.

[115] Diod. 33. 4ᵃ.

mentioned by Pliny, where it is just a name in a list[116] and later, in AD 92, some rare coins report the city's adoption of a new dating era in that year.[117] It is quite possible that Chalkis never escaped from the Arab grip, and that the new era of AD 92 celebrated the removal of an Arab dynasty established in 145. This is only a suggestion, and the evidence is negative, but the possibility must exist that Chalkis ceased to be a Greek city.

On the other hand, Antioch's importance was enhanced. It was already the largest city in Syria and it functioned as the capital of the Seleukid state. In the civil wars the possession of Antioch became the mark of legitimacy for a king or a pretender. This function had appeared first in 163, when the city was the main bone of contention between the two rival regents of Antiochos V.[118] In the same year Demetrios I was recognized as king at some point between landing at Tripolis and setting out to fight Timarchos—and two events, the killing of Antiochos V and Demetrios' occupation of Antioch are, together, the signs of his success.[119] Alexander Balas based himself at Ptolemais-Ake, and used Hierax and Diodotos to rule Antioch for him, with the result that he lost Antioch and the war and his life. The connection is not fortuitous, for it was at Antioch that the decision was made as to his successor.[120] It was Demetrios II's treatment of Antioch which proved to be the catalyst for other cities in their rejection of him in favour of the non-Seleukid army officer Diodotos.[121] Thus it is clear that Antioch was the main prize in these civil wars and that its possession carried with it a moral legitimation such as the possession of no other city provided.

The long civil war compelled the adoption of measures of protection and self-protection by various cities, with varied effectiveness. Seleukeia-in-Pieria became 'holy' in the early 140s, and was given the right to call itself '*asylos*' by 138,[122]

---

[116] Pliny, *NH* 5. 19. 81.

[117] Head, *HN* 779.

[118] Jos. *AJ* 12. 9. 2 and 9. 7; 1 Macc. 6: 63.

[119] App. *Syr.* 47; Justin 34. 3; 1 Macc. 7: 1–4; Jos. *AJ* 12. 10. 1.

[120] Diod. 32. 9[c].

[121] 1 Macc. 11: 56; Jos. *AJ* 13. 3.

[122] A letter from Newell quoted by R. C. Welles, *Royal Correspondence of the Hellenistic Period* (New Haven, 1934), 292 n. 3.

though the main movement for *asylia* was among the Phoenician cities further south.[123] Arados was not one of them, but instead it took rather more active measures. A letter recorded in 1 Maccabees,[124] from the Roman 'Consul' to 'king Ptolemy', which is to be dated *c.*140 BC, included Arados in its distribution list. This list comprises six kings and fifteen cities and peoples in Asia Minor, Cyprus, and Cyrenaica. Some of the peoples are distinctly odd, and it looks as though the list has been altered or perhaps concocted later.[125] But Arados is the only place in Syria which is on the list; even if the list is a concoction, it still gives some indication that Arados was thought of—either in Rome or in Judaea—as an independent state at the time. It is significant, also, that very shortly afterwards, in 138/137, Arados resumed its minting of silver coins, for the first time for thirty years.[126] It is a reasonable assumption, given previous similar events in Arados' past, that this was the city's price for supporting Antiochos VII. He arrived in Syria in 138 and established himself as the successor to his brother Demetrios II, who had been captured by the Parthians. Antiochos was in competition with Tryphon, and so this seems to be another example of Arados using a dynastic crisis to enlarge its area of political autonomy.

The grant of *asylos* to Seleukeia-in-Pieria which is first recorded in 138, may also have been part of the price Antiochos VII paid for his throne—though the larger price was marriage to Kleopatra Thea, who controlled that city.[127] Antiochos, in fact, was able to claim the Seleukid throne with little difficulty because he was not subject to the dislike engendered by his brother, and that meant, in turn, that support for Diodotos-Tryphon weakened rapidly. Concessions to Arados, a grant to Seleukeia, and marriage to Kleopatra Thea were not really very great prices to pay for the kingship. There is, in other words, little or no evidence to show that

---

[123] See the list compiled by E. Bikerman, *Institutions des Séleukides* (Paris, 1938), 150.

[124] 1 Macc. 15: 16–24.

[125] Almost everything about this letter is problematic; see now E. S. Gruen, *The Hellenistic Monarchies and the Coming of Rome*, vol. ii, Appendix iii, pp. 748–751, where references are given, and where authenticity and the date 142 are both accepted.

[126] Seyrig, 'Aradus', p. 220.

[127] Jos. *AJ* 13. 7. 2.

there was any change in the status or fortunes of any of the cities of Syria—with the exception of Arados, of course.

In this case it may be that the argument from silence has more force than usual. Any change in a Syrian city's circumstances can only have been in one of two directions— either physical destruction or a grant of privilege by the king. Examples of both of these are known—Arados' and Seleukeia's grants, Berytos' destruction—but there is nothing concerning the other cities. Destruction of a city makes a big noise, and seems likely to have been noted somewhere, as well as leaving physical evidence to be discerned in the archaeological record, even though the archaeological exploration of Syrian cities is poor. Chalkis may have fallen to the local Arab king, but there is no sign of physical destruction. On the other hand, royal grants were advertised, particularly on coins, as in the case of cities which became 'holy' and *asylos*. This was a necessary advertisement for it was the only way that the fact of a city's new and protected status could be kept before the eyes of any potential enemies. This is how we know of Seleukeia's status. But none of the other cities produced the coins which would advertise such a development. The most economical explanation of this is that they had nothing to advertise, that they had not received any royal grant. The fate of Berytos— which was *asylos* when it suffered destruction[128]—will have demonstrated the essential uselessness of such royal concessions, and will have encouraged all the cities to cling close to one king, so long as he was acceptable, for proper protection.

Antiochos VII, like his brother, attacked Parthia and lost,[129] dying in the process. Demetrios II was released from his prison, to return to his kingdom and his wife.[130] In the shock of the losses of Antiochos' expedition, Demetrios was accepted as king once more. He immediately attacked Egypt,[131] but

---

[128] E. Bikerman, *Institutions des Séleukides*, p. 150; Str. 15. 2. 19.

[129] Justin 38. 10; Diod. 34. 35. 15–16; App. *Syr.* 68; Jos. *AJ* 13. 9. 4.

[130] Justin 38. 10; App. *Syr.* 68.

[131] This act has usually provoked condemnation (e.g. Bevan, *House*, ii. 248) on the grounds that the kingdom deserved a period of rest after the losses in the east. This is no doubt true enough, but Demetrios must have been able to see that even more clearly than modern historians. Thus Demetrios will have had overriding reasons, and the obvious one is that, after his decade in a Parthian prison, he realised that only

was stopped in mid-campaign by the news of the rebellion of Antioch and Apamea in his rear.[132] He died in the course of the subsequent civil war against another non-Seleukid king, Alexander II Zabinas.[133]

The actual sequence of events reveals, once more, the relationship of the king and the cities. The cities accepted Demetrios as king for several months, then they were provoked into revolt by Ptolemaic agents,[134] who then foisted Zabinas on to the kingdom.[135] The sequence can best be understood in the light of the internal Syrian reaction to the loss of Antiochos VII's army. The grief in almost every household in Antioch, and hence presumably in the other cities of the kingdom as well, and to the same degree, is reported by Diodoros.[136] This may have dulled the old resentment of Demetrios, but only temporarily. After some months, past animosities reawakened. Antioch and Apamea had been the main cities which had rejected Demetrios in the 140s. Six months of him, plus Ptolemaic promptings and promises, were enough to bring them to the point of rebellion again. Alexander II appears to have been cynically open about his origins, and earned his nickname Zabinas, 'the Bought', as a result.[137] And once more, when Demetrios was out of the way, support for his supplanter faded away. Like Diodotos-Tryphon before him, Zabinas was dumped when he ceased to be of use.

The behaviour of the Syrian cities remained quite consistent. Only Arados, with its particular past, was interested in independence, and in this crisis, as in the others, it was Arados which alone made an attempt to further enlarge its area of autonomy. The exact sequence of events is not known,

---

a union of Syria and Egypt, the two major Hellenistic kingdoms still surviving, would ensure that they continued to survive. The concentration on dynastic history has meant that such policies have tended to be ignored, or have been seen in purely personal terms.

[132] Justin 39. 1. 3.

[133] Justin 39. 1. 7.

[134] Demetrios returned early in 129, but the revolt of the cities did not take place until he was almost in Egypt in 128.

[135] It is clear that the revolt came first, and Zabinas was produced as a substitute king only afterwards.

[136] Diod. 34. 35. 17. 1.

[137] Justin 39. 1.

though the approximate date is clear enough. Arados, at last, 'destroyed' Marathos and Simyra,[138] but the destruction was not physical but political. The two places were incorporated into Arados' own territory.[139] There is no suggestion that this act was approved of by the Seleukid government, and it is difficult to see the circumstances when it would be given royal approval, since it clearly involved a sensible reduction of royal authority. It was, that is to say, an action taken by the city of Arados itself. The precise date is not known, but it was presumably the news of the destruction of Antiochos VII's army, which reached Syria in the late spring of 129, which was the occasion for the deed.[140] The result, however, is quite clear. Arados was an independent state now, with the island-city controlling its *peraia* from the mouth of the Eleutheros river (the old Ptolemaic boundary) as far as the southern edge of the territory of Gabala.

There is another possible dimension to this crisis of 129–126. A fragment of Diodoros reports events at 'Laodikeia', which is presumably Laodikeia-ad-Mare.[141] The city rebelled against Demetrios II in 128, as did Antioch and Apamea, and for once we know the actual names of the leaders of the rebellion: Antipater, Klonios, and Aeropos. The city was then attacked by Zabinas, who captured it and pardoned these leaders. Once again a rebellion against one king simply led to his replacement by another. The brief report of this event by Diodoros also contains a remark which is very suggestive. Diodoros comments that Zabinas was 'deeply beloved by the common people',[142] and this implies that the city-rulers held a different opinion, perhaps favouring Demetrios. In this connection it is worth noting the action of Arados, just to the south of Laodikeia. Having 'destroyed' Marathos and Simyra, the lands so acquired by Arados were then distributed among

---

[138] Archaeologically the site of Marathos demonstrates a gradual decline rather than any destruction (Rey-Coquais, *Arados*, pp. 135–6).

[139] Str. 16. 2. 12.

[140] Str. 16. 2. 14.

[141] Diod. 34. 35. 22. The other possible Laodikeias are Laodikeia-ad-Libanum and Berytos, which had the dynastic name of Laodikeia. But neither was known as Laodikeia pure and simple, and the first was small and the second had been destroyed only twelve years before by Tryphon. Laodikeia-ad-Mare, on the other hand, was a large and important city, and was the original bearer of the dynastic name in Syria.

[142] Diod. 34. 35. 22. 1; he uses the word *pollon*.

her own people. One of the traditional demands of the revolutionaries of old Greece was for a redistribution of lands.[143] There is no suggestion of a social revolution at Arados, but the acquisition of the mainland may have allowed the rulers of the city to distribute the new lands and so short-circuit the revolution at someone else's expense. The suggestion of internal divisions at Laodikeia at the same time is thus perhaps likely enough. If such internal divisions did exist the civil war would certainly exacerbate them, and the willingness of the rulers of cities such as Laodikeia to cling closely to the monarchy would be as great as ever.

Zabinas' attraction for the common people would suggest that the normal Seleukid policy was to favour the city-rulers where internal tensions existed. Since the rulers were presumably the wealthy, the landowners, and the rich merchants, this would make sense. The royal Friends who were the channels of communication between king and city would be of the same general class as the city oligarchs, as would the *epistatai*. In the rest of the Greek world, this period, the third quarter of the second century BC, was one of considerable social tension and agitation. There are numerous examples from old Greece, from Asia Minor, from Sicily—two great slave revolts—of revolts, rebellions, revolutions.[144] There is no reason to suppose that Syria was immune from this. At Arados land was redistributed. In Palestine the Jewish revolt and conquests dominated the local scene, but its revolutionary origins are clear.[145] Laodikeia, a seaport in contact with the general Mediterranean world, in a country where civil war is likely to have disrupted trade and so inflicted hardship, is a place very likely to receive and react to revolutionary impulses. Antioch's

---

[143] W. W. Tarn, 'The Social Question in the Third Century', in J. B. Bury, *et al.*, *The Hellenistic Age* (Cambridge, 1923), and W. W. Tarn and G. T. Griffith, *Hellenistic Civilisation*, 3rd edn., (1952), 120–5.

[144] A. Fuks, 'Social Revolution in Greece in the Hellenistic Age', *La Parola del Passato* 111. (1966), pp. 437–448, and 'Patterns and Types of Social-Economic Revolution in Greece from the Fourth to the Second Century BC', *Ancient Society* 5 (1974), 51–81. G. E. M. de Ste. Croix, *The Class Struggle in the Ancient Greek World* (1981), does not deal seriously with this matter or this period.

[145] The Maccabean revolt began as a movement of conservative rural-dwelling Jews against the innovative urban society, though, of course, it had other ingredients than this social one, and was much more than that; cf. M. Hengel, *Judaism and Hellenism*, trans J. Bowden (1974).

behaviour in the 140s may well be partly explained in the same way. It is quite possible that the civil wars had stimulated revolutionary demands from the 140s onwards. Once more, however, the dearth of source material renders proof impossible.[146]

The civil war begun in 128 by the revolt of the cities against Demetrios II continued until the establishment of Antiochos VIII Grypos as sole king in 121. There followed a period of peace, of which nothing is known (hence it is assumed to be a period of peace) before a further bout of internal warfare. It is thus convenient to halt at this point to take stock of the situation.

Since 153, there had been only one period of internal peace in Syria, the reign of Antiochos VII between 138 and 130.[147] The civil wars before and after that period of peace had revolved around the control of the cities of Syria, for they were physically and socially dominant in the land. In particular, the possession of Antioch had come to be the mark of legitimacy for a king. A number of the cities had suffered in the wars—massacre at Antioch, war at Larissa and Apamea, a royal oppression at Laodikeia—but there were remarkably few occasions when cities, as corporate political entities, had undertaken political actions. Excluding Arados for the moment, Antioch had been the scene of political riots in the 140s, and Antioch and Apamea had defected from Demetrios

---

[146] One other tantalizing datum may be mentioned here. In the ancient world only two kings bore the name Tryphon: one was the rebel Diodotos in Syria between 142 and 138, whose first appearance was as a Ptolemaic governor at Antioch, and who raised the most formidable anti-Seleukid revolt ever seen in Syria; the second was the leader of the second slave rebellion in Sicily in 104–100, originally called Salvius, who took the throne name Tryphon, apparently by popular acclamation (Diod. 36. 1). The connections are sufficiently close to cause comment (J. Vogt, 'The Structure of Ancient Slave Wars', in *Ancient Slavery and the Ideal of Man*, trans. T. Wiedeman, (Oxford, 1974), 58). The connection is closer still when it is recalled that many of these slaves in Sicily came from the east. It is quite possible that the first revolt in Sicily (136–132) involved men who had been enslaved and sold overseas because they had supported Tryphon in Syria. This seems sufficient to suggest a more revolutionary programme for the Syrian Tryphon than is sometimes allowed. If slaves remembered him and used his name a full generation (138–104) after his death, then his name and achievement and programme must have meant something to them.

[147] *Internal* peace only; the period was partly occupied with external warfare, including a major campaign into Judaea (Jos. *AJ* 13. 7. 3 and 9. 2; 1 Macca. 15: 38–16: 24), and the preparations for and early stages of the Parthian war (Justin 38. 10) even if exaggerated, imply a huge effort by Antiochos VII.

II in 128, and they were followed by Laodikeia. Other changes at individual cities were the result of capture or campaign—at Laodikeia in 128, Chalkis and Larissa in 145. And even the rebellions of Antioch and Apamea in 128 were prompted by Ptolemaic agents, who soon produced an alternative king for the cities.

When the actions and reactions of these cities are compared with what happened at Arados, the contrast is, once again, stark. Arados consistently worked for two things: autonomy and control of its own *peraia*, neither of which was viable without the other. After two centuries, it finally succeeded. But the example of Arados was not infectious. Its success did not stimulate any of the other cities of Syria to work for their own autonomy.

The reasons for this difference are no doubt much the same as before: the need felt by the Greek cities for alliance with the king in their joint exploitation of the surrounding peasantry—though this, it must be emphasized, is only a theory.

The political system of Seleukos I had survived the test of a generation of intermittent civil warfare. The system had not ensured the continued and active loyalty of the cities to his house, as he had no doubt wanted, but it had shown their continued need for monarchy. The misbehaviour of a king, however, as in the case of Demetrios II and the two usurping Alexanders, could cause resentment to the point of rebellion, and, as the two Alexanders and Tryphon had shown, there were alternatives to Seleukid kings.

7

THE SURVIVAL OF THE CITIES

THE long period of civil warfare between 153 and 138 had been accompanied by invasions from outside the Seleukid kingdom, and by rebellions within, and gradually more territory had been lost. Asia Minor had gone already, in 188, and now the eastern provinces were taken by the Parthians. Two Seleukid armies were destroyed, in 139 and 129, and the Parthian king conquered as far as Babylonia and Mesopotamia. The Ptolemies invaded, but failed to annex any territory permanently. Inside the kingdom, the Jewish rebellion which began in 166 eventually organized itself into a state and was accorded a semi-independent status by the Seleukid kings; other areas more quietly detached themselves, Osrhoene and Kommagene as kingdoms under the rule of self-promoted former satraps, Arados as an independent city.

By 128 the Seleukid state was reduced to Syria and some appendages. The civil wars of the 120s made recovery impossible. Antiochos VIII Grypos emerged as sole king by 121 and ruled his kingdom for eight years without—so far as we know—any challenge, but then a further civil war began when his half-brother Antiochos IX Kyzikenos made a bid for the kingship. Neither king ever wholly succeeded in beating the other, and so for the next thirty years, from 113 to 83, civil war was institutionalized, first between the half-brothers, and then between their various heirs.

Discerning what was happening in these years is even more difficult than usual. There are occasional anecdotes, but the only continuous sources for the period are the coins. These have been investigated by Bellinger,[1] who has been able to discern an outline of the course of the civil wars, for the numismatic evidence provides a record of which king controlled which city mint. But where there were no mints in

---

[1] Bellinger 'End', considers the literary references as well as the numismatic. There is nothing to add to his account.

operation, as at Laodikeia-ad-Mare, royal control is simply not known.

In these conditions it is very difficult to discern the effects which these wars had on the various cities. There can be no doubt that the breakdown of the monarchy hurt the cities; the problem is to find out how, since such sources as there are can be deceptive. This is the case with the source which seems to provide the clearest information. An inscription from Cyprus,[2] indicates that, in 109 BC, Seleukeia-in-Pieria was granted autonomy by one of the kings, probably Grypos. This is the first grant of its kind in Syria, and it would seem on the surface that it was a result of the civil wars, perhaps an example of a city extracting its price from one of the kings in return for its support. Yet in reality this apparent autonomy made little or no difference to the city. The Seleukid king at no time relinquished physical control over the city, and at times it was the only base he possessed.[3] At one point a refugee Ptolemy from Cyprus was received into the city along with his army,[4] but the city itself had no voice in the matter. The grant of autonomy was not a recognition of the city's independence by the king, although the very fact of its being granted should have some significance. Instead, the grant has all the appearance of being a mask for continued royal control.

Since the only grant of 'autonomy' to a Syrian city by a Seleukid king turns out, in effect, to mean nothing, it reinforces the point that it is necessary, as before, to look at what cities actually did, rather than what theory or legalism might suggest. In this situation of civil war, it was quite possible for a city to be effectively independent without any formal grant, just as the formal grant of autonomy was effectively meaningless. The position of Arados was one of effective independence. No evidence exists that any formal grant of autonomy was made to that city by any king, but it is clear that the city behaved in a completely independent way from 128 onwards. Cities which were truly independent had no need of a grant.

The other three great cities, Antioch, Apamea, and

---

[2] *OGIS* 257.
[3] Bellinger, 'End', p. 69.
[4] Justin 39. 3. 3; Jos. *AJ* 13. 12. 2.

Laodikeia, each reacted to the prolonged civil wars in a different way. Antioch was the main prize in all the civil wars because of its size and reputation, and so it was usually the host to the king and his court and army. The presence of these powerful institutions would inhibit any expressions of dissent, while at the same time they would guarantee some protection and provide a certain prosperity. Until the end of the civil wars there is no sign of Antioch's disaffection from the various kings who ruled it. Laodikeia-ad-Mare scarcely enters the story of these years. It will have been at this time that the economic development was taking place which became the established prosperity of Strabo's time.[5] The city may or may not have been under royal control. Since the evidence is numismatic, and there appears to have been no royal Laodikeian coins, the question must remain open. Apamea did remain, however, under firm royal control, since a fort built by a 'king Antiochos', otherwise unspecified, dominated the city.[6] The king in question was probably Grypos, since he controlled Antioch all the time from 109/108 to his death in 96,[7] and was able to send expeditions to the south—to Damascus in 104/103, for instance.[8] To do so, he must have held Apamea, whose possession also blocked the way north for his rival. The fort became a symbol of the city's subjection, and was razed by Pompeius as a token of its freedom, though we do not know the attitude of the citizens. In Grypos' kingdom the city had once more taken on the role which Seleukos Nikator had originally intended for it, as a fortified block on the main inland route between northern and southern Syria.

These great cities were thus to a large degree at the mercy of royal actions; only Arados seems immune. The smaller cities were correspondingly even more vulnerable. A fragment of Poseidonios gives a sight of what was happening in the north, for once.[9] Grypos was murdered in 96 by his chief minister and commander, Herakleon of Beroia, who then claimed the

---

[5] Str. 14. 2. 9

[6] Jos. *AJ* 14. 3. 2.

[7] Bellinger, 'End', pp. 68–69 and the chart on p. 87.

[8] Bellinger, 'End', p. 87.

[9] Athenaeus, 4. 153 B—C, quoting Poseidonios (L. Edelstein and I. G. Kidd, *Posidonius: The Fragments* (1972), no. 75).

kingship for himself. Herakleon is said to have been a martinet, so it is scarcely surprising that his claim was unsuccessful. Instead he withdrew to his home city, and established it as a separate principality which included Hierapolis and a place called Herakleia whose location is not known. Eight years later, in 88, Beroia was under the rule of a man called Strato when it was besieged by the Seleukid king then ruling in Antioch, Demetrios III.[10] Later again, perhaps in 69, or when Pompeius arrived in 64, the three places were under the rule of Dionysios son of Herakleon.[11] It would seem, therefore, that Herakleon established Beroia as the seat of a minor dynasty, which was capable of dominating the area around that city for some distance,[12] and which existed for thirty years at least.

This, then, is a further option, one which had been available to other, but usually larger, fragments of the Seleukid state: independence as a separate kingdom. In a sense it was the option already taken up by Kommagene and Osrhoene when they had become independent kingdoms.[13] It is true that Beroia is never referred to as an independent kingdom—the rulers did not, it seems, call themselves kings, despite Herakleon's initial claim, nor did they coin—and its dynasty did not survive (so far as we know) to become a client state of the Roman empire; nevertheless the actions of Herakleon, Strato and Dionysios between 96 and 69 are those of independent kings, whatever they themselves or their neighbours or subjects called them.

---

[10] Jos. *AJ* 13. 14. 3.

[11] Str. 14. 2. 7.

[12] U. Kahrstedt, *Syrische Territorien in Hellenistischer Zeit* (Göttingen,1923), 92, suggested that Beroia was under the rule of a Semitic state at Pompeius' arrival; the existence of Dionysios' principality in 69 makes this unlikely.

[13] Osrhoene became independent after the disaster to the army of Antiochos VII in the east in 130/129: the Abgarid dynasty of Osrhoene dated from either 132 or 127 BC (Jones, *CERP* 443, n. 9; A. Segal, *Edessa, the Blessed City*, (Oxford, 1970), ch. 1). Kommagene's satrap, Ptolemaios, had attempted a break for independence in 162, in the confusion following the death of Antiochos IV, also in the east (Diod. 31. 19ᵃ). The 'era of Kommagene' commemorated this event (H. Seyrig, 'Sur quelques eres syriennes: I, L'ere des rois de Kommagene', *Rev. Num.* (1964), 51–2). Yet one cannot help feeling that until Antiochos VII's disaster in 129 this independence was on Seleukid sufferance; the foundation of Samosata by king Samos (acceded *c*.130) is just as definitive a sign of independence, and a clearer sign of security (see also R. D. Sullivan, 'The Dynasty of Kommagene', *ANRW* 12/8 (1977)).

Since the rulers of Beroia survived for thirty years, it seems reasonable to conclude that they were able to establish their rule on a firm basis, which presumably included attracting a degree of loyalty from the citizens. The major test came under Strato, who was besieged in Beroia by Demetrios III, the current Seleukid king based at Antioch. Strato was assisted by an Arab king, Azizos, and by a Parthian satrap.[14] But this help did not reach Beroia for some time. The Seleukid siege had lasted long enough by the time help did arrive for any disaffected Beroians to betray the city had they wished to. They did not. The conclusion must be drawn either that the citizens were actively supporting Strato, or that his military power was great enough to ensure his domination of the city without their goodwill. In either case it is clear that he, and presumably his predecessor Herakleon and his successor Dionysios, were politically quite secure. That is, they were successfully ruling a city state, which must mean that dynastic civic independence was a viable option as an alternative to the rule of the Seleukid king.

Strato's Parthian alliance brought a Parthian army across the Euphrates to help relieve the siege of Beroia, and this in turn suggests what had happened to the city of the bridge, Seleukeia-Zeugma. The only way a Parthian army could have reached Beroia is by way of that bridge, which in turn means that the city itself had been taken, or was then taken, by the Parthians. This fits in with the cemetery of Parthian soldiers at Deve Huyuk, north of Hierapolis, between Zeugma and Beroia.[15] This is the only time that a Parthian outpost could have been established at that point. Zeugma was thus the first Syrian city to fall to the Parthians, and it gave them a major bridgehead over the river.

It is not clear what happened to Kyrrhos. The only possible source is a corrupt passage of Strabo,[16] which appears, as it stands, to refer to Gindaros as 'the acropolis of Kyrrhestike and a natural stronghold for robbers', but this is a description which can scarcely apply to a town in the valley of the Afrin.

[14] Jos. *AJ* 13. 14. 3.

[15] P. R. S. Moorey, *Cemeteries of the First Millenium BC at Deve Huyuk near Carchemish, salvaged by T. E. Lawrence and C. L. Woolley in 1913*, BAR S 87 (Oxford, 1980).

[16] Str. 14. 2. 8.

More probably it was applied to Kyrrhos itself, on its hilltop. Whichever place is referred to, Kyrrhos itself was clearly in a bad way, for it and Gindaros were on the northern route which connected Antioch with the bridge at Zeugma. This route was open to harassment from the independent kingdom of Kommagene to the north, and at some point the next station east beyond Kyrrhos, Doliche, became part of that kingdom.[17] With Parthians controlling Zeugma, and Kommageneans at Doliche, it seems very likely that this northern route was in steep decline, and so Kyrrhos, without any local wealth or other advantages, can only have declined as well. The city was revived temporarily in the Roman period by becoming the headquarters of a Roman legion,[18] but in the late Hellenistic period it was of little account. It may even have been deserted in favour of Gindaros, which had better local resources, and was closer to Antioch, which could have afforded it some protection. The whole area is very obscure, but the geographical and historical situation suggests strongly that Kyrrhos had failed.

When Philip I died in 84/83, he seems to have controlled only Antioch and Apamea and perhaps Laodikeia. After his death, the magistrates of Antioch met to consider what to do. They discussed the merits of the various kings of the region and chose to subject themselves and their city to the authority of Tigranes of Armenia.[19] There can be no clearer indication of the need of the Syrian cities to be part of a kingdom. Over the next few years others of the cities accepted Tigranes as king. Usually the process seems to have been more or less voluntary and involved negotiations. Laodikeia was granted autonomy in 81,[20] which was perhaps only a formal recognition of the *de facto* position—the city scarcely appears in any of the civil wars after the time of Alexander Zabinas in the 120s. Apamea was made 'holy' and *asylos* in 76;[21] since these

---

[17] It was one of the four cities of Kommagene which were established by the Roman Imperial government when the dynasty was suppressed in AD 72 (*IGLS* 38–44). Kommagene gained Zeugma at Pompeius' hands and it is possible that Doliche was acquired at the same time, that is, in 66–64. Even so this suggests that Seleukid power had already withdrawn from Doliche.

[18] Tacitus, *Annals*, 2. 57. 2.

[19] Justin 40. 1. 1–4; Bellinger, 'End', pp. 79–80.

[20] Beginning a new era then: Seyrig, 'Ères', p. 31.

[21] Seyrig, 'Ères', pp. 15–18.

were royal grants, presumably Tigranes was the grantor. At Apamea, however, the fort remained in existence under Tigranes. In contrast neither Beroia nor Arados appear to have been affected by Tigranes' operations and it must be presumed that both of them retained the independence which they had established earlier. Tigranes' interests were mainly in the lands to the north and east of Syria, in Asia Minor and Parthia. His control over both Kommagene and Mesopotamia clearly implies also his control of Zeugma.

There were contradictory traditions about Tigranes' rule in Syria. One emphasized the peaceful nature of his authority,[22] the other claimed that it was essentially violent.[23] Certainly some force was involved, as one would expect, for Tigranes was besieging Ptolemais-Ake in 69 when he was recalled by the news that a Roman army under Lucullus was invading his homeland.[24] Yet the evidence of violence in the rest of Syria is absent; instead the emphasis is on the slow, negotiated extension of his authority, beginning with the invitation from the magistrates of Antioch which first brought him to Syria. One city, Seleukeia-in-Pieria, which may have sheltered a pair of Seleukid princes,[25] was apparently not attacked,[26] and the Herakleonid dynasty at Beroia appears not to have been disturbed.

Antioch's invitation to Tigranes puts him firmly into the same position as his Seleukid predecessors. He ruled Syria as the ally of the Greek cities, and it is through these cities that his power was expanded. The cities had always required the assistance of the power of the king to support them. Their common enemy appears to have been the local non-Greek

---

[22] This tradition appears in Justin 40. 1.

[23] App. *Syr*, 48; Str. 11. 14. 15.

[24] Jos. *AJ* 13. 16. 4.

[25] These two, Antiochos and Philip, were based somewhere; their mother Kleopatra Selene sent them to Rome in 75 (Cicero, *In Verram*, 4. 27–30) and she was captured by Tigranes in Ptolemais-Ake in 69 (Str. 16. 2. 3). Seleukeia-in-Pieria, as the only north Syrian city which did not succumb to Tigranes is likely to have seen her and her sons at some time between 83 and 69.

[26] Seleukeia's survival outside Tigranes' area of rule was put down to the strength of its walls, which is due to Pompeius' comment that it was too strong to attack (Str. 16. 2. 8). In fact, there is no evidence that the city was attacked by anyone. It is equally reasonable to assume that Tigranes extended his power through diplomacy rather than force, for the two traditions are equally likely. After all, his Syrian power began through diplomacy.

population. In the last century of Seleukid history, this enemy developed an organized political life which threatened the destruction of both the kingship and the cities.

Arados had struggled for two centuries to separate itself from Seleukid rule and this struggle was finally successful in 129. This independence was the result of the city's own efforts, but it was also a consequence of the breakdown of Seleukid authority. There were others in Syria who wished to escape in the same way. They were, inevitably, people who did not live in the cities, and so it is necessary to look at the rural areas, the desert lands and the mountains. The extension of occupation in many rural areas of Syria, suggested by the archaeological evidence, no doubt took a long while to have much effect, but by 100 BC the evidence suggests greater activity than for centuries in the hills and in the desert lands and margins.

The signs of political organization are clearest concerning the peoples of the desert. In 145 an Arab chieftain called either Malchos or Iamblichos helped Diodotos to capture Chalkis.[27] It is thus evident that the nomad peoples of the desert were organized into relatively powerful political groups. This fits in with evidence from further south, where, in the lands east of the Jordan, the Nabataeans' development is traceable in outline from the time of a raid upon them by Demetrios Poliorketes in 312.[28] At that time the Nabataeans were nomadic, but also deeply involved in trade. Their numbers were augmented by a northward drift of nomadic peoples, and at the same time they settled in the thinly populated lands east of the Jordan.[29] This combination coalesced into a kingdom by c.150.[30] In the Syrian desert region to the north, this process cannot be observed so easily, but the archaeological evidence shows that there was settlement in the empty steppeland to the east and south of the Greek cities of Syria during that same period.

[27] Diod. 33. 4ª; Jos. *AJ* 13. 5. 1.
[28] Diod. 19. 94. 1–97. 6.
[29] J. R. Bartlett, 'From Edomites to Nabataeans: A Study in Continuity', *Palestine Exploration Quarterly* 111 (1979), especially pp. 53–6.
[30] G. W. Bowersock, *Roman Arabia*, Cambridge, Mass., (1983), ch. 2, who even refers to the Nabataeans as a 'great power' in the second century BC (p. 21), which is an exaggeration, to say the least.

The Arab chief called Malchos or Iamblichos in 145 was thus likely to be the ruler of a mixed nomadic and sedentary population. Nomads are always likely to settle down if they can get land, or work, or resources.[31] The openness of the steppe, together with the demand for food from the new cities—food which would include meat—would be sufficient inducements to desert nomads to settle. Yet they also retained their tribal membership, which meant that the authority of the sheikh continued to be recognized by villagers of nomad origin, probably in preference to the authority of the nearby city or of the king. Thus the chieftain would be attracted to the steppeland, since his people who had settled there were wealthier in food and resources than those still in the desert. Yet the desert-dwellers were still tough and fierce and bred to fighting. The combination of nomads and farmers was thus a formidable one, and one which was clearly antagonistic towards the cities, though, if the relations of Alexander I Balas with Malchos/Iamblichos are anything to go by, it was possible for the Syrian king to neutralize this hostility.

It is by some such process as this that Emesa became the headquarters of the dynasty of Samsigeramos. Emesa lay in the area which was reoccupied during the Hellenistic period, yet the site itself was apparently not occupied by the Seleukids.[32] It was both available and fortifiable, and yet at the same time it was in contact with the desert to the east. (In the Roman period, Emesa's city-territory stretched deep into the desert.) It was, in the circumstances, an excellent base from which to raid the weakening Seleukids, and for storing the looted wealth.

---

[31] The process by which nomads settle is one which has been the subject of considerable sociological study. One of the clearest representations, because it is based on a study of an actual historical process, is in D. Nir, *The Semi-Arid World*, trans. R. Gottlieb, (1974).

[32] On the face of it, Emesa was a good candidate for use as a garrison by the Seleukid forces. In fact, the tell is some distance from the river, and is on the *east* bank. Compared with Laodikeia-ad-Libanum, which is in the west bank and is protected by two rivers and the lake, and with Arethusa, which is a naturally powerful site, Emesa had nothing to recommend it to the Seleukid military planners. Similarly, the distance from Arethusa to Laodikeia-ad-Libanum is about the same as from Larissa to Arethusa, that is, a day's march. The garrisoning of Emesa was not necessary for a Seleukid army thinking in terms of attack from the south. An archaeological *sondage* is reported to have found Iron Age, Hellenistic, and Roman remains in the tell (Aurenche, 'Chronique archéologique', *Syria* 62 (1984)), but details are not published.

Another method of domesticating the nomads was to recruit
them into the Seleukid army. In 217, at the battle of Raphia,
Antiochos III had a force of 10,000 Arabs, who were beaten
back by a somewhat smaller group of phalangites in the
Ptolemaic force.[33] At Magnesia, a generation later, he had a
force of Arab archers, probably a good deal smaller in
number.[34] Both of these groups are generally reckoned to be
mercenaries, but there is really no way of telling.[35] In the
parade at Daphne in 167 Antiochos IV had no Arabs, but this
was a special case, designed to display wealth, and there
would be little call for extra, non-Greek contingents.[36]

The Arab archers at Magnesia (but not present, it seems, at
Raphia) call to mind the fact that the Roman army recruited a
corps of archers from Emesa, and, unusually, the Emesan
regiments posted overseas were brought up to strength by
drafts of recruits from Emesa rather than being recruited
locally.[37] The 10,000 Arabs at Raphia could have been
recruited at any part of the desert margin all the way round
from Damascus to the Gulf, and from within Arabia; these
archers, however, seem to localize recruiting to the Emesa
region.

Now, Emesa was the centre of an Arab kingdom which
comes more or less clearly into view when Pompeius, on his
journey south through Syria, confirmed king Samsigeramos in
possession of Emesa and Arethusa.[38] The kingdom lasted for
well over a century after then, being suppressed by Vespasian
in AD 72,[39] which was, no doubt, when the corps of archers
became Roman troops. The king confirmed in office by
Pompeius had been a potential successor to the Seleukids in
the years between the withdrawal of Tigranes' power and the

[33] Pol. 5. 79. 8 and 85. 2.
[34] Livy 37. 40. Their number is unspecified. They were employed as skirmishers
and mounted on dromedaries.
[35] G. T. Griffith, *The Mercenaries of the Hellenistic World* (Cambridge, 1935), 144–6.
B. Bar-Kockva, *The Seleukid Army* (Cambridge, 1976), 48–53, calls them 'national
contingents'.
[36] Pol.30. 26–8.
[37] G. L. Cheesman, *The Auxilia of the Roman Army* (Oxford, 1914). A. Mocsy, *Upper
Moesia and Pannonia*, (1974), 195, makes the point about the continued recruitment
from Syria, in connection with the Syrian archers stationed at Intercisa
(Dunaujvaros).
[38] Str. 16. 2. 10.
[39] J.–P. Rey-Coquais, 'Syrie romaine de Pompée à Dioclétien', *JRS* 68 (1978), 50.

arrival of Pompeius himself (69–64 BC). A king whose base
was at Emesa and whose reach could extend almost to
Antioch was clearly well rooted both territorially and historically. In dealing with Syria, Pompeius had no compunction
about eliminating recent upstarts, such as Silas at Lysias,[40]
but Samsigeramos was much more carefully handled: his
kingdom was reduced in extent, certainly, but it was neither
eliminated nor broken up.

In the 60s, therefore, Samsigeramos' kingdom was firmly
established, though its origins are obscure. Samsigeramos
himself could have been active for thirty years before
Pompeius. The names employed in the dynasty included
Samsigeramos and Iamblichos,[41] and this fact suggests a
connection backwards in time with the Arab chief called
either Malchos or Iamblichos who was allied with Diodotos-
Tryphon in the capture of Chalkis in 145.[42] 'Malchos' is
clearly a graecization of 'Malik', the Aramaic and Arabic for
'king'; this was the result, no doubt, of Greeks confusing the
title with the man.[43] Iamblichos would thus be the king's own
name. It is tempting to associate him with the dynasty which
became established at Emesa. There are difficulties, however.
The Iamblichos of 145 was operating well to the north of
Emesa. This may not be an insuperable obstacle to identification, since the Arabs he controlled were presumably at least
partly nomadic. If it is correct that Chalkis remained under
Arab control after 145, then Iamblichos would be its ruler,
and so he would be unlikely to father a dynasty which ruled at
Emesa. The name is really the only evidence, and it is not
strong enough by itself. Nevertheless, given Samsigeramos'

[40] Jos. *AJ* 14. 13. 2.

[41] R. D. Sullivan, 'The Dynasty of Emesa', *ANRW* 2/8 (1977), 198–219. This
article appears to assume that Samsigeramos was the first of the dynasty. There is no
discussion about his origins and antecedents. C. Chad, *Les Dynastes d'Emèse*
(Beyrouth, 1972), 33–35, claims that the connection of Iamblichos with Diodotos 'of
Apameé' puts Iamblichos 'dans les pays d'Apamée', but even he cannot demonstrate
a clear connection with Emesa.

[42] 'Malchos' in Jos. *AJ* 13. 5. 1; 'Iamblichos' in Diod. 33. 4ᵃ.

[43] 'Malchos' was also a popular personal name, but the records are essentially of
Roman date, and mainly epigraphic, as any superficial view of local inscriptions
reveals. The author Porphyry had the Semitic name Malchos (F. Millar, 'The
Phoenician Cities: A Case Study in Hellenisation', *Proceedings of the Cambridge
Philological Society* (1983), 64.

obvious power in the 60s, solidly established at Emesa and
Arethusa, one would expect that it had originated some time
before. The Seleukid civil wars of the 120s and from 113
onwards would provide an excellent opportunity for raiders
from the desert to become established in such places.

Samsigeramos was only one of two Arab kings competing to
succeed the Seleukids in Syria in the 60s; the other was
Azizos.[44] Twenty years before, in 88, the Arab chief who
operated in the north as the ally of Strato of Beroia was
'Zizon', and he appeared at the siege of Beroia in that year.[45]
They were presumably either the same man or related. It may
be that their tribe was the Rhambaei, which had a long
history in the steppe of the north, tracking back and forth
south of the Jabboul lake and across the Euphrates.[46] It is this
tribe which is most likely to have gained control of Chalkis, if
any did, and it is here that the Iamblichos of 145 is perhaps
best located, as a likely ancestor of 'Zizon' and Azizos.

Deeper in the desert than these kings, who were operating
on the margins, it is just at this time that Palmyra begins to
rise to wealth. It is a commonplace to point out that the city
owed its wealth to its control of the desert route between the
middle Orontes and the middle Euphrates.[47] This, however,
was not the obvious route for any non-desert dweller to take.
For Syrians there were two better routes, in the sense of being
less arduous and less dangerous. They were both in the north,
beginning at Antioch and crossing the Euphrates at Zeugma.
Both of these routes became difficult in the first century BC,
and it was just at that time that the desert route through
Palmyra grew to importance. The choice between the
northern routes and that by Palmyra would partly depend on
the point of origin of the traveller, partly on his destination
and partly on his preference for a desert route or a route
through well-watered lands. But it could also be a choice

[44] Diod. 40. 1ᵃ—6.
[45] Jos. *AJ* 14. 14. 3.
[46] Jos. calls Zizon 'the ruler of the Arabian tribes' (*AJ* 14. 14. 3) which in that
context of northern Syria would seem to be the confederation which is called, in
Caesar's time, the Rhambaei (M. C. Astour, 'The Rabbaeans: A Tribal Society on
the Euphrates from Yahdu-Lim to Julius Caesar', *Syro-Mesopotamian Studies* 2/1 (Jan.
1978)).
[47] Jones, *CERP* 265, for example.

between, so to say, a 'Greek' route and a 'Syrian' route. In the
north one would travel from Antioch to Zeugma through
Kyrrhos or Beroia and Hierapolis, all Greek cities. The southern
route, through the desert, connected Emesa and Palmyra; to the
eastward it reached to the middle Euphrates, to the west of
Emesa was Arados. All three, Arados, Emesa and Palmyra,
were Syrian cities, in the sense of originating among the Syrian
'native' population, and the first two had gained their power and
importance in defiance of the Seleukid kings.

Palmyra's history in the Seleukid period is even more
obscure than Emesa's. It was attacked by M. Antonius in 40
BC for its wealth,[48] which suggests a preceding history of a
reasonable length. Yet the place is not mentioned in any text
from the fourth century BC until the first.[49] This contrasts with
the Nabataeans who were subjected to a similar raid by
Demetrios Poliorketes as early as 312.[50] Had the place been
large or wealthy or important in the Seleukid period, one
would have expected some indication of Seleukid interest, if
not actual control. As it is, the only sign of such interest is a
pair of inscriptions with lettering of a Hellenistic date, noted
by Seyrig.[51] Both of them came from the foundations of the
Bel temple, and one was a fragment of a dedication by a king
with the surname Epiphanes. Seyrig argued between a
Parthian or a Kommagenean king, but there were at least four
Seleukids in the 90s and 80s with such a surname.[52] The only
firm fact is that one king at least showed an interest in the city
in the late Hellenistic period. But there seems nothing earlier,
at least so far. The preliminary conclusion is therefore that
Palmyra only reaches more than local, oasis importance
from *c.* 100 BC.[53]

---

[48] App. *Civil Wars*, 5. 9.

[49] Jones, *CERP* 231, claims Palmyra as 'important' in the fourth century BC on the
grounds that its foundation is attributed by the author of Chronicles to Solomon.
Jones' reasoning is difficult to accept. The mention in *2 Chron.*, 8: 4 does show that the
place existed, but its importance may have been no more than that it was the only
oasis in the whole area which had permanent inhabitants.

[50] Diod. 19. 94. 1–98. 1.

[51] H. Seyrig, 'Inscriptions', *Syria* 20 (1933), 302–23, nos. 27 and 28.

[52] These kings, whose surnames are noted by Bellinger, 'End', are Seleukos VI,
Antiochus XI, Philip I, and Antiochos XII, all sons of Antiochos IX Grypos, and
who all reigned briefly and died young between 95 and 83.

[53] E. Will, 'Le Développement urbain de Palmyre: Témoignages épigraphiques
anciens et nouveaux', *Syria* 60 (1983), 69–81, is not concerned with the city's origins.

It does not seem too fanciful, therefore, to see here a commercial alliance symbolized by the new importance of the desert route, and perhaps also a political alliance between these three Semitic powers. At a guess, one would suggest that the impulse came from Arados, once Emesa had become established and politically stable. Emesa's nomad connections would inevitably include a knowledge of the desert routes and of the Palmyrene oasis. In Roman times, the boundaries of Emesa and Palmyra marched together in the midst of the desert.[54]

There are therefore at least four political authorities in Syria—Arados, the two Arab kings, Palmyra—who can be seen to act independently of the Seleukid state in the generation after 128. There are also others, this time in the mountains.

In the Lebanon mountains the Ituraean Arabs emerged as a political power during the last fifty years of the Seleukids. They were an Arab tribe who began by raiding from the mountains into the Biqaa valley and towards the coast, and then moved into those areas as conquerors. There were two principalities of Ituraeans, a small one in the northern Lebanon mountains, and a larger one to the east, in the Biqaa valley.[55] A very similar process had happened further south, for the Maccabean uprising in Judaea was also, in part, a rising of hillmen against the people of the plains.[56] And in the north, in the Bargylos mountains behind Arados and Gabala and Laodikeia-ad-Mare, the same process was at work, though here it is much less visible.

The hillmen of the Bargylos do not intrude on the surviving sources at all, but they cannot have been ignored. They did have some resources, and so they were taxable; they also produced young men, who could be taken for soldiers.[57] The Seleukid impact is likely therefore to have been limited to

---

[54] *IGLS* 2552.

[55] Str. 16. 2. 18; A. H. M. Jones, 'The Urbanisation of the Ituraean Principality', *JRS* 21 (1931), 265–75.

[56] See the geographical interpretation of M. Avi-Yonah, *The Holy Land from the Persian to the Arab Conquests (536 BC—AD 640), A Historical Geography* (Grand Rapids, Mich., 1966), 55–9, and his map of 'Hasmonean Palestine' on p. 75.

[57] The young male population of these mountains has today been much reduced by military conscription, for they are of the same sect as President Assad of the modern Republic, that is, Alawites, and so are presumed to be loyal.

these essentially predatory effects in most of the area. The
road from Antioch to Laodikeia-ad-Mare, with staging posts,
inns and villages, radiated Greek influence of a more positive
sort. Further than this it is not possible to go, in the absence of
any archaeological evidence. There is, however, one item of
literary information which can be exploited. When the
hillmen of the Bargylos actually obtrude into the historical
record, they are organized as the tetrarchy of the Nazerini,
who are named by Pliny from an official list, apparently of the
Augustan period.[58]

This tetrarchy's size is unclear, and it must be admitted
that its location in the Bargylos mountains rests on the
assumption that 'Nazerini' is a term ancestral to 'Nosairi', a
people later known of in those hills. For the purpose of this
argument, however, the precise location is not important. For
this tetrarchy to be in existence in Augustus' time, it must
have existed beforehand. No new monarchies were created in
Syria in the Roman period, but those already in existence
were often maintained. This means that their origins lay in the
Hellenistic period. The mountain Nazerini, then, organized
themselves into a principality in the same way as had their
fellow mountain-men, the Ituraeans of the Lebanon.

Pliny's list is jumbled and incomplete, but it does reveal—
as in the case of the Nazerini—that there were a number of
political communities in Syria in Augustus' time which did
not rank as cities. Many of them cannot be located, and Pliny
himself fails to name seventeen of them, which he dismisses as
'having barbarian names'. But enough are traceable to show
that these non-urban communities were interspersed between
the cities and were thus separate from them. Those whose
identification seems secure are, besides the Nazerini: the
Gindareni, who can be connected with Gindaros, south-west
of Kyrrhos, though Gindaros itself is listed separately; the
Mariamnitai are clearly the people in or around Mariamme,
which was on the road inland from Arados towards Emesa;
the Hemeseni were obviously the people of Emesa. Less
certain identifications are: the Gabeni, who were perhaps the
people of the Ghab valley and marshes; the Tardytenses, who

---

[58] Pliny, *NH* 5, 81–2.

have been suggested as the people of Tarutia east of Apamea; the Gazetae, who were possibly the people of the town of Azaz, between Kyrrhos and Beroia.[59] Some on the list are called 'tetrarchies' by Pliny, the Nazerini being one, but most of the names are simply those of peoples (see Map 4).

These peoples and statelets had been originally, in most cases, part of the territory of one or other of the cities of Syria. Gindaros had been part of Kyrrhos' territory, as had the Gazetae, if they were located at Azaz. The Gabeni, if they were in the Ghab, were originally in Apamea's lands, and so were the Tardytenses, and likely enough the Mariamnitai as well. The cities had effectively divided up lowland Syria between them from the start, and their boundaries seem to have marched one with another. In one clear case, the mutual boundary of Antioch and Apamea in the Roman period has been plotted over a considerable distance by reference to dated inscriptions,[60] and this boundary presumably originated in the Hellenistic period. Yet the tetrarchies and peoples listed by Pliny were not part of any city's land. They have, therefore, become politically separate at some stage, and, as in the case of the Nazerini, this can only have occurred during the Seleukid troubles.

Pliny's source listed the situation as it had been at some time during the reign of Augustus.[61] From that time onwards, and perhaps for some time earlier, the smaller political units in Syria were progressively absorbed into the Roman province of Syria, a process which eventually culminated in the annexations of the Emesan and Kommagenean kingdoms in AD 72 (and that of Chalkis in AD 92). Pliny's list, therefore, reflects the political situation in Syria midway between two periods of unity. In the period when the Seleukids were in full control, the only permitted political authorities were the king and the cities, and most of the land was divided up among the latter. From about 100 AD the only political authorities were the cities and the Roman governor. The two centuries or so

---

[59] For many of these identifications see Jones *CERP* 260–3, where the list is discussed in detail.

[60] H. Seyrig, Appendix II of vol. iii of G. Tchalenko, *Villages antiques de la Syrie du Nord* (Paris, 1958), 2–62.

[61] This is established by Jones, *CERP* 260.

between were years of political fragmentation, and it is this which Pliny's list reflects. It can also reveal the process by which Seleukid Syria broke up.

Most of the Greek cities are included in the list: they were usually too strongly fortified to be captured by their Syrian enemies, still less destroyed. There had been exceptions: Chalkis captured by Iamblichos; Arethusa was in Samsigeramos' kingdom in 64; Kyrrhos had probably expired; Laodikeia-ad-Libanum can scarcely have survived; all these are likely victims. As a general rule, however, the Syrian cities do not appear to have been captured or capturable by local Syrian forces. The one certain exception is Arethusa, taken at some point by the Emesan king; it was small and isolated and very close geographically to its conqueror. Other cities were more distant and stronger.

The names on Pliny's list which were not cities will therefore in most cases be those of peoples who had detached themselves from one of the cities; that is, they were groups of Syriac-speaking peoples who had seceded from the Seleukid kingdom when they got the chance, and had therefore set up their own political communities, some of which still existed when the list was drawn up.

At the same time, as royal authority weakened, the desert chiefs were able to extend their power into the steppeland over some of the sedentary communities in the borderland. Similarly, the men of the hills, perhaps never fully part of any city's territory, detached themselves and the tetrarchy of the Nazerini may thus be directly analogous to the kingdom of Samsigeramos: the chiefs will have extended their authority into the lowlands when that of the Seleukid kings broke down. None of the secessionist groups was notably powerful in itself. In 88 the Seleukid king who controlled Antioch—but not much else—was able to put 10,000 men into the field.[62] This is probably a larger army than any of the Semitic states could raise, yet even that army was unable to capture Beroia, a relatively small city. Nevertheless the constant raids by hillmen and desert tribes will have weakened all of the cities by ravaging their lands. So the cities' authority over their

---

[62] Jos. *AJ* 14. 14. 1.

more distant territories declined, in some cases to vanishing point. This permitted some of these distant territories to secede.

In Pliny's list the peoples who can be located on the ground were all at some distance from the cities. The Gindareni, for example, were midway between Kyrrhos and Antioch; the Gazetae, if located at Azaz, were similarly equidistant from Kyrrhos and Beroia. Apamea's territory had been very large from the start, and it is not surprising that it produced correspondingly more examples of these secessions: the Ghab, if that was the home of the Gabeni, was difficult territory, Mariamme (of the Mariamnitai) was on Apamea's southern boundary, Tarutia (of the Tardytenses, perhaps) was on the desert fringe. These communities may have done no more than refuse to pay their customary rents and taxes to the cities, but this effectively made them independent. No doubt they paid blackmail to any more powerful political authority which was within reach. They were undoubtedly small and weak, no more than village groups or small towns. Nevertheless the fact that they were in Pliny's list, and were thus recognized as political entities in the time of Augustus, means that they had established themselves as political entities in the Seleukid period. There was no opportunity later. Pompeius had revived the cities, and no more independent non-city groups would be permitted to appear in the Roman period.

Amid all this, the cities will have felt that they were being slowly strangled. Their control over territory close under their walls remained, and so they will have been able to maintain a certain level of food supplies, but the more distant or inaccessible territories defied or escaped their authority. Beyond those there were the fully independent and hostile kingdoms, based in the deserts or the steppe or the hills. The Seleukid kings had repelled or dominated those enemies for two centuries, but after the destruction of the army of Antiochos VII in Parthia in 129 and the failure of Demetrios II in Egypt in 128, this domination became increasingly difficult. When they were left to fend largely for themselves, during the collapse of the dynasty after 113, the cities were unable to hold on to their large territories. Thus the cities eventually looked outside Syria for a king who would assume the role which the last Seleukids were not fulfilling and who could be both powerful and supportive.

When the magistrates of Antioch met in 83 to consider the available candidates the list comprised Mithridates of Pontos, Tigranes of Armenia, Parthia, and Rome.[63] The absentees from this list are as interesting as the candidates. The Ptolemies were as far gone as the Seleukids by this time, and a union with them would scarcely have strengthened Syria. Nor was the lord of Beroia on the list. If he was a relative of the Herakleon who had tried to seize the throne in 96/95, then the Beroian (presumably Strato, the survivor of the siege of 88) might be said to have had a claim. But perhaps local enmities were too powerful. The local Syrian (that is, Arab) kings were not considered either: it was against their depradations that the new king must defend the cities.

The final choice of the Antiochene magistrates was dictated largely by international politics. Rome was too distant, too erratic, and had too long a history of enmity to the Seleukids to be seriously considered, quite apart from being involved in its own internal quarrels at the time. Parthia was an ally of the ruler of Beroia, who was the enemy of Antioch and had not been considered. Mithridates of Pontos was a distant monarch and was also so deeply involved with Rome that his attention would be constantly distracted.[64] That left Tigranes, who at least was Syria's neighbour. Perhaps by some such process of elimination as this, he was chosen.

Tigranes' extended his authority in Syria in stages, marked by the cities he acquired. First, Antioch, at the start; then Laodikeia in 81, Apamea in 76. He was thus the cities' king, a true successor to the Seleukids. Thus Laodikeia's acceptance of his authority in 81 meant that Tigranes accepted the responsibility of defending the city against external attack. Given Laodikeia's geographical situation these external enemies can only have been the hillmen of the Bargylos. Tigranes no doubt had little or no authority in the hills.

We do not have any record of relations between him and the

---

[63] Justin 40. 1.

[64] For the general background to all this see A. N. Sherwin-White, *Roman Foreign Policy in the East* (1984), and Will *Hist. pol.*, vol. ii.

Semitic states—Samsigeramos, Arados, Azizos, and Palmyra—nor with the much lesser known statelets such as the
Tardytenses and the Gazetae. But since Pompeius accepted
them a few years later, it seems reasonable to presume that
they existed through the 80s and 70s. Their survival and
continued existence was in fact in Tigranes' own interest,
since it was fear of these secessionists which had led the cities
to accept his authority in the first place. The slow expansion of
his power in Syria strongly suggests that he was accepted with
considerable reluctance, which culminated in the need to
exert force at Ptolemais-Ake in 69.[65]

The practical effect of Tigranes' kingship in Syria was thus
to freeze the political situation as it was when he found it. He
had been invited into Syria by the hard-pressed Greek cities,
and it was through them that his power expanded, yet he
could not do what they no doubt wanted, which was to
eliminate all the local threats to the cities, for the continued
existence of these enemies of the cities was necessary to him as
a hold over the allegiance of the cities. Yet at the same time he
could not allow these local non-Greek powers to continue to
expand as they had been doing before his arrival. Hence he
will have preserved the situation as he found it, suppressing
conflict without removing its causes. It is this which is
perhaps at the root of the tradition preserved by Justin[66] that
his rule was peaceful.

Tigranes' authority evaporated in 69, when his ancestral
kingdom was attacked, and the peaceful period ended. The
cities were once more under threat. The Armenian episode
had not weakened their enemies, but its failure weakened the
cities. The search began again for a protector. The cities were
plainly incapable of surviving, either singly or in combination,
without support. Tigranes had provided it for a time, but now
another co-ordinator was required. There were still adult
Seleukids available, but their rivalry was ineradicable, and
was used by the Arab kings for their own purposes;
Mithridates of Pontos was in the process of going down before
the Roman attacks at long last; Parthia was too distant and

[65] Jos. *AJ* 13. 16. 4.
[66] Justin 40. 1.

too ill-organized to be acceptable, and it had retreated eastwards before the temporary power of Tigranes. Only Rome was left. So the magistrates contacted the conqueror of Tigranes, Q. Pompeius Magnus, then in Armenia.

Pompeius marched south through the Taurus in late 65, entering Syria after a brief fight in Kommagene. He already had much information about the state of things there. His sources included the diplomatic archives at Rome, which will have included a report on the visit in 73 to the city by a couple of claimant Seleukids.[67] Several Roman magistrates had visited the land itself or had meddled in its affairs in recent years, and Pompeius himself had insisted that Syria was at his disposal in his conversation with king Tigranes after the latter's surrender in 66.[68] Two of his naval commanders, Q. Caecilius Metellus Nepos and L. Lollius, had reached Damascus in their hunt for pirates. They had been superseded there by M. Aemilius Scaurus who had been specifically sent by Pompeius to investigate the situation.[69] So Pompeius had information from three men about the situation in the mid-Syrian area, and Scaurus had had to travel through north Syria to get to Damascus. L. Licinius Lucullus, Pompeius' predecessor in the great eastern command, had briefly concerned himself with Syria in 69.[70] Q. Marcius Rex, proconsul in Kilikia in 67, had been drawn, not unwillingly, into the problem of the area, and he had sent P. Clodius into Syria.[71] Between them these two Romans had only muddled matters even more, by choosing to support a loser. Thus Pompeius had plenty of information about Syria, and this could be supplemented by other, less highly placed informants.

And then, of course, there were the Syrians themselves. The withdrawal of Armenian authority after Tigranes' defeat in 69

---

[67] Cicero, *In Verrem* 2. 2. 4. 61.

[68] Plut. *Pompeius* 33. 5; App. *Syr.* 49 and *Mith.* 106. There is disagreement among modern historians as to whether Pompeius deprived Tigranes of his Parthian conquests, but there is no doubt about Syria.

[69] Jos. *AJ* 14. 2. 3; *BJ* 1. 6. 2; App. *Mith.* 95.

[70] App. *Syr.* 49.

[71] Dio Cassius 36. 17. 3; Mal. 225. 4–11; G. Downey, 'Q. Marcius Rex at Antioch', *CPP* 32 (1937), 144–51; correction to Downey in A. N. Sherwin-White, *Roman Foreign Policy in the East*, 211, n. 65.

had released all the various competitors for power who had been held in restraint for the past decade and more. There were just two surviving Seleukids: Antiochos XIII was based in Seleukeia-in-Pieria,[72], and Philip II, his cousin, was in an unspecified corner of Kilikia.[73] Philip had been sponsored by Marcius and Clodius, whereas Antiochos had been to Rome in 73 and had secured some sort of recognition from the Senate, and from Lucullus in 69. Neither of these two had the actual physical power on the ground which alone would convince Pompeius of their worth.

The two Seleukids had each allied themselves with rival Arab kings: Philip with Azizos, Antiochos with Samsigeramos, but each of these was effectively a claimant to the kingship of all Syria. The two Arab kings agreed to kill off their Seleukid stooges and take power for themselves.[74] This agreement was not implemented, and the two Seleukids escaped.[75] That the agreement should have been made at all is a clear indication that it was the two Arab kings who had the power in Syria rather than the hapless Seleukids.

These four were the major protagonists, each of them aiming to achieve complete control of all Syria, but there were also others, whose aims were more modest. Dionysios son of Herakleon ruled Beroia, Hierapolis and Herakleia in 69[76] and his principality presumably still existed in 65. Antiochos of Kommagene was pressing down from the north and very quickly came to terms with Pompeius as the latter passed

---

[72] Cicero, *In Verrem*, 2. 2. 4. 61; Bellinger, 'End', p. 91.

[73] Justin 40. 2. Kilikia's position is not at all clear, and the pirates, Pompeius, and Marcius were all involved in it, as well as cities which had been the source of men gathered for Tigranes' city-building at Tigranocerta. There was clearly plenty of scope for a man like Philip, who Justin says was 'hiding in Kilikia'. By the time the dust had settled, Alexandria-by-Issos and most of the Amanus mountains and even Nikopolis were counted as parts of Kilikia.

[74] Diod. 40. 1ᵃ—1ᵇ; Eusebius, *Chronicon*, ed. Schoene, p. 261; Hieronymos, *Chron.*, ed. Helm, p. 150. Attempts to unravel the confusion: Downey, *Antioch*, chs. 6 and 7, and 'Q. Marcius Rex at Antioch', *TAPA* 32 (1937), 144–51; Bevan, *House*, ch. 31; Will, *Hist. Pol.* ii. 426–430; Bellinger, 'End', pp. 82–86; Sherwin-White, *Roman Foreign Policy in the East*, (1984), 211–12. The confusion is probably unsolvable, but the general chaos is clear enough, and the predominance of the Arab kings comes out well from the sources, even though it is not always recognized in the modern interpretations.

[75] Diod. 40. 1ᵇ.

[76] Str. 16. 2. 7.

through his kingdom.[77] The hillmen of the Bargylos were by now organized into the tetrarchy of the Nazerini.[78] The town of Lysias, whose precise location is unknown, was the base for Silas the Jew, called, since he was executed by Pompeius, a brigand.[79] Had he been more fortunate, he could have been a tetrarch at least. There were others. Pliny's list of half a century later shows only the survivors.[80]

Then there were the cities. Circumstances might have compelled them to act independently, but there is no evidence that they enjoyed possessing such a privilege. Arados, of course, did, and had sent ships to co-operate with Lucullus in his campaign against the pirates in 87;[81] no doubt Aradian co-operation was similarly forthcoming in Pompeius' anti-pirate campaign. Seleukeia-in-Pieria had resisted all the blandishments of Tigranes and his viceroy, and had held, or had been held, to the Seleukid cause, specifically that of Antiochos XIII.[82] Antioch had been the prime mover in calling in Tigranes in 83, and was still the barometer for those who chose to claim to rule all Syria. Both Philip II and Antiochos XIII had held the city more than once between 69 and 65,[83] and Antiochos is said to have met Pompeius there.[84] The fates of other cities are less obvious; some were parts of principalities, some were probably expiring, one at least—Laodikeia-ad-Mare, appears to have been flourishing.[85]

It is impossible to know if Pompeius had decided on his approach to Syria before he arrived, or whether he made up his mind once he got there. During the previous year he had been busy establishing cities in Pontos in place of the kingdom of Mithridates, and he had reconciled many of the pirates to the loss of their freedom by placing them in cities.[86] And he

[77] Dio Cassius 36. 2. 5; Str. 16. 2. 3; App. *Mith.* 114; Kommagene was later reckoned to have been conquered, according to Pompeius' triumph, so there was presumably some fighting between Romans and Kommageneans. But Antiochos was recognized as king and was rewarded with land, so his resistance was not serious.

[78] Pliny *NH* V. 81.   [79] Jos. *AJ* 14. 3. 2.

[80] Pliny, *NH* 5. 82.   [81] Str. 16. 2. 14.

[82] Jos. *AJ* 14. 3. 2.

[83] Downey, *Antioch*, pp. 139–42; Bevan, *House*, ii. 266–7; Bellinger, 'End', pp. 82–6.

[84] Justin 40. 2.

[85] Assuming that Str.'s description of its prosperity applies to this period almost as much as to later in the century (16. 2. 9).

[86] Plut. *Pompeius*, 28; see also R. Seager, *Pompey, A Political Biography*, (Oxford, 1979), 38.

was a Roman, with a built-in prejudice for cities as against kings. There were plenty of cities in Syria. Yet only one of those cities had ever demonstrated any eagerness for autonomy, and a king had been proved to be necessary for the cities to survive. So, if the cities were to be presented with their unsought autonomy, they had also to be protected against the manifold enemies around them. The kings in and around Syria had demonstrated their willingness, indeed their eagerness, to acquire the lands and riches of the cities. They could scarcely be trusted to refrain from continuing their attacks once Pompeius had gone home.

The crucial decision, therefore, came at the meeting of Pompeius and Antiochos XIII. It is to some extent surprising that Antiochos should be in Antioch and be available. Previously he is said to have been Samsigeramos' prisoner, while Philip was in possession of Antioch—or, at least, resident there, as the ally of Azizos[87]—and Antiochos is said to have escaped to Parthia and then returned to Antioch.[88] If so, this may imply that he was Parthia's candidate. He had the better claim from the Roman point of view, for he had been one of the Seleukid princes who had been given some sort of recognition by the Senate in 73[89] and he had also gained recognition from Lucullus in 69.[90] Philip, on the other hand, had only been supported by Marcius and his subordinate Clodius,[91] both of whom were operating outside their province in this instance (though Philip does seem to have had a base in Kilikia,[92] Marcius' province). It may be that Samsigeramos, Azizos, the Parthians, and Antiochos had all got together to put Antiochos forward on the assumption that Pompeius would simply go along with the preceding Roman policy. It was in the interests of all of these to keep the Romans out of Syria, and the best way to do that was to get

---

[87] Philip appears to have got to Antioch after escaping from Azizos' assassination plot, so presumably the alliance no longer operated. This is, of course, not necessarily the case.

[88] Eusebius, *Chronicon*, ed. Schoene, p. 261.

[89] Cicero, *In Verrem*, 4. 27–30.

[90] Justin 40. 2.

[91] G. Downey, 'Q. Marcius Rex at Antioch', pp. 144–51, and 'The Occupation of Syria by the Romans', *TAPA* 82 (1951), 149–63.

[92] J. Keil and A. Wilhelm, *Monumenta Asiae Minoris Antiqua*, vol. iii (Manchester, 1931), no. 62; Mal. 225.

Pompeius to recognize one particular king. Then Pompeius would go home, and the game could continue.

This is why the information Pompeius had gathered is important. Neither the Senate nor Lucullus, Marcius nor Clodius, had a detailed knowledge of conditions within Syria; instead they had their information from only one of the interested parties. Nor had the Senate or Lucullus been seriously interested in Syria when they had extended recognition to Antiochos.[93] But now Pompeius was both well informed and on the spot. It was in his own interest to produce a settlement which would last for some time, long enough for him to get the Senate's ratification. Thus the settlement had to last for several years at least, otherwise its breakdown would be a stick with which his enemies could beat him.[94]

Therefore Pompeius' answer to Antiochos' request for recognition was an uncompromising refusal. His reason was essentially that Antiochos was quite unable to control Syria. He also stated that Antiochos' subjects did not want him, but this was only saying the same thing again. He remarked that he had no intention of leaving Syria a prey to Arabs and Jews,[95] and this is precisely what it had been in the previous four years, since 69. Thus the refusal to accept Antiochos as king automatically also ruled out Philip, Azizos, and Samsigeramos as candidates.

This left Pompeius with the need to establish the cities and principalities as autonomous states, and, since they were incapable in most cases of maintaining their authority alone, they had to be protected. This now had to be done by Rome, since no other authority had the military and political power required, and that in turn meant the creation of a province, with a governor and an army. And, given a province, the various constituent parts of Syria would have to be reduced to

[93] Antiochos and his brother had originally gone to Rome to lay claim to the kingship of *Egypt*, not Syria (Cicero, *In Verram*, 4. 27). This hardly suggests an active campaign to recover Syria, and it also implies that Syria was 'awarded' to them as a consolation after the refusal of Egypt.

[94] The contemptuous tone which Cicero adopts when discussing Pompeius in the East (e.g., nicknaming him 'Samsiceramus') gives a hint of one Roman attitude (Cicero, *Ad Atticum*, 2. 14. 1). Pompeius' later difficulties in getting Senatorial authorization for his whole programme are too well known to need emphasis.

[95] Justin 40. 2. 2–5; App. *Syr*, 49; Plut. *Pompeius*, 39. 3.

a fairly uniform size, with no single entity being predominant over the rest.

When Pompeius set off southwards through Syria, therefore, dealing out justice right and left, the cities received the most favoured treatment, at least in Pompeius' view. The five great cities were given autonomy, or had their existing autonomy confirmed. Seleukeia-in-Pieria was granted autonomy, Pompeius apparently remarking that the city was too strong to be attacked.[96] Maybe it really was too strong, but there is no sign of Pompeius wishing to attack it, nor would there be any reason for him to do so, unless perhaps it had continued to stand by the Seleukids. But Antiochos XIII had been the city's man, and he soon vanished, murdered at last, it seems, by Samsigeramos, to whom his usefulness was now ended.[97] So Seleukeia's autonomy was confirmed, this time with perhaps rather more sincerity than the kings had displayed. Antioch, inevitably, became formally autonomous, and adopted a Pompeian era.[98] Apamea's fort was razed by Pompeius as he passed, and this is clearly a sign of increased local authority for the city,[99] but it is also a sign of the essential impotence of the city as compared with either a royal or a Roman dynast. Laodikeia-ad-Mare and Arados were both secure and strong, and both had their autonomy confirmed, by implication if not by an actual known grant. Arados, uncharacteristically, was sufficiently grateful to Pompeius to fall foul of Caesar fifteen years later.[100]

The second rank of cities are more difficult to pin down. None of them are known to have adopted a Pompeian era,[101] which would be one sign that he had favoured them, but this is not definitive. What evidence there is suggests that they did not get much in the way of independence. It is known that Seleukeia-Zeugma was presented to Antiochos of Kommagene by Pompeius.[102] It had been, presumably, under

[96] Str. 16. 2. 8.
[97] Diod. 40. 1[b].
[98] Seyrig, 'Ères', pp. 10–14.
[99] Jos. *AJ* 14. 3. 2.
[100] In 46 Arados ceased producing tetradrachms, a sure sign of loss of power by the city (Rey-Coquais, *Arados*, p. 162). The city also fell foul of Antonius a few years later.
[101] Seyrig, 'Eres', pp. 15–20.
[102] Wagner, *Zeugma*, pp. 44–5.

Parthian control from *c*.88 BC until Tigranes had taken control of Mesopotamia, so the city had been out of Seleukid hands for a quarter of a century by the time Pompeius arrived in Syria. Pompeius' relations with Parthia, formed in the course of the wars in Asia Minor, seem to have convinced him that Parthia was a somewhat different proposition than, say, Armenia or Kommagene. Thus Phraates of Parthia got most of what he claimed from the wreckage of Tigranes' empire, but Pompeius did ensure that there was a string of buffer states between Syria and the Parthians: Osrhoene in the western part of Mesopotamia, and Kommagene to the north and east of Syria. Zeugma, the link between the two, became Kommagenean, but its trans-Euphratean suburb, Apamea, presumably went to Abgar of Osrhoene.[103]

Between Antioch and Kommagene were Kyrrhos and the Beroian principality. The fate of neither is known. Kyrrhos had probably died by now. It seems likely that the Beroian principality was suppressed though this is no more than an assumption from the general political situation. Herakleon's claim to the Seleukid kingship thirty years before may have been enough to ensure the elimination of his family's power. If so, Beroia and Hierapolis could have become autonomous cities within the new province. Hierapolis was one of three towns presented by M. Antonius to a refugee Parthian prince in the 30s,[104] but this does not necessarily mean that the principality of Herakleon had disappeared. Another of the three towns was Arethusa, which had been Samsigeramos', whose kingdom certainly continued. A generation later, Strabo refers to them by the enigmatic term 'small towns'.[105] They thus existed, but their political status is quite obscure. Nikopolis became part of Kilikia at about his time,[106] as did Alexandria-by-Issos. Again, both continued in existence, and Alexandria coined,[107] but information about neither of them emerges from the sources.

In the southern sector, the situation was just as various, if

---

[103] Discussion of Pompey's relations with Parthia in Sherwin-White, *Roman Foreign Policy in the East*, pp. 218–26.
[104] Plut. *Antonius*, 37.
[105] Str. 16. 2. 7; he uses the word *polichnia*.
[106] Str. 16. 4. 19, though he imagines it to be on the coast.
[107] Head, *HN* 716.

not more so. Again, there were both cities and principalities to deal with, while the sheer size of Apamea's original territory meant that the independent fragments of it were more numerous. The Gabeni, the Mariamnitai, the Tardytenses, and probably other fragments were in this area. The fact that they were in Pliny's list means that Pompeius recognised their effective autonomy. Samsigeramos was restricted to a defined territory which included the urban centres of Emesa and Arethusa, but his rural desert lands could not be so easily defined.[108] The territory of Arados was unaffected, which means that Pompeius confirmed it. The overall result was a patchwork of varying political entities, kings, tetrarchs, cities, and autonomous village communities.

Any military strongpoint which was not an actual city was liable to be destroyed. It is this military strength which perhaps best accounts for the elimination of Silas' stronghold at Lysias and of the castle at Apamea rather than any Pompeian animus towards them or his possible love of civic freedom. Pompeius' whole policy in Syria seems to be aimed at a reduction in the power of the strong and a recognition of autonomy for the weak. A future Roman governor would therefore have no over-mighty subjects to deal with. Arados, yet again, might be said to be the exception here, for it must have ranked with the more powerful entities in the whole area, yet it was not reduced. But Arados had demonstrated consistently that it was not interested in any extension of its territory beyond the *peraia* it had acquired in 130/129. It was a 'sated' power, and a friend of Rome—of Rome in its guise as a law-enforcer, that is. So Arados proves the rule: its lack of territorial ambition made it safe, whereas Samsigeramos' devouring ambition made him dangerous. So Arados was treated as a friend and ally and its territory was confirmed and maintained, while Samsigeramos was cut down, both in power and in pretensions.

Among those which can be classified with the weak powers were most of the cities. Laodikeia and Apamea demonstrated a certain strength during the Roman civil wars by standing

---

[108] Arethusa: Str. 16. 2. 11. It was later taken from Samsigeramos by Antonius and given to a Parthian prince (Plut. *Antonius*, 37). Emesene, the later territory of Emesa, is discussed by H. Seyrig, 'Caractères de l'histoire d'Emèse', *Syria* 36 (1959), 184–92.

substantial sieges, but that was not by their own choice.[109]
Antioch might be thought strong through its sheer size, and
Seleukeia-in-Pieria gained a reputation for strength from that
offhand remark of Pompeius'. But their strength was not
based on deeds. The ease with which Antioch changed hands
in the period between the departure of Tigranes and the
arrival of Pompeius suggests once more a basic weakness in
the city's political will. It was no more an independent
political force in Syria in the 60s than it had been in the
previous two-and-a-half-centuries—with the single exception
of the 140s.

If the great cities were quietist, how much more so were the
smaller ones. None of them shows any political initiative of
any sort, with the usual exception of Arados. The only
political vigour in the area came from the Arab kings, the
Roman governors, and the various dynasts. There was no *civic*
vigour. Just as they had relied on the political initiative of the
Seleukid kings in every major political act, so they now relied
on the will and judgement of kings, chiefs, and governors.
Pompeius' grant of some sort of autonomy was in this
tradition: a gift from above. This was the essential legacy of
the Seleukids to the cities of the dynasty's founder: the cities
were no more than urban agglomerations, without serious
civic or political purposes other than those endowed them by
the royal government. Now the Roman Republic had become
the king, and the cities did as they were told, once more.

The Roman annexation of Syria—'conquest' is too strong a
word—did not by itself save the cities. True, by reducing the
power of the enemies of the cities, the Roman presence
reduced the pressure on them; but the future of the cities was
not secure until the Roman state itself was secure, and in Syria
this took another generation. There were more civil wars and
invasions. Arados, Laodikeia-ad-Mare and Apamea were all
damaged by the civil wars.[110] The Parthians raided across the
Euphrates more than once,[111] even to Antioch.

Nevertheless the Roman state was basically friendly towards the cities, whereas its opponents were not, so in the long

---

[109] Laodikeia: Str. 16. 2. 9; Apamea: Str. 16. 2. 10.
[110] Str. 16. 2. 9; 2, 10; Rey-Coquais, *Arados*, p. 169.
[111] Str. 16. 1. 28; Jos. *AJ* 14. 13. 3.

run the cities were safe. As part of the Roman Empire they flourished even more than they had at the height of Seleukid power, and even the anti-city Semitic states yielded: Kommagene was annexed and became city-land;[112] Emesa became a city when the monarchy was eliminated,[113] and Arethusa became free and a city at last.[114] Those cities who had survived all through the troubles now blossomed. Antioch grew again, getting new walls in Tiberius' reign;[115] Laodikeia-ad-Mare was exceptionally prosperous to Strabo's eyes;[116] Seleukeia-in-Pieria was Rome's naval base in the east.[117]

Yet conditions had not changed in any basic way. The cities were still parasitic on the peasant economy, and the antagonism of Greek citizens and Syriac peasantry continued throughout the Roman and Byzantine periods; it was noted by Libanios in the fourth century.[118]

The internal conflict was mitigated by the power of the central government, in the persons of the Roman governor and the Roman army. They took the place, in Syrian terms, of the Seleukid king and his army, and so the cities survived for six centuries and more after the end of the Seleukid state. When, in turn, the Roman-Byzantine state was displaced from Syria by the Islamic Arabs, the Seleukid cities rapidly slid down into ruin and desertion and decay. They were valued for their fortifications at times, but not as cities. Those places which flourished as cities in the Islamic period were those which were not Greek in origin: Emesa became Arabic Homs; Beroia, Strabo's small town, became the great Aleppo; Birejik replaced Zeugma; Antioch, revived briefly by the Crusades, was deserted by the fourteenth century;[119] Apamea shrank to the fort of Qalat al-Mudiq.

Once the support of the central government was removed,

[112] *IGLS* 43, 44.

[113] H. Seyrig, 'Caractères de l'histoire d'Emèse', *Syria* 36 (1959), 184–92.

[114] Seyrig, 'Éres', pp. 20–1.

[115] Downey, *Antioch*, pp. 176–7.

[116] Str. 16. 2. 9.

[117] H. Seyrig, 'La Cimitière des Marins à Séleucie de Pierie', *Mélanges syriens offerts à René Dussaud* (Paris, 1939), 451–9.

[118] J. H. W. C. Liebeschuetz, *Antioch, City and Imperial Administration in the Later Roman Empire* (Oxford, 1972), ch. 1.

[119] S. Runciman, *History of the Crusades*, vol. iii (1954), 325–6.

the cities died. In the longer term—longer than the Roman Empire, that is—the cities of Seleukos I could not stand on their own feet; they were artificial. Yet it is not an inconsiderable achievement for a king to have founded a double handful of cities which existed for a thousand years.

APPENDIX I

Concordance of City-Names

Pre-Greek Name	GREEK NAME	Modern Name
—	ALEXANDRIA-BY-ISSOS	Iskenderun
—	ANTIOCH-ON-ORONTES	Antakya
Urima	ANTIOCH-ON-EUPHRATES	Horum Huyuk(?)
Niya	APAMEA (PELLA)	Qalat al-Mudiq
Arvad	ARADOS	Arad
?	ARETHUSA	Ar-Restan
?	BALANAIA	Baniyas
Halab	BEROIA	Aleppo
Qinnesrin	CHALKIS-AD-BELUM	Nebi Is
Duluk	DOLICHE	Tell Duluk
Emesa	EMESA	Homs
Hamath	EPIPHANEIA	Hama
Carchemish	EUROPOS	Gargamis
Gabala	GABALA	Jeblé
Bambyke	HIERAPOLIS	Membij
—	KYRRHOS	—
?	LARISSA	Shaizar
Qadesh	LAODIKEIA-AD-LIBANUM	Tell Nebi Mend
—	LAODIKEIA-AD-MARE	Latakia
Marathus(?)	MARATHOS	Amrit
Mariamme	MARIAMME	Mariamin
—	NIKOPOLIS	Islahiyé
?	PALTOS	Arab el-Mulk
Rhosos (?)	RHOSOS	Arsuz
—	SELEUKEIA-IN-PIERIA	—
—	SELEUKEIA-ZEUGMA	Balqis
—	SELEUKOBELOS	Sqalbiyé (?)
Simyra	SIMYRA	Tell Kazel

Notes:
 — = No settlement.
 ? = Name not known.
 (?) = Name not certain.

APPENDIX 2

Hellenistic Kings of Syria

THE following list contains the names of all those who ruled in Syria as kings between the Persians and the Romans. Dates are those of their exercise of power. Asterisks mark non-Seleukids. Only brief surnames are given.

333–323	*ALEXANDER III the Great
323–316	*PHILIP III Arrhidaios
323–310	*ALEXANDER IV
306–301	*ANTIGONOS I Monophthalmos (satrap from 318)
301–281	SELEUKOS I Nikator
292–261	ANTIOCHOS I Soter
261–246	ANTIOCHOS II Theos
246–244	*(?) PTOLEMY III
246–226	SELEUKOS II Kallinikos
226–223	SELEUKOS III Soter
223–187	ANTIOCHOS III Megas
187–175	SELEUKOS IV Philopator
175–170	(?) ANTIOCHOS
175–164	ANTIOCHOS IV Epiphanes
164–162	ANTIOCHOS V Eupator
162–150	DEMETRIOS I Soter
153–145	*ALEXANDER I Balas
146–139	DEMETRIOS II Kallinikos (1st reign)
145–142	ANTIOCHOS VI Dionysos
142–138	*TRYPHON (Diodotos)
138–129	ANTIOCHOS VII Sidetes
129–126	DEMETRIOS II Kallinikos (2nd reign)
128–123	*ALEXANDER II Zabinas
125	SELEUKOS V
125–96	ANTIOCHOS VIII Grypos
113–95	ANTIOCHOS IX Kyzikenos
96–95	SELEUKOS VI
95–88	DEMETRIOS III
94–83	ANTIOCHOS X
92–83	PHILIP I

92	ANTIOCHOS XI
89–94	ANTIOCHOS XII
83–69	*TIGRANES
69–64	ANTIOCHOS XIII
69–64	PHILIP II

APPENDIX 3

Evidence for Persian and Hellenistic Period Occupation

THE evidence has been gathered either by excavation or by archaeological survey. Clearly the former is preferable, and the contrast is made all the greater by some of the surveys' methods. In the following tables excavations are listed individually, and in each case only occupation in the two periods in question is noted (P = Persian, H = Hellenistic), together with the major references (full references are in the Bibliography). Occupation in the Persian period but not in the Hellenistic means that occupation *ended* at some point in the Persian, usually fairly early; similarly no occupation in the Persian but occupation recorded for the Hellenistic means that occupation *began* in the Hellenistic, usually in the second half of the period.

The survey evidence is summmarized on the maps 5(*a*)–(*c*); numbered sites correspond to those in the lists. Open circles indicate Persian period occupation; crosses Hellenistic. If the site is not numbered the evidence is purely from a survey. Survey areas are delineated on the maps and comments on the quality of the surveys are appended after the excavation lists.

A. THE NORTH WEST

Excavations

Site	Occ'n	References
1 Alexandria-by-Issos	H	—
2 Antioch	H	*Antioch-on-the-Orontes.*
3 Ayin Dara	H	Seirafi and Kirichian, *AAAS* 15.
4 Catal Huyuk	P H	Haines, *Plain of Antioch*, vol. ii.
5 al Mina-Sabouni	P	Woolley, *Alalakh.*.

6 Seleukeia-in-Pieria	H	*Antioch-on-the-Orontes*, vol. iii.
7 Tell el-Judaidah	P H	Haines, *Plain of Antioch* vol. ii.
8 Tell Masin	H	du Mesnil de Buisson, *Berytus*, 2 (1935).
9 Tell Tainat	?P	Haines, *Plain of Antioch* vol. ii.
10 Zincirli		von Luschan, *Sendschirli*.

Surveys.

I. *Kilikia.*

A small part of a survey of the whole of the Kilikian plain by Seton Williams, published in 1951. No Persian period remains were found, but occupied sites are known for Myriandros and Rhosos and a Persian fortification existed at the Syrian Gates, the northern entrance to the plain of Iskenderun.

II. *The Amuk Plain.*

A survey of the whole plain by an expedition from Chicago led by R. J. Braidwood in the 1930s, combined with the excavation of three sites in the south-eastern Amuq plain (Tell el-Judaidah, Tell Tainat, and Catal Huyuk). The excavations produced a clear sequence of pottery, which was then applied to the findings of the survey. Careful and detailed, the survey was a pioneer effort, and this shows in the periodization adopted. Period II is the Roman and III comprises the Persian and Hellenistic periods combined. II and III are distinguished by red-glazed Antiochene ware. The preceding period (IV) is called 'Syro-Hittite', and corresponds to what would now be called the Iron Age, c.1000 to c.500 BC, thus including the Assyrian and Babylonian periods and the beginning of the Persian. The map therefore cannot separate Persian and Hellenistic occupation, though the excavations can—but excavations have been relatively few.

B. THE NORTH EAST

Excavations.

Site	Occ'n	References
1 Atcherine	H	Meer, *AAS* 1 (1951).
2 Beroia	H	Sauvaget, *Alep.*

3 Chalkis	H	Monceaux and Brossé, *Syria* 6 (1925).
4 Deve Huyuk	P H	Woolley, *Annals of Archeology and Anthropology 7* (1914–6); Moorey, *Levant* 7 (1975).
5 Doliche	P H	Cumont, *Études syriennes*; Perkins, Braidwood, *AJA* (1947).
6 Europos	H	Woolley, *Carchemish* ii.
7 Gedikli	H	Alkim, *Belleten* 30 (1966).
8 Hierapolis	P H	Goossens, *Hierapolis de Syrie*.
9 Kyrrhos	H	Frézouls, *AAS* 4 and 5 (1954–5), and Balty, *Apamée de Syrie* (1972).
10 Neirab	PH	Abel and Barrois, *Syria* 6 (1927) and Carrière and Barrois, *Syria* 7 (1928).
11 Tell el-Abd	H	Freedman, *AASOR* 4 (1977).
12 Tell Abu Danné	P H	Tefnin, *et al*, *Syro-Mesopotamian Studies* 3/3, and *AAAS* 33/2 (1983).
13 Tell Frey	H	*Exposition Alep* (1979).
14 Tell el-Hajj	H	Krause *et al.*, *Tell el-Hajj in Syrien*.
15 Tell es-Suweyhat	H	Holland, *Levant* 8 (1976).
16 Umm el-Mara	H	*LIEAO* II.
17 Zeugma	H	Wagner, *Zeugma*.

Surveys.

III. The Gaziantep Region

A very rapid, wide-ranging, and superficial survey by an Italian team in 1969; only the most obvious or outstanding periods of occupation were recorded. Periods of weak occupation are understated, periods of intense occupation are exaggerated by contrast. (A. Archi, F. E. Pecorella, M. Salvini, *Gaziantep e sua Regione*, Rome (1971).)

IV. Sakce Gozu and Gaziantep Areas

Two small areas surveyed by the excavators of Sakce Gozu in 1948, one near the excavation site, the other near the city of Gaziantep. This is almost the only survey to appreciate that there were other sites than tells which give evidence of past occupation. It is thus

important more for that hint than for the finds it made. (J. du Plat
Taylor, M. V. Seton Williams, J. Waechter, 'The Excavations at
Sakce Gozu', *Iraq* 12 (1950), 53–138.)

V. The Qoueiq Valley.

A survey by a British team in 1975. The sites visited were selected in
advance by place-name or because they were known to have a tell.
In its periodization, the survey was able to divide the Hellenistic
into 'Early' and 'Late', but the Persian period was lumped in with
the Iron Age. (J. Matthers (ed.), *The River Qoueiq, Northern Syria, and
its Catchment: Studies arising from the Tell Rifaat Survey, 1977–1979*
(Oxford, 1981).)

VI. North of Membij

Two surveys in 1977 and 1979 covering a small area near
Hierapolis. The first was a 'pilot' survey, done by visiting sites by
car; the second was a slightly more detailed version. Again the
Persian period was consumed by the whole Iron Age, though only
five sites of that long period were found; ten sites of the Hellenistic
were located; one site was common to both. (P. Sanlaville (ed.),
Holocene Settlement in North Syria (Oxford 1985).)

VII. The Jabboul Area.

Survey conducted in 1938 by a team from the Palestine Exploration
Society. Attention was overwhelmingly directed to the Bronze Age
and earlier, and the later periods are only perfunctorily recorded. No
pottery for the Persian period was recognized, yet four sites are said
to be 'Persian', and twenty-six to begin or end as Persian. Also
Greek black-glaze pottery of the fourth century BC is recorded at
three places, all on the road from Aleppo to Bab. Hellenistic pottery
is said to be 'far more common' than this, but only sixteen sites out
of the 114 listed are specifically said to have produced Hellenistic
pottery. It is therefore very difficult to draw dependable conclusions
for the Hellenistic and Persian periods from the published information. (R. Maxwell Hyslop, J. du Plat Taylor, M. V. Seton
Williams, J. d'A. Waechter, 'An Archaeological Survey of the Plain
of Jabboul, 1939', *Palestine Exploration Quarterly* (1942).)

VIII. The Tabqa Dam/Lake Assad Survey

A systematic programme of survey and excavation in advance of
flooding behind the Tabqa Dam. Eighteen sites identified by the
survey have been excavated. The lowest point of occupation is the
Persian period, with only one site; there is then a slight recovery in
the Hellenistic, when there are four sites. (*Exposition des découvertes de*

la Campagne Internationale de Sauvegarde des Antiqités de l'Euphrate,
Musée Nationale d'Alep (1974); D. N. Freedman (ed.), 'Archaeo-
logical Reports from the Tabqa Dam Project, Euphrates Valley,
Syria', *AASOR* 44 (1977).)

C. THE SOUTH

Excavations

Site	Occ'n	References
1 Apamea	H	Balty, *Apamée de Syrie* (1969 and 1972).
2 Arab el-Mulk	H	Oldenburg and Rohweder
3 Arados	P H	Rey-Coquais, *Arados*.
4 Arjouné	H	Parr, *AAAS* 33 (1983).
5 Dehes	H?	Sodini *et al.*, *Syria* 57 (1980).
6 Emesa	H	Aurenche, 'Chronique archéologiqué', *Syria* 62, (1985)
7 Gabala	H	Aurenche, 'Chronique archéologiqué', *Syria* 62 (1985).
8 Hama	H	Fugman, *Hama* 2, Ploug 1 and Christencen and Johansen, 3/2
9 Huarte	H	Canivet 'Huarté', *AAAS* 27–8, 1977–8.
10 Khan Sheikhoun	P	du Mesnil de Buisson, *Syria* 13 (1932).
11 Laodikeia-ad-Mare	H	Sauvaget, 'Plan'; Saadé, *AAAS*, 29 (1979).
12 Laodikeia-ad-Libanum	H	Parr, *Archiv für Orient-forschung, 26 (1978/9)*, and *AAAS* 33 (1983).
13 Marathos	P H	Dunand *et al.*, *AAS* 4–5, (1954–5), 6 (1956), Saliby, *AAAS* 21 (1971).
14 Mishrifé	H	du Mesnil de Buisson, *Mishrefé-Qatna*.
15 Ras el-Basit	H	Courbin, *AAAS* 27–8 (1977–8) and 33 (1983).

16	Ras Ibn Hani	H	Lagarce, *CRAI* 1978.
17	Ras Shamra	P	Schaeffer, *Ugaritica* 4; Stucky, *Leukos Limen*
18	Simyra	P H	Dunand *et al.*, *AAAS* 14 (1964).
19	Sukas	P H	Riis, *Sukas* i.
20	Tabbat el-Hammam	P H	Braidwood, *Syria* 21 (1940).
21	Tell Afis	P H	Matthiae, *Akkadica* 14 (1979).
22	Tell Deinit	P H	Aurenche, 'Chroniques archéologiques', *Syria* 62 (1985).
23	Tell Durak	P H	Oldenburg and Rohweder.
24	Tell et-Tin	H	Gautier, *CRAI* 1895.
25	Tell Hana	P	du Mesnil de Buisson, *Syria* 11 (1930).
26	Tell Mardikh	P H	Matthiae, *Ebla.*
27	Tell Qarqur	H	Lundquist *AAAS* 33/2 (1983).
28	Tell Tuqun	P H	Matthiae, *Akkadica* 14 (1979).

Surveys

IX. *Tell Mardikh Survey.*

Survey of the area west of the Madkh marsh conducted as a preliminary to the excavation at Tell Mardikh. Published in two parts, between which the Persian and Hellenistic periods tend to fall. (A. de Maigret, 'Fluttuazioni territoriali e caratteristiche tipologiche degli Insediementi nella regione del Matah (Siria): nota preliminare', *Orientis Antiquo Collectio* 13 (1964), pp. 83–94; F. S. Pericoli Ridolfini, 'La rovine romano-bizantine', *Missione Archeologia Italiana in Siria: rapporto preliminare della campagna 1964* (Rome, 1965), 135–155.)

X. *Jebel Sbet Survey*

Small area survey, published in outline only. No Persian or Hellenistic remains are reported. (G. P. Haase, 'Ein Archäologischer Survey in Gabal Sbet und in Gabal al-Ahass', *Damascener Mitteilungen* 1 (1983), 69–76.)

XI. *North-East of Hama.*

An early survey, done primarily to locate sites; well published, but does not provide any systematic evidence of occupation. (J. Lassus,

Inventaire archéologique de la region au nord-est de Hama (Paris, 1935).)

Several other surveys in the south and on the coast do no more than list the names of tells, information which can be gleaned from the map.

BIBLIOGRAPHY

AALDERS, G. J. D. 'City-State and World-Power in Hellenistic Political Thought', in J. Harmatta (ed.), *Proceedings of the VII Congress of International Federation of the Societies of Classical Studies* (Budapest, 1984), i, 293–301.

A (BDUL-HAK), S., 'Chronique des fouilles en Syrie: III. Les fouilles de la Direction Général des Antiquités dans la Nécropole de Tell Nebi Mind', *AAS* I (1951), 121–6.

—— 'Découvertes archéologiques récentes dans les sites greco-romains de Syrie', *Atti del VII Congresso Internazionale de Archeologia Classica*, 3, (Rome 1961). 32–3.

ABEL, M., Alexandre le Grand en Syrie et en Palestine', *Revue biblique* 43 (1934), 528–45 and 44 (1935) 42–61.

—— 'La Syrie et la Palestine au temps de Ptolemée Ier Soter', *Revue biblique* 44 (1935), 559–69.

—— and M. BARROIS, 'Fouilles de l'école archéologique français de Jérusalem effectuées à Neirab', *Syria* 8 (1928), 187–206 and 303–19.

ADAMS, R., McC., *Heartland of Cities* (Chicago, 1981).

ADMIRALITY, *Turkey*, Geographical Handbook Series (London, 1942).

—— *Syria and Palestine*, Geographical Handbook Series (London, 1943).

ALBRIGHT, W. F. 'Archaeological and Topographical Explorations in Palestine and Syria', *BASOR* 49 (1933), 23–32.

—— and R. P. DOUGHTY, 'From Jerusalem to Baghdad down the Euphrates: I, From Jerusalem to Aleppo', *BASOR* 21 (1926) 1–10.

ALKIM H., 'Explorations and Excavations in Turkey in 1970, 1971 and 1972', *Anatolica* (1973–6), 3–140.

ALKIM, U. BAHADUR 'The Road from Samal to Asitawandawa', *Anadolu Arastirmalari* 2 (1965), 1–45.

—— 'Excavations at Gedikli (Karahuyuk), First Preliminary Report', *Belleten* 30 (1966) 1–57.

—— 'The Amanus Region in Turkey', *Archaeology* 22 (1969), 280–9.

ARCHI, A., F. E. PECORELLA, and M. SALIVINI, *Gaziantep e sua Regione* (Rome, 1971).

ASHTON, B. S., 'The Geography of Syria', *Journal of Geography* 27/5 (May 1928), 167–77.

ASHTOR, E., *A Social and Economic History of the Near East in the Middle Ages* (1976).

ASTOUR, M. C., 'The Rabbaeans: A Tribal Society on the Euphrates from Yahdu-Lim to Julius Caesar', *Syro-Mesopotamian Studies* 2/1 (Jan. 1978), 1–12.

ASWAD, B. C., *Property Control and Social Strategies: Settlers on a Middle Eastern Plain*, University of Michigan Museum of Anthropology, Anthropological Papers 54 (1971).

ATHANASSIOU, H., 'Rasm et-Tanjera: A Recently Discovered Syrian Tell in the Ghab', Ph.D. thesis, University of Mississippi, Columbia 1977.

AURENCHIE, O. (ed.), 'Chronique archéologique', *Syria* 62 (1985), 125–69.

AUSTIN, M. M., *The Hellenistic World from Alexander to the Roman Conquest* (Cambridge, 1981).

AVI-YONAH, M. *The Holy Land from the Persian to the Arab Conquests (536 B.C. to A.D. 640), A Historical Geography* (Grand Rapids, Mich. 1966).

AYMARD, A., 'Autour de l'avènement d'Antiochos IV', *Historia* 2 (1953), 49–73.

—— 'Du nouveau sur la chronologie des Séleucides', *Revue des études anciennes* 57 (1955) 102–12.

BADIAN, E., 'The Administration of the Empire', *Greece and Rome* N.S. 12 (1965) 166–82.

BAGNALL, R. S., *The Administration of the Ptolemaic Possessions outside Egypt* (Leiden, 1976).

BALDUS, H. R. 'Der Helm des Tryphon und die seleukidische Chronologie der Jahre 146–138 v. Chr.', *Jahrbruch des Numismatik Geldsgeschichte* 20 (1970) 218–39.

BALTY, J. *Apamée de Syrie, bilan des recherches archéologigues, 1969-71* (Brussels, 1972).

—— 'Apamée de Syrie, archéologie et histoire: I, Des origines a la Tetrarchie', *ANRW* 2/8 (1977) 1; 3–34.

—— 'L'Apamène antique et les limites de la Syria Secunda', *La Geographie administrative et politique d'Alexandre à Mahomet* (Strasbourg, n.d.) 41–75.

BALTY, J.-C., 'Les Grandes Étapes de l'urbanisme d'Apamée-sur-l'Oronte', *Ktema* (1977), 3–16.

—— 'Le Bélus de Chalcis et les fleuves de Ba'al de Syrie-Palestine', *Archéologie au Levant, Recueil R. Saidah* (Lyon, 1982), 287–98.

BAR-KOCKVA, B. *The Seleucid Army* (Cambridge, 1976).

BARONI, A., 'I terreni e i privilegi del tempio di Zeus a Baitokaike', in B. Virgilio (ed.), *Studi ellenestici* (Turin, 1984), 135–67.

BARTLETT, J. R. 'From Edomites to Nabataeans: A Study in Continuity', *Palestine Exploration Quarterly* III (1979) 53–66.

BATES, D. G. *Nomads and Farmers, A Study of the Yoruk of Southeastern*

Turkey, University of Michigan Museum of Anthropology, Anthropological Papers 52 (1973).

BELLINGER, A. R. 'The End of the Seleucids', *Transactions of the Connecticut Academy of Arts and Sciences* (1949).

—— 'Notes on Some Coins from Antioch in Syria', *American Numismatic Society Museum Notes* 5 (1952), 52–5.

BEVAN, E. R. *The House of Seleucus* 2 vols. (London, 1902).

BI(C)KERMAN, E. J. *Institutions des séleucides* (Paris, 1938).

—— 'La Cité grecque dans les monarchies hellénistiques', *Revue de philologie*, 3rd ser., 13 (1939) 335–49.

—— 'Notes on Seleucid and Parthian Chronology', *Berytus* 8 (1944) 73–83.

—— 'La Coele Syrie: notes de géographie historiques', *Revue Biblique* 54 (1947) 256–68.

BINTLIFF, J. T. and W. VON ZEIST, *Palaeoclimate, Palaeoenvironments and Human Communities in the Eastern Mediterranean in later Prehistory*, BAR S 133 (Oxford, 1982).

BIRAN, A., 'Chronique archéologique—Tell Dan', *Revue Biblique* 84 (1977) 256–63.

BOSWORTH, A. B., 'The Government of Syria under Alexander the Great', *Classical Quarterly* 24 (1974) 46–64.

—— *A Historical Commentary on Arrian's History of Alexander*, vol. i (Oxford, 1980).

BOUCHE-LECLERCQ, L., *Histoire des Séleucides* 2 vols. (Paris, 1913).

BOUISSON, Comte du Mesnil de, 'Comte rendu de la quatrième campagne de fouilles des quelques sites des environs de Mishrifé', *Syria* 11 (1930), 160–3.

—— 'Une campagne de fouilles à Khan Sheikhoun', *Syria* 13 (1932) 171–88.

—— *La Site archéologique de Mishrifé Qatna* (Paris, 1935).

—— 'Souran et Tell Masin', *Berytus* 2 (1935).

BOUNNI, A., 'La Quatrième Campagne de Fouilles (1978) à Ras Ibn Hani', *CRAI* (1979) 277–94.

BOWERSOCK G. W., *Roman Arabia* (Cambridge, Mass. 1983).

—— 'Antipater Chaldeaus', *Classical Quarterly* 33 (1983), 491.

BRAIDWOOD, R. J., *Mounds in the Plain of Antioch* (Chicago, 1937).

—— 'Report on two Sondages on the coast of Syria', *Syria* 21 (1940), 183–226.

BRIANT, P., 'Villages et communautés villageoises d'Asie achémenide et hellénistique', *Journal of the Economic and Social History of the Orient* 18 (1975), 165–88.

—— 'Colonisation hellénistique et populations indigènes: I, La Phase d'installation', *Klio* 60 (1978) 57–92.

—— 'Colonisation hellénistique et populations indigènes: II, renforts grecs dans les cités hellénistiques d'Orient' *Klio* 64 (1982) 83–94.

—— 'Des Achémenides aux rois hellénistiques: continuités et ruptures (bilan et propositions)', in *Rois, tributs et paysans* (Paris, 1982), 291–330.

BRICE, W. C. (ed.) *The Environmental History of the Near and Middle East since the last Ice Age* (1978).

BROSSÉ, L., 'La Dique du Lac de Homs', *Syria* 4 (1922) 234–40.

BROWN, K. S. O., *Central Place Theory* (London, 1977).

BUHL, M. L. 'The Near Eastern Pottery and Objects of Other Materials from the Upper Strata', *Sukas* vii (Copenhagen, 1983).

BULOW-JACOBSEN, A., 'P. Haun 6: An Inspection of the Original', *Zeitschrift für Papyrologie und Epigrafik* 36 (1979) 91–100.

BURFORD, A., 'Heavy Transport in Classical Antiquity', *Economic History Review* 13 (1960) 1–18.

BUTZER, K. W. 'Physical Conditions in Eastern Europe, Western Asia and Egypt before the period of Agricultural and Urban Settlement', *CAH* 2nd edn. (Cambridge, 1970) vol. i, part 1, pp. 35–69.

Cambridge Ancient History, vol, i, part 1, (3rd edn., 1970): vol. ii, (1st edn., 1924); vol. vii, part 1 (2nd edn., 1984).

CANIVET, M.-T. and P., 'Sites chrétiens d'Apamène', *Syria* 48 (1971). 295–321.

—— 'Deux campagnes archéologiques à Huarté d'Apamène', *AAAS* 27-28 (197-8) 141–64.

CANIVET P. and M. T. FORTUNA, 'Recherches sur le site de Nikertai', *AAAS* 18 (1968) 37–54.

CARRIÈRE B. and BARROIS, A. 'Fouilles de l'école archéologique français de Jérusalem effectuées à Neirab', *Syria* 7 (1927) 126–42 and 201–12.

CAVAIGNAC, E., 'A propos des monnaies de Tryphon: L'Ambassade de Scipion Emilien', *Rev. Num.* (1951), 131–38.

CAWKWELL, G., *Philip of Macedon* (1978).

CHAD, C., *Les Dynastes d'Emèse* (Beyrouth, 1972).

CHAPOT, V., 'Séleucie de Pierie', *Mémoires de la Société des Antiquaires de France* 66 (1906), 149–224.

—— *La Frontière de l'Euphrate* (Paris, 1907).

CHEESMAN, G. L. *The Auxilia of the Roman Army* (Oxford, 1914).

CHESNEY, F. D. *Narrative of the Euphrates Expedition* (London, 1868).

CHRISTALLER, W., *Die Zentralen Orte in Suddeutschland* (Jena, 1933).

CHRISTENSEN, A. P. and C. F. JOHANSEN, 'Les Poteries hellénistiques et les terres sigillées orientales', *Hama* 3/2 (Copenhagen, 1971).

CLAIRMONT, C., 'Greek Pottery from the Near East', *Berytus* 11/2 (1955), 85–141.

—— 'Poterie grecque provenant de Ras Shamra', *Ugaritica* 4 (1962), 631–6.

CLAYTON, P. A. 'The Coins from Tell Rifaat', *Iraq* 29 (1967), 143–54.

COHEN, G. M. The Seleucid Colonies: Studies in Founding, Administration and Organisation, *Historia* Einzelschriften 30 (Wiesbaden, 1978).

—— 'Colonisation and Population Transfer', in W. Peremans (ed.) *Egypt and the Hellenistic World*, Studi Hellenistica 27 (Louvain, 1983) 63–74.

—— 'Property Rights of Hellenistic Colonists', in J. Harmatta (ed.), *Proceedings of the VII Congress of the International Federation of the Societies of Classical Studies* (Budapest, 1984), 323–5.

COOK, R. M. *The Persian Empire* (London, 1984).

COURBIN, P. 'Rapport sur la sixième campagne de fouilles (1976) à Ras El-Bassit (Syrie)', *AAAS* 27–8 (1977–8), 29–39.

—— 'Les Premiers Grecs à Ras el-Basit', *11th International Congress of Classical Archaeologists* (London, 1979), 198–9.

—— 'Bassit', *AAAS* 33/2 (1983) 119–27.

COURTOIS, J. C. 'Prospection archéologique dans la moyenne vallée de l'Oronte', *Syria* 50 (1973), 53–99.

CROWFOOT, J. M., K. M. KENYON, and E. L. SUKENIK, *The Buildings at Samaria* (London, 1942).

CUMONT, F., 'Doliché et le Zeus Dolichenus', *Études Syriennes* (Paris, 1917), 173–202.

DHORMÉ, P. 'Les Tablettes babyloniennes de Neirab', *Revue d'assyriologie* 25 (1928), 53–67.

DIEUDONNÉ, A., Les Monnaies grecque de Syrie au Cabinet des Médailles', *Rev. Num.* (1927) 1–50.

DILLER, A., *The Textual Tradition of Strabo's Geography* (Amsterdam, 1975).

DOBIAS, J., 'Séleucie sur l'Euphrate', *Syria* 6 (1925) 253–68.

G. L. DOWNEY, 'Q. Marcius Rex at Antioch', *Cl.Ph.* 32, (1937), 144–51.

—— 'Strabo on Antioch: Notes on his Methods', *TAPA* 72 (1941).

—— 'The City Plan of Antioch', *AJA* 55 (1951).

—— 'The Water Supply of Antioch on the Orantes in Antiquity', *AAS* 1 (1951), 171–87.

—— 'The Occupation of Syria by the Romans', *TAPA* 82 (1951) 149–63.

—— 'The Size of the Population of Antioch', *TAPA* 89 (1958), 84–91.

—— *A History of Antioch in Syria* (Princeton, NJ, 1961).

—— *Ancient Antioch*, (Princeton, NJ, 1963).

DUNAND, M. 'Les Sculptures de la Favissa du Temple d'Amrith', *Bulletin du Musée de Beyrouth* 7 (1944–5), 99–107; and 8 (1946–8), 81–107.

—— 'Défence du front mediterranéan de l'empire Achémenide', in W. A. Ward (ed.), *The Role of the Phoenicians in the Interaction of Mediterranean Civilisations* (Beirut, 1968), 43–52.

—— A. BOUNNI, and N. SALIBY, 'Fouilles de Tell Kazel, rapport préliminaire', *AAAS* 14 (1964) 3–14.

—— and N. SALIBY, 'Rapport préliminaire sur les fouilles d'Amrith en 1955', *AAS* 6 (1956) 3–8.

—— 'A la recherche de Simyra', *AAAS* 7 (1965), 3–16.

—— 'Le Sanctuaire d'Amrith: rapport préliminaire', *AAS* 11 (1961–2), 3–12.

—— and A. KHIRICHIAN, 'Les Fouilles d'Amrith en 1954: Rapport préliminaire', *AAS* 4–5 (1954–5), 181–204.

DUSSAUD, R. *Topographie historique de la Syrie ancienne et Médiévale* (Paris, 1927).

—— 'La Dique du Lac de Homs et le "Mur Egyptien" de Strabon', *Foundation Eugène Piot, monuments et mémoires* 25 (1921–2), 135–42.

EDDY, S. K. *The King is Dead* (Lincoln, Neb. 1961).

EDELSTEIN L. and I. G. KIDD, *Posidonius: The Fragments* (London, 1972).

EDSON C. 'The Antigonids, Heracles and Beroea', *Harvard Studies in Classical Philology* 41 (1934) 213–46.

—— 'Imperium Macedonicum: The Seleucid Empire and the Literary Evidence', *Cl. Ph.* 53 (1958) 153–70.

EGAMI, N. and S. MASUDA, *Tell Mastuma, Excavations in the Idlib District, Syria, 1989* (Tokyo, 1982 and 1984).

—— and T. IWASAKI, *Rumeilah and Mishrifat* (Tokyo, 1979).

EL-ZEIN, M., 'Geschichte der Stadt Apameia am Orontes von den Anfangen bis Augustus', dissertation, Heidelberg, 1972.

Exposition des découvertes de la Campagne Internationale de Sauvegarde des Antiquités de l'Euphrate, Musée Nationale d'Alep (1974).

FARRELL, W. J. 'A Revised Itinerary of the Route followed by Cyrus the Younger through Syria, 401 B.C.', *Journal of Hellenic Studies* 81 (1960) 153–5.

FISHER, W. B., *The Middle East* (London, 1956).

FORBES, R. J., *Metallurgy in Antiquity* (Leiden, 1950).

FRASER, P. M., *Ptolemaic Alexandria* (Oxford, 1972).

FREEDMAN, D. N., (ed.). 'Archaeological Reports from the Tabqa Dam Project, Euphrates Valley, Syria', *AASOR* 44 (1977).

FRÉZOULS, E., 'Recherches historiques et archéologiques sur la ville de Cyrrhus', *AAS* 4 and 5 (1954–5). 89–128.

—— 'Sur les divisions de la Séleucide à propos de Strabon XVI, 2', *MUSJ* 37 (1960) 221–34.

—— 'Les Théâtres antiques de l'Orient Syrien', *Atti del VIII Congresso Internazionale de Archeologia Classica* (Paris, 1963), 339–51.

—— 'La Toponymie de l'Orient Syrien et l'apport des élements macedoniens', *La Toponymie antique* (Strasbourg, 1977), 219–48.

FROST, H., 'The Arwad Plans, 1964: A Photogrammetric Survey of Marine Installations', *AAAS* 16 (1966) 13–28.

FUGMAN, E., 'L'Architecture des périodes pre-Hellénistiques', *Hana* 2/1 (Copenhagen, 1958).

FUKS, A., 'Social Revolution in Greece in the Hellenistic Age', *La Parola del Passato* 111 (1966), 437–48.

—— 'Patterns and Types of Social-Economic Revolution in Greece from the Fourth to the Second Century B.C.', *Ancient Society* 5 (1974) 51–81.

GAUTIER, J-E., 'Note sur les fouilles entreprises dans la Haute Vallée de l'Oronte . . . pour retrouver l'emplacement de l'ancienne ville de Kadech', *CRAI* 4th ser., 26 (1895), 441–64.

GOODCHILD, R. G. 'The Coast Road of Phoenicia and its Roman Milestones', *Berytus* 9 (1948) 91–128.

GOOSSENS, G., *Hierapolis de Syrie* (Louvain, 1943).

GRANT, M., *The Etruscans* (1980).

GRIFFITH, G. T. *The Mercenaries of the Hellenistic World* (Cambridge, 1935).

GRUEN, E. S. *The Hellenistic Monarchies and the Coming of Rome* (Berkeley and Los Angeles, Calif. 1984).

HAASE, G. P. 'Ein archäologischer Survey in Gabal Sbet und in Gabal al-Ahass', *Damascener Mitteilungen* 1 (1983), 69–76.

HADDAD, G., 'The Population of Antioch in the Hellenistic-Roman Period', *AAS* 1 (1951) 19–31.

HAINES R. C., *Excavations in the Plain of Antioch: II, The Structural Remains of the Later Phases* (Chicago, 1971).

HAMMOND, N. G. L. *Alexander the Great* (London, 1980).

—— and G. T. GRIFFITH, *History of Macedonia*, vol. ii (Oxford, 1979).

HARPER R. P., 'Excavations on the Euphrates Frontier, 1968–1974', *Studien zu den Militargrenzen Roms* 2 (Cologne, 1977), 454–60.

HEAD, B. V., *Historia Numorum* (Oxford, 1911).

HEICHELHEIM, F., *Roman Syria* (vol iv, part II of T. Frank (ed.), *An Economic Survey of Ancient Rome* (Baltimore, 1938)).

HELLIESEN, J. M. 'Demetrius I Soter: A Seleucid King with an Antigonid Name', in H. J. Dell (ed.) *Ancient Macedonian Studies in Honour of Charles F. Edson* (Thessalonika, 1981).

HENGEL, M., *Judaism and Hellenism*, trans. J. Bowden (London, 1974).

—— *Jews, Greeks and Barbarians* (London, 1980).

HERRMANN, P., 'Antiochos der Grosse und Teos', *Anadolu* 9 (1965). 29–160.

HERZFELD, E., *The Persian Empire* (Wiesbaden, 1968).

HEUSS, A., 'Stadt und Herrscher des Hellenismus', *Klio* Beiheft XXXIX (1937).

HITTI, P. K. *History of Syria* (London, 1951).

HOGARTH, D. G. *A Wandering Scholar*, 2 edn. (London, 1896).

—— 'Hierapolis Syriae', *Annual of the British School at Athens* 14 (1908) 183–96.

—— *Carchemish*, vol. i (London, 1914).

HOLLAND, T. A. 'Preliminary Report on the Excavations at Tell es-Suweyhat', *Levant* 8 (1976) 36–70.

HOLLEAUX M., 'Remarques sur le Papyrus de Gourob', *Bulletin de correspondance hellénique* 30 (1906) 330–48.

—— *Études d'épigraphie et d'histoire grecques*, vol, ii (Paris, 1942).

HONIGMANN, E., 'Historische Topographie von Nordsyrien in Altertum', *ZDPV* 46 (1923) 149–93 and 47 (1924), 1–64.

—— 'Notes de géographie syrienne', *Mélanges syriens offerts à René Dussaud* (Paris, 1939) 129–33.

HOOD, S. 'Excavations at Tabara el-Akrad', *Anatolian Studies* 1 (1951) 13–47.

HYSLOP, R. MAXWELL, J. DU PLAT TAYLOR, M. V. SETON WILLIAMS, J. D'A. WAECHTER, 'An Archaeological Survey of the Plain of Jabboul, 1939', *Palestine Exploration Quarterly* (1942) 8–40.

INGHOLT, H., *Rapport préliminaire sur sept campagnes de fouilles à Hama en Syrie (1932–1938)* (Copenhagen, 1940).

JACOBY, F., (ed.), *Die Fragments des Greichischen Historiker* (Berlin and Leiden, 1923–58).

JACQUOT, P., *Antioche, Centre du Tourisme* (Antioch, 1931).

JAHNE, A., 'Die "Syrische Frage", Seleukeia in Pierien und die Ptolemaer', *Klio* 56 (1974), 501–19.

JONES, A. H. M. 'The Urbanisation of the Ituraean Principality', *JRS* 21 (1931) 265–75.

—— 'The Urbanisation of Palestine', *JRS* 21 (1931), 78–85.

—— *The Greek City from Alexander to Justinian* (Oxford, 1940).

—— *The Cities of the Eastern Roman Provinces*, 2nd. edn. (Oxford, 1971).

—— 'Taxation in Antiquity', in P. A. Brunt (ed.) *The Roman Economy* (Oxford, 1974), 151–85.

KAHRSTEDT, U., *Syrische Territorien in Hellenistischer Zeit* (Göttingen, 1923).

KAN, A. H. *Juppiter Dolichenus* (Leiden, 1943).

KEIL, J. and A. WILHELM, *Monumenta Asiae Minoris Antiqua*, vol. iii (Manchester, 1931).

KOOIJ, G. VAN DER, 'Some Ethnographical Observations of Archaeological Import at the Village of Hodeidi, Syria', *LIEAO* 5 (July, 1982), 80–4.

KRAELING, C. H., (ed.), *Gerasa, City of the Decapolis* (New Haven, Conn., 1938).

KRAUSE, C., K. SCHULER, and R. A. STUCKY, *Tell el-Hajj in Syrien* (Berne, 1972).

KREISSIG, H., 'Prolegomena zu einer Wirtschaftsgeschichte des Seleukidenreiches', *Klio* 56 (1974) 521–8.

—— 'Tempelland, Katoiken, Hierodulen in Seleukidenreich', *Klio* 59 (1977) 375–80.

KRENCKER, D. and W. ZCHIETZSCHMANN, *Romische Tempel in Syrien* (Leipzig, 1938).

KUSCHKE A., S. MITTMANN and U. MULLER, *Archäologischer Survey in der nordlichen Biqa', Herbst, 1972* (Wiesbaden, 1976).

LACOSTE, H., 'La VIIe Campagne de fouilles à Apamée', *L'Antiquité classique* 10 (1941) 115–22.

LAGARCE, J. and E., 'Decouvertes archéologiques à Ras Ibn Hani', *CRAI* (1978) 45–65.

LASSUS, J., *Inventaire archéologique de la region au nord-est de Hama* (Paris, 1935).

LEHMANN-HARTLEBEN, K., *Die antiken Hafenanlagen des Mittelmeeres* (Leipzig, 1923).

LERICHE P., 'La Fouille des fortifications de la ville hellénistique d'Ibn Hani', *Archéologie au Levant, Recueil R. Saidah* (Lyon, 1982), 271–9.

LEUZE, O., *Die Satrapieneinteilung in Syrien und in Zweitromsland von 520–320* (Königsberg, 1935).

LEWIS, N. N., 'The Frontier of Settlement in Syria, 1800–1950', *International Affairs* 31 (1955) 48–60.

—— *Settlers and Nomads in Syria and Jordan, 1800–1980* (Cambridge, 1987).

LIEBESCHUETZ, J. H. W. C. *Antioch, City and Imperial Administration in the Later Roman Empire* (Oxford, 1972).

LIERE, W. J. VAN. 'Ager Centuriatus of the Roman Colonia of Emesa (Homs)', *AAS* 8–9 (1958–9), 54–7.

LIFSHITZ B., 'Études sur l'histoires de la province romaine de Syrie', *ANRW* 2/8 (1977), 3–30.

LIMBREY, S., *Soil Science and Archaeology* (London, 1975).

LIVERANI M., 'I tell pre-classici', *Missione Archeologica Italiana in Siria: rapporto preliminare della campagna 1964* (Rome, 1965), 107–33.

LOON, M. N. VAN, *The Tabqa Dam Survey, 1964* (Damascus, 1967).

LORTON, D., 'An Alleged Expedition of Ptolemy II to Persia', *Journal of Egyptian Archaeology* 57 (1971) 160–4.

LUNDQUIST, J. M. 'Tell Qarqur, the 1983 Season', *AAS* 33/2 (1983), 273–88.

LUSCHAN, F. VON. et al., *Ausgrabungen in Sendschirli* (Berlin, 1893–1943).

MacDonald, G. 'The Coinage of Tigranes I', *Numismatic Chronicle* (1902), 193–201.

MacEwan, C. W. 'The Syrian Expedition of the Oriental Institute of the University of Chicago', *AJA* 41 (1937) 8–16.

McNicoll, A., 'Some Developments in Hellenistic Siege Warfare with Special Reference to Asia Minor', *Proceedings of the 10th International Congress of Classical Archaeologists*, vol. i (Ankara, 1978), 405–20.

Maigret, A. de, 'Fluttuazioni territoriali e caratteristiche tipoligiche degli insediement nella regione del Matah (Siria): nota preliminare', *Orientis Antiquo Collectio* 13 (1964) 83–94.

Marfoe, L., L. Copeland, and P. J. Parr, 'Arjoune 1978: Preliminary Investigation of a Prehistoric Site in the Homs Basin, Syria', *Levant* 13 (1982), 1–27.

Maricq, A., 'Le Plus Ancien Inscription syriaque: Celle de Birejik', *Syria* 39 (1961), 88–100.

Marinoni, E., 'La Capitale del regno di Seleuco I', *Rendiconit Istituto Lombardo* 106 (1972) 579–631.

Marsden, E. W., *The Campaign of Gaugamela* (Liverpool, 1964).

Matthers, J., *et al.*, 'Tell Rifaat, 1977: Preliminary Report of an Archaeological Survey', *Iraq* 40 (1978).

—— (ed.), *The River Qoueiq, Northern Syria, and its Catchment: Studies arising from the Tell Rifaat Survey, 1977–1979* BAR S 98 (Oxford, 1981).

Matthiae, P., 'Sondages à Tell Afis (Syrie), 1978', *Akkadica* 14 (1979) 2–5.

—— 'Sondages à Tell Touqan (Syrie), 1978', *Akkadica* 14 (1979), 6–10.

—— *Ebla, an Empire Rediscovered*, trans C. Holme (London, 1980).

Mayence, F., 'La Quatrième Campagne de fouilles à Apamée', *L'Antiquité classique* 4 (1935), 199–204.

Mazloum, S., *L'Ancien Canalisation d'eau d'Alep* (Damascus, n.d.).

Mazur, B., 'The Aramaean Empire in its Relations with Israel', *The Biblical Archaeologist* 25 (1962), 98–120.

Meer, P. V. D. 'Sondage à Atcherine', *AAS* 1 (1951) 126–8.

Merlat, P., *Jupiter Dolichenus: Essai d'interpretation et de Synthèse* (Paris, 1960).

Mertens, J., 'Sondages dans la Grande Colonnade et sur l'Enceinte', *Colloque d'Apamée* 1 (Brussels, 1968), 68–71.

Metheny, J. R., 'Road Notes from Cilicia and North Syria', *Journal of the American Oriental Society* 28 (1907).

Millar, F., 'The Phoenician Cities: A Case Study in Hellenisation', *Proceedings of the Cambridge Philolgical Society* (1983), 55–71.

Milne, J. G., 'The Coinage of Aradus', *Iraq* 5 (1938).

MITTMANN, S., *Beitrage zur Ziedlungs- und Territorialgeschichte des nordlichen Ostjordanlandes* (Wiesbaden, 1970).

MOCSY, A., *Upper Pannonia and Moesia* (1974).

MONCEAU, P. and L. BROSSÉ, 'Chalcis ad Belum: notes sur l'histoire et les ruines de la ville', *Syria* 6 (1925), 339–50.

MOOREY, P. R. S., 'Iranian Troops at Deve Huyuk in Syria in the earlier fifth century B.C.', *Levant* 7 (1975), 108–17.

—— *Cemeteries of the First Millenium B.C. at Deve Huyuk near Carchemish, salvaged by T. E. Lawrence and C. L. Woolley in 1913*, BAR S 87 (Oxford, 1980).

MORKHOLM, O., 'A Posthumous Issue of Antiochus IV of Syria', *Numismatic Chronicle* (1960), 25–30.

—— *Studies in the Coinage of Antiochus IV* (Copenhagen, 1963).

—— 'The Municipal Coinages with Portrait of Antiochus IV of Syria', *Atti di Congresso Internazionale de Numismatica, Roma 1961* (Rome 1965), 63–7.

—— *Antiochus IV of Syria* (Copenhagen, 1966).

—— 'The Monetary System of the Seleucid Kings until 129 B.C.', in A. Kindler (ed.), *Proceedings of the International Numismatic Convention, Jerusalem 1963* (Tel Aviv–Jerusalem, 1967), 75–87.

MORROW, G. R. *Plato's Cretan City* (Princeton, NJ 1960).

MOUTERDE, R., 'A travers l'Apamène: II, Mesta Blouné, Apollonia?', *MUSJ* (1949–50) 16–21, and ' . . . IX, Massyaf', p. 36.

—— and A. POIDEBARD, *Le Limes de Chalcis* (Paris, 1945).

MUHLY, J. D. 'Copper and Tin: The Distribution of Mineral Resources and the Nature of the Metals Trade in the Bronze Age', *Transactions of the Connecticut Academy of Arts and Sciences* 43 (1973), 208–14.

MUIR, A., 'Notes on the Soils of Syria', *Journal of Soil Science* 2 (1951) 163–82.

MULLER, C., *Geographi Graeci Minores*, vol. i (Paris, 1855).

MURISON, C. L. 'Darius III and the Battle of Issus', *Historia* 21 (1972), 399–423.

NAVEH, J., 'An Aramaic Inscription from el-Mal—a Survival of "Seleucid Aramaic" Script', *Israel Exploration Journal* 25 (1975), 117–23.

NEWELL, E. T., 'The Seleucid Mint of Antioch', *American Journal of Numismatics* 51 (1917), 1–152.

—— *Myriandros kat' Isson* (New York, 1920).

—— *Western Seleucid Mints*, 2nd edn., revised by O. Morkholm (New York, 1977).

NIR, D., *The Semi-Arid World*, trans. R. Gottlieb (London, 1974).

OATES, D. and J., 'Nimrud, the Hellensitic Settlement', *Iraq* 20 (1958), 114–57.

ODED, B., *Mass Deportations and Deportees in the Neo-Assyrian Empire* (Wiesbaden, 1979).

OLDENBURG E. and J. ROHWEDER, *The Excavations at Tell Durak (Usnu?) and Arab el-Mulk (Paltos)* (Copenhagen, 1981).

OLMSTEAD, A. T., *History of Assyria* (Chicago, 1923).

—— *A History of Palestine and Syria to the Macedonian Conquest* (Westport, Conn. 1931).

—— *History of the Persian Empire* (Chicago, 1948).

OPPENHEIM, A. L., *Ancient Mesopotamia*, 2nd edn. (Chicago, 1977).

OTTO, W., *Beitrage zur Seleukidengeschichte des 3 Jahrh, v. Chr.* (Munich, 1928).

OWEN, R., *The Middle East in the World Economy, 1800–1914* (1981).

PARR, P. J. 'Tell Nebi Mend—Qadesh', *Archiv für Orientforschung* 26 (1978/9), 160–2.

—— 'Tell Nebi Mend Project', *AAAS* 33/2 (1983), 99–117.

PERDRIZET, P., 'Syriaca', *Revue archéologique*, 3rd ser., 32/1 (Jan.–June 1898), 34–49.

—— and C. FOSSEY, 'Voyage dans la Syrie du Nord' *Bulletin du correspondance hellénique* 21 (1897), 66–91.

PERKINS, A. and R. J. BRAIDWOOD (eds.), 'Archaeological News: The Near East', *AJA* 51 (1947).

PETERS, R. E. 'City-Planning in Greco-Roman Syria: Some New Considerations', *Damaszener Mitteilungen* 1 (1983), 269–78.

PETRAN, T., *Syria, a Modern History* (London, 1972).

PEZARD, M., *Qadesh* (Paris, 1931).

PIEJEKO, F., 'Ptolemies in a list of Deified Seleucids from Teos', *Zeitschrift für Papyrologie und Epigrafik* 49 (1982) 129–31.

PIQUET-PELLORCE Capt. and R. MOUTERDE. 'Magarataricha', *Syria* 9 (1928), 207–15.

PLANHOL, X de, *Les Fondements géographiques de l'histoire d'Islam* (Paris, 1968).

PLOUG, G., 'The Greco-Roman Town', *Hama* 3/1 (Copenhagen, 1985).

POIDEBARD A. and J. LAUFFRAY, *Sidon: Aménagements antiques du Port de Saida* (Beyrouth, 1951).

PRÉAUX, C., *Le Monde hellénistique* 2 vols (Paris, 1978).

RABIN, A. (ed.) *Harbour Archaeology*, BAR S 257 (Oxford, 1986).

REIFENBERG, A., 'The Soils of Syria and the Lebanon', *Journal of Soil Science* 3 (1952) 68–88.

REX COQUAIS, J.-P., 'Notes de geographie syrienne antique', *MUSJ* 40 (1964), 289–312.

—— *Arados et sa Perée* (Paris, 1974).

—— 'Inscription grecque découverte à Ras Ibn Hani', *AAAS* 26 (1976), 51–61.

—— 'Syrie romaine de Pompée à Dioclétien', *JRS* 68 (1978), 44–73.

RIDOLFINI, F. S. PERICOLI 'La rovine romano-bizantine', *Missione Archeologia Italiana in Siria: rapporto preliminare della campagna 1964* (Rome, 1965), 135–55.

RIGSBY, K. J., 'Seleucid Notes', *TAPA* 110 (1980), 233–54.

RIIS, P. J., *Sukas* i, (Copenhagen, 1970).

—— 'The First Greeks in Phoenicia and their Settlement at Sukas', *Ugaritica* 6, pp 435–50.

—— *Temple, Church and Mosque* (Copenhagen, 1965).

ROBERT, L., *Le Sanctuaire de Sinuri près de Mylasa: I, Les Inscriptions grecque* (Paris, 1945).

—— *Hellenica* 7 (Paris, 1949), 5–22.

ROBINSON, E. S. G., 'Coins from the Excavations at al-Mina', *Numismatic Chronicle* ser. 5, vol. 17 (1937), 182–96.

RODINSON, M., 'De l'archéologie à la sociologie historique: notes methodologiques sur le dernier ouvrage de G. Tchalenko', *Syria* 38 (1961), 170–200.

RONZEVALLE, S., 'Les Monnaies de la dynastie de Abd-Hadad et les cultes de Hierapolis-Bambyke', *MUSJ* (1940) 1–82.

ROSCISZEWSKI, M., 'Quelques remarques sur la géographie agraire de la Syrie', *Mediterranée* 6 (1965), 171–84.

ROSTOVTZEFF, M. I., *Dura-Europus and its Art* (Oxford, 1938).

—— 'The Foundation of Dura-Europus', Annales de l'Institut Kondakov 10 (1938), 99–106.

—— *Social and Economic History of the Hellenistic World* (Oxford, 1941).

—— *Caravan Cities* (Oxford, 1932).

—— A. R. BELLINGER, F. E. BROWN, and C. B. WELLES (EDS.), *The Excavations at Dura Europos, Preliminary Report, Ninth Season*, Part 1 (New Haven, Conn., 1944).

ROUGÉ, J., *Ships and Fleets of the Ancient Mediterranean*, trans. S. Freezer (Middletown, Conn., 1981).

ROUSSEL, P. 'Un Syrien au service de Rome et d'Octave', *Syria* 15 (1934) 33–74.

—— 'Décret des Péliganes de Laodicée sur Mer', *Syria* 23 (1942–3), 21–32.

ROWTON, M. B., 'The Woodlands of Ancient Western Asia', *JNES* (1967), 261–77.

RUNCIMAN S., *History of the Crusades*, 3 vols. (London, 1952–4).

SAADÉ, G., 'Explorations archéologiques de Lattaquié', *AAAS* 26 (1979), 9–29.

SACHS, A. J., and D. J. WISEMAN, 'A Babylonian King List of the Hellenistic Period', *Iraq* 16 202–11.

SAGGS, H. W. F., *The Might that was Assyria* (London, 1984).

STE. CROIX, G. E. M., *The Class Struggle in the Ancient Greek World*, (London, 1981).

SALIBY, N., 'Essai de restitution du Temple d'Amrit', *AAAS* 21 (1971), 283–8.

SAMMAN, M. L. 'La Situation démographique de la Syrie', *Population* (1976), 1253–88.

SANLAVILLE, P., (ed.), *Holocene Settlement in North Syria*, BAR S 238 (Oxford, 1985).

SAUVAGET, J., *Alep*, 2 vols. (Paris, 1941).

—— 'Le Plan de Laodicée-sur-Mer', *Bulletin des études orientales* 4 (1934) 81-114 and 6 (1936), 51–2.

—— 'Le Plan antique de Damas', *Syria* 26 (1947) 314–58.

SCHAEFFER, C. F. A., 'Preface et résumé', *Ugaritica* 4 (1962), xi-xxxvi.

—— 'La XXIVe Campagne de fouilles à Ras Shamra-Ugarit, 1961', *AAAS* 13 (1963), 123–34.

SCHIFFMANN, I. 'Griechische und orientalische Quellen der hellenistischen Polisorganisation im vorderasiatischen Reich', *Klio* 60 (1978), 203–16.

SCHLUMBERGER, D., 'Bornes milliaires de la Palmyrène', *Melanges syriens offerts à René Dussaud* (Paris, 1939), 547–55.

—— 'Triparadisos', *Bulletin du Musée de Beyrouth* 22 (1972), 147–9.

SCHMITT, H. H., *Untersuchungen zur Geschichte Antiochos des Grossen und seiner Zeit*, Historia Einzelschriften 6 (Wiesbaden, 1964).

SCHURER. E., *The History of the Jewish People in the Age of Jesus Christ*, rev. edn. by G. Vermes *et al.*, 3 vols. (Edinburgh) 1976–86.

SCULLARD, H. H., *The Elephant in the Greek and Roman World* (London, 1974).

SEIRAFI, F., and A. KIRICHIAN, 'Recherches archéologiques à Ayin-Dara au Nord-Ouest d'Alep', *AAAS* 15 (1965), part II, pp. 3–20.

SEAGAR, R., *Pompey, a Political Biography* (Oxford, 1979).

SEGAL, A., *Edessa, the Blessed City* (Oxford, 1970).

SEYRIG, H., 'Demetrias de Phenicie (ou de Palestine)', *Syria* 9 (1928), 207–15.

—— 'Décret de Séleucie et ordonnance de Séleucus IV', *Syria* 13 (1932), 255–8.

—— 'Inscriptions', *Syria* 12 (1933), 302–23.

—— 'Les rois séleucides et la Concession de l'Asylie', *Syria* 12 (1933), 35–39.

—— 'La Cimitière des Marins à Séleucie de Pierie', *Mélanges syriens offerts à René Dussaud* (Paris, 1939), ii, 451–9.

—— 'Cachets d'Archives Publiques de quelques villes de la Syrie Romaine', *MUSJ* 23 (1940), 83–108.

—— 'Scène historique sur un chapiteau du Musée de Beyrouth', *Revue des études anciennes* 42 (1940), 340–4.
—— 'Ères de quelques villes de Syrie', *Syria* 27 (1950), 5–50.
—— 'The Khan el-Abde Find and the Coinage of Tryphon', *Numismatic Notes and Monographs* 119 (1950), 1–23.
—— 'Aradus et Baetocaecé', *Syria* 28 (1951), 191–206.
—— 'Aradus et sa Perée sous les rois séleucides', *Syria* 28 (1951) 206–17.
—— 'Le Phare de Laodicée', *Syria* 29 (1952), 54–9.
—— 'Charactères de l'histoire d'Emèse', *Syria* 36 (1959), 184–92.
—— 'Zeus de Berée', *Syria* 40 (1963), 28–30.
—— 'Questions aradiennes: I, Gabala', *Rev. Num.* 4 (1964), 9–28.
—— Sur quelques éres syriennes: l'ère des rois de Commagene', *Rev. Num.* 11 (1971), 11–21.
—— 'Deux pièces énigmatiques', *Syria* 42 (1965), 28–34.
—— 'Alexandre le Grand, fondateur de Gerasa', *Syria* 42 (1965), 25–8.
—— Séleucos I et la fondation de la monarchie syrienne', *Syria* 47 (1970), 290–311.
—— 'Monnaies hellénistiques: XVIII, Séleucus III et Simyra', *Rev. Num.* 11 (1971), 7–11.
—— 'Le Monnayage de Hierapolis de Syrie à l'époque d'Alexandre', *Rev. Num.* 11 (1971), 11–21.
—— *Trésors du Levant anciens et nouveaux* (Paris, 1973).
SHERWIN-WHITE, A. N. *The Roman Citizenship*, 2nd edn., (Oxford, 1973).
—— *Roman Foreign Policy in the East* (London, 1984).
SMITH, S., *Babylonian Historical Texts* (London, 1924).
—— 'O Myriandros kolpos o pros Phoinike keimenos', *Mélanges syriens offerts à René Dussaud* (Paris, 1939), 27–31.
SODINI J.-P. *et al.*, 'Déhès (Syrie du Nord), Campagnes I–III (1976–1978): Recherches sur l'habitat rurales', *Syria* 57 (1980), 1–302.
STARCKY, J., 'Stèle d'Elahgabal', *MUSJ* 49 (1975–6), 502–520.
STILLWELL R., *et al.* (eds.), *Antioch-on-the-Orontes, Preliminary Reports on the Excavations*, 6 vols. Princeton, NJ, 1933.
STRONG H. A., and J. GARSTANG, *The Syrian Goddess* (London, 1913).
STUCKY, R. A., *Ras Shamra Leukos Limen* (Paris, 1983).
SULLIVAN, R. D., 'The Dynasty of Commagene', *ANRW* 2/8 (1977) 732–798.
—— 'The Dynasty of Emesa', *ANRW* 2/8 (1977) 198–219.
TARN, W. W., 'The Social Question in the Third Century', in J. B. Bury *et al.*, *The Hellenistic Age* (Cambridge, 1923), 120–5.

—— 'The Proposed New Date for Ipsus', *Classical Review* 40 (1926) 13–15.

—— *Alexander the Great*, 2 vols. (Cambridge, 1948).

—— *Hellenistic Civilisation*, 3rd edn., revised by G. T. Griffith (London, 1951).

TAYLOR J. DU PLAT, M. V. SETON WILLIAMS, J. WAECHTER, 'The Excavations at Sakce Gozu', *Iraq* 12 (1950), 53–138.

TAYLOR, J. E. 'Seleucid Rule in Palestine', dissertation, Duke University, North Carolina, 1979.

TCHALENKO, G., *Villages antiques de la Syrie du Nord*, 3 vols. (Paris, 1953–8).

—— 'Travaux en cours dans la Syrie du Nord: I, Le Sanctuaire de Seih Baraket', *Syria* 50 (1970), 115–27.

TCHERIKOVER, V., 'Die Hellenistische Stadtegrundungen von Alexander der Grosse bis auf die Romerzeit', *Philologos* Supplement 19 (1927).

—— *Hellenistic Civilisation and the Jews* (New York, 1970).

TEFNIN, R., 'L'Or et le sel, notre sur l'écologie d'une region de l'ancienne Syrie', *AAAS* 27–8, (1977–8)m 197–206.

—— 'Aperçu sur neuf compagnes de fouilles belges aux Tells Abou Danné et Oumm el-Marra (1975–1983)', *AAAS* 33/2 (1983), 141–52.

—— DOYEN, J.-M. and E. WAREMBOL, 'Les Niveaux supérieure de Tell Abou Danné, Chantier A, 1978/79', *Syro-Mesopotamian Studies* 3/3 (Oct. 1980), 109–68.

TEIXIDOR, J., *The Pagan God: Popular Religion in the Greco-Roman Near East* (Princeton, NJ, 1977).

THOMAS, D. W., *Documents from Old Testament Times* (1953).

TOYNBEE, J. M. C. 'Some Notes on Artists in the Roman World', *Latomus* 4 (1951), 307–16.

VAGGI, G., 'Siria e Siri nei documenti dell'Egitto greco-romano', *Aegyptus* 17 (1937), pp. 29–51.

VAUMUS E. DE, 'Montagnes du Proche Orient: L'Amanus et le Djebel Ansarieh, étude morphologique', *Revue de géographie alpine* 42 (1954), 11–42.

—— 'Plateaux, plaines et depressions de la Syrie intérieure septentrionale, étude morphologique', *Bulletin de la Société Géographique d'Égypt* 30 (1957), 97–235.

—— 'Le Djebel Ansarieh, études de géographie humaine', *Revue de géographie alpine* 48 (1960), 267–311.

VOGT, J., 'The Structure of Ancient Slave Wars', *Ancient Slavery and the Ideal of Man*, trans. T. Wiedeman, (Oxford, 1974).

VOLKMANN, H., 'Demetrius I und Alexander I von Syrien', *Klio* 19 (1925), 373–93.

VOLNEY, Comte de, *Voyages en Egypte et en Syrie* (Paris, 1787).

VOUTE, C., 'Climate or Tectonics; some Remarks on the Evolution of the Valley of the Orontes (Nahr el Aassi) between Homs and the marshy plain of the Ghab (Syria)', *Geologie en Mijnbouw* NS 17, no. 9 (Aug. 1955), 197–206.

VOUTE, P. H. E. 'Chronique des fouilles et prospections en Syrie de 1965 à 1970', *Anatolica* 4 (1971–2), 83–132.

WAGNER, J., *Seleukeia am Euphrat/Zeugma* (Wiesbaden 1974).

—— 'Legio IIII Scythica in Zeugma am Euphrat', *Studien zu den Militargrenzen Roms* (Cologne, 1977), ii. 517–39.

WALBANK, F. W., *A Historical Commentary on Polybius*, 3 vols. (Cambridge, 1957–79).

—— *The Hellenistic World* (London, 1981).

WALKER, D. S., *The Mediterranean Lands* (London, 1956).

WARD, W. A, (ed.), *The Role of the Phoenicians in the Interaction of Mediterranean Civilisations* (Beirut, 1968).

WATZINGER, C. and K. WITZINGER, *Damaskus: Die antike stadt* (Berlin, 1921).

WELLES, R. C., *Royal Correspondence of the Hellenistic Period*, New Haven, Conn. 1934).

WEST, L. C., 'Commercial Syria under the Roman Empire', *Transactions and Proceedings of the American Philological Association* 55 (1924), 159–89.

WESTLAKE, H. D., 'Eumenes of Cardia', *Essays on the Greek Historians and Greek History* (Manchester, 1969), 313–30.

WEULERSSE, J., 'Antioche, essai de géographie urbaine', *Bulletin des études orientales* 4 (1934), 27–79.

—— *L'Oronte* (Tours, 1940).

WIEGAND, T., *Milet*, vol. i. (Berlin, 1906).

WILD, J. P., *Textile Manufacture in the Northern Roman Provinces* (Cambridge, 1970).

WILL, E., 'Les Premiers Années du regne d'Antiochos III (223–219 av. J-C)', *Revue des études grecques* 75 (1962), 72–129.

—— *Histoire politique du monde hellénistique*, 2 vols., 2nd ed., (Nancy, 1979–82).

—— 'Le Dévelopment urbaine de Palmyre: Témoignages épigraphiques anciens et nouveaux', *Syria* 60 (1983), 69–81.

WILLIAMS, G., *Eastern Turkey* (1976).

WILLIAMS, M. V. SETON, 'Cilician Survey', *Anatolian Studies* 4 (1954), 121–174.

—— 'Preliminary Report on the Excavations at Tell Rifaat', *Iraq* 23 (1961) 68–87.

WINTER, F. E., *Greek Fortifications* (Toronto, 1971).

WIRGIN, W., 'On the Right of Asylum in Hellenistic Syria', *Numismatic Chronicle* (1982), 137–48.

WIRTH, E., *Syrien* (Darmstadt, 1972).

WISEMAN, D. J., *Chronicles of the Chaldaean Kings in the British Museum* (London, 1956).

WOOLLEY, C. L., 'A North Syrian Cemetery of the Persian Period', *Annals of Archaeology and Anthropology* 7 (1914–16), 115–128.

—— *Carchemish*, vols ii (1921) and iii (1954).

—— *A Forgotten Kingdom* (London, 1953).

—— *Alalakh-Tell Atchana* (Oxford, 1955).

WROTH, W., *Catalogue of the Greek Coins in the British Museum: Galatia, Cappadocia and Syria* (London, 1878).

ZOUDHI, B., 'Monnaies antiques et plus récentes trouvées à Ras Shamra et dans les environs', *Ugaritica* 7 (1968) 183–4.

MAPS AND PLANS

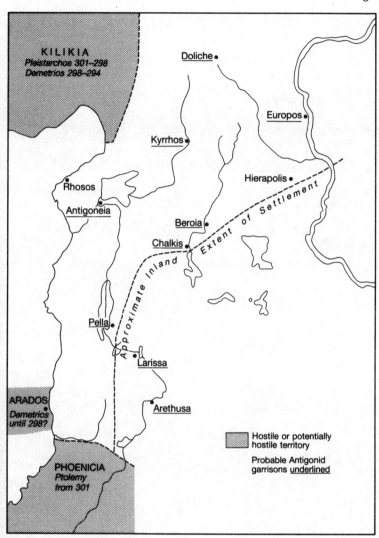

MAP I. SYRIA IN 301 BC

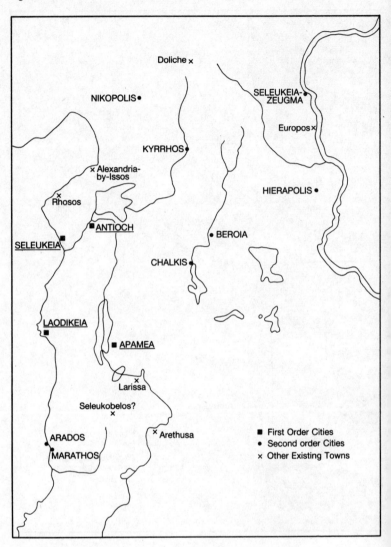

MAP 2. THE CITIES OF SELEUKOS

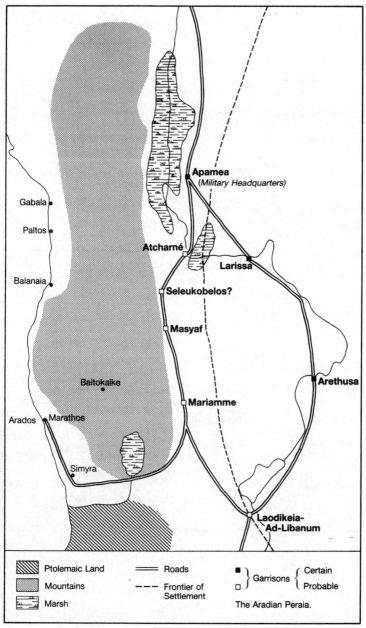

MAP 3. THE SOUTHERN FRONTIER ZONE

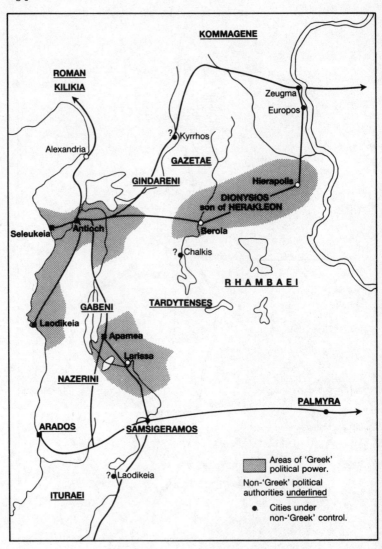

MAP 4. SYRIA IN 66 BC

Maps 5 (a)–(c). Persian and Hellenistic Occupation.
For details of the Survey areas (Roman numbers) and excavated
sites (Arabic numbers) see Appendix 3.

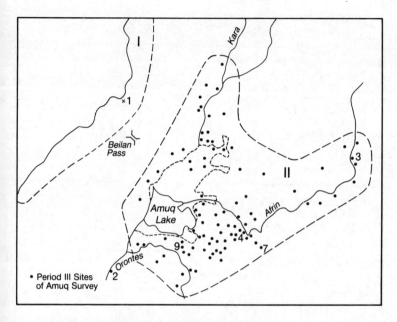

MAP 5 (A). THE NORTH-WEST

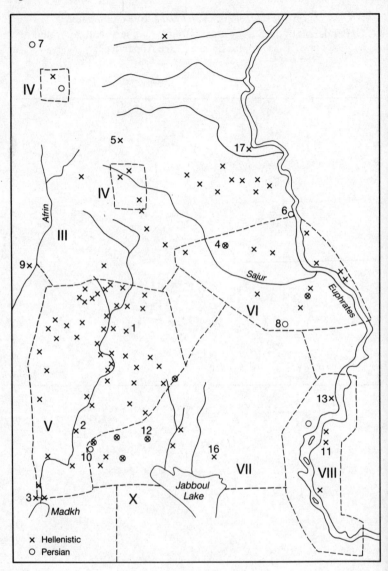

MAP 5 (B). THE NORTH-EAST

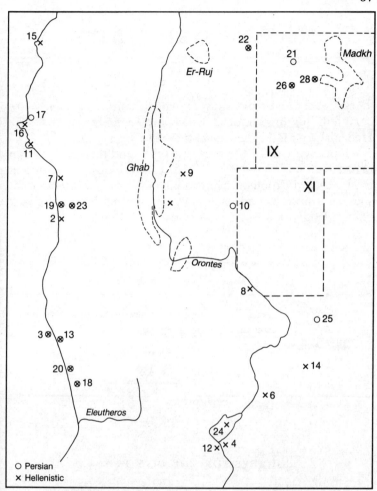

MAP 5 (C). THE SOUTH

PLANS OF SYRIAN CITIES

These plans are deliberately drawn without detail. There are very few buildings indeed which are securely dated to the Hellenistic period. They have, therefore, been omitted.

All plans are drawn to the same scale, and three non-Syrian urban communities—Rome, Miletos, and Cosa—are added to give an indication of the meaning of the sizes. Sites omitted, such as Marathos and Nikopolis, are omitted because of lack of knowledge.

KEY TO THE PLANS:

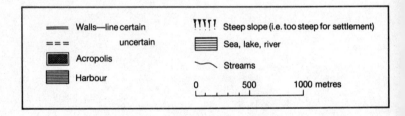

SOURCES FOR THE CITY PLANS

All these maps have been redrawn to a standard scale. Only selected Hellenistic period features are shown. The sources of the plans are as follows, giving, in most cases, a short reference; full references are in the Abbreviations or Bibliography.

Antioch—*Antioch-on-the-Orontes.*
Apamea—J.-C. Balty, *Guide d'Apamée* (by permission).
Arados—H. Frost, *AAAS* 16 (1966) (by permission).
Arethusa, Beroia—Sauvaget, *Alep* (by permission).
Chalkis—Monceau and Brossé, *Syria* 6 (1925).

Cosa—E. T. Salmon, *Roman Colonisation under the Republic,* (London, 1969) (*by permission*).

Epiphaneia-Hamath—*Hama 2.*

Europos-Carchemish—*Carchemish ii.*

Kyrrhos—Frezouls, *AAS* 4 and 5 (1954–5) (by permission).

Laodikeia-as-Libanum—S. A(bdul-Hak), *AAS* 1 (1951) (by permission).

Miletos A. von Gerkan, *Griechische Stadteantigan* (Berlin, 1924), ill. 6. Rome—I. A. Richmond, *The City Wall of Imperial Rome* (Oxford, 1930), fig. 2.

Seleukeia-in-Pieria—Chapot, *Mémoires* . . . 66 (1906).

Seleukeia-Zeugma—Wagner, *Zeugma* (by permission).

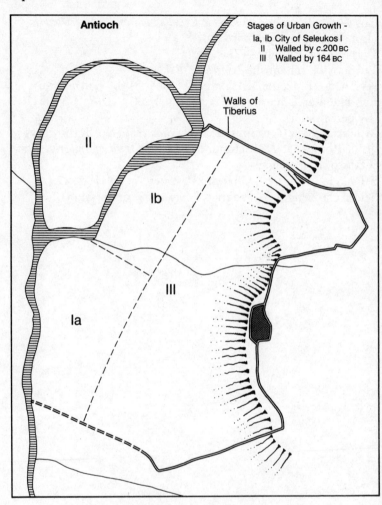

MAP 6 (A). ANTIOCH

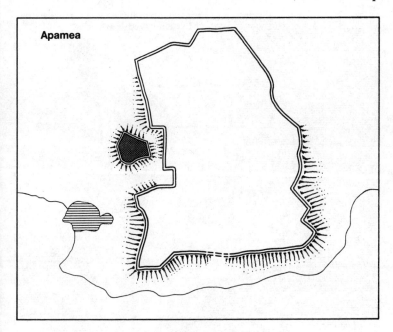

MAP 6 (B). APAMEA

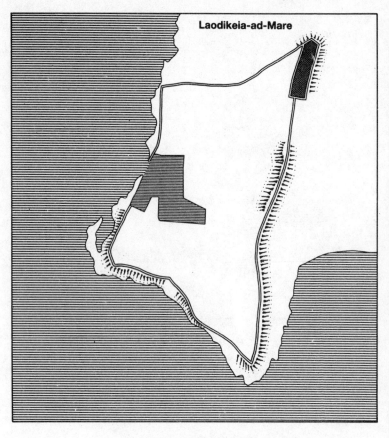

MAP 6 (C). LAODKEIA-AD-MARE

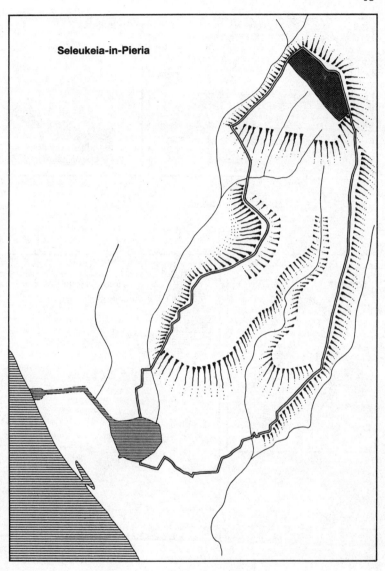

Seleukeia-in-Pieria

MAP 6 (D). SELEUKEIA-IN-PIERIA

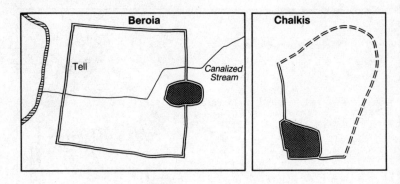

MAP 6 (E). BEROIA, CHALKIS

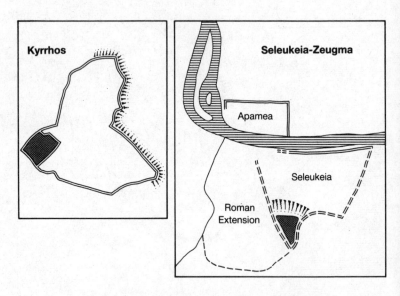

MAP 6 (F). KYRRHOS, SELEUKEIA-ZEUGMA

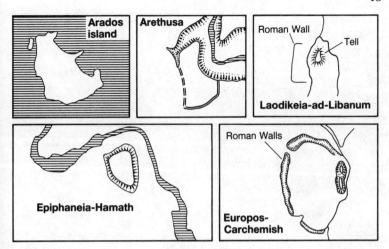

MAP 6 (G). ARADOS, ARETHUSA, EPIPHANEIA-HAMATH,
LAODIKEIA-AD-LIBANUM, EUROPOS-CARCHEMISH

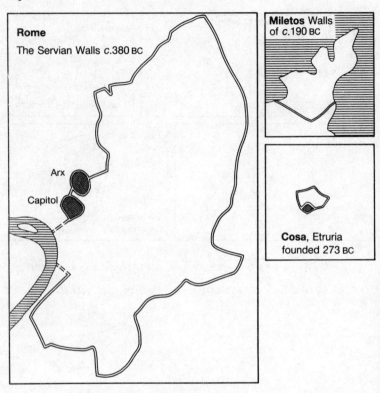

MAP 6 (H). ROME, MILEOTS, COSA

INDEX

Abd-Hadad, king? 26, 53
Abgar, king of Osrhoene 196
acropolis/eis 58, 61–2, 86–7
Ada Tepe 24, 108, 117
Aegean Sea 17
Aemilius Scaurus, M. 190
Aeropos, Laodikeian leader 166
Afrin, river 10, 174
agriculture in Syria 9, 11–12
Aigai 45, 46
Ainos 43
Aleppo 19, 24n, 27, 79, 199; *see also* Beroia
Alexander I Balas, king 134, 155, 156–9, 169
Alexander II Zabinas, king 165–7, 169, 175
Alexander III the Great, king 7, 17, 23, 24, 26, 28, 31, 50–1, 66, 104; rule in Syria 32–3, 46; supposed foundations of 34–7, 45
Alexander IV, Macedonian king 37
Alexandria-by-Egypt 35, 100, 125, 135
Alexandria-by-Issos 24, 25, 46, 68, 80, 117, 131, 140, 196; communications 105; development 108–9, 129, 135; supposed foundation by Alexander 36–7, 137
Amanus, mountains 8, 9, 25, 35–6, 71, 78, 80, 104; as Seleukos' boundary 41; confrontation in 52–3, 55
Ammonios, Seleukid minister 159
Amphipolis 45
Amuq basin and lake 10, 38, 41, 69, 117–18, 123
Andriskos, Macedonian pretender 156
Antarados 94, 117
Anthedon 45
Anthemos 45
Antigoneia 39, 49, 57, 74; destruction 37, 47–8, 53, 55–6, 67, 82, 98; population 95–6, 99, 152; site 56; situation 69–70; Tyche 35 n, 56, 98
Antigonos I Monophthalamos, king 1, 30, 32, 51, 57, 58; founder of Antigoneia 37–8, 47, 152; possible

foundations 40, 44, 45–6; settles Macedonians in Syria 44–5, 46–7, 54; war with Seleukos 51, 57
Antioch 79, 82, 86, 91, 108, 152–3, 160, 173–4, 180, 186, 193; as a capital 35, 99, 120, 122–6, 155, 162, 192, 198; attacked by Parthians 38, 198; autonomy 195; coins 49, 154, 157; communications 80, 104–7, 181–2, 184; foundation 48, 56–7, 112, 118; government 64, 152; growth 60, 100, 121–8, 135, 141; history 122–6, 142, 144, 155–9, 161, 168–9, 171–2, 175–6, 188, 199; inhabitants 60, 124, 152; population 95–6, 99, 100, 124; reception of Ptolemy III 142, 150–1, 152; revolts 124, 142, 165; satrapy 41; settlers 97–9; site 56, 58, 69, 85, 86, 91, 95, 97; situation 59–60, 67, 69, 74–5; supposed foundation by Alexander 34–5; temples 35 n, 60
Antioch-on-Euphrates 138, 141
Antiochos I Soter, king 50, 53, 143, 149, 154
Antiochos II Theos, king 50, 142, 143, 150
Antiochos III Megas, king 59, 104, 122, 126, 130, 133, 134, 179; and Antioch 125, 141; and Arados 128, 146–7; and Seleukeia-in-Pieria 96, 123
Antiochos IV Epiphanes, king 36, 109, 125, 129, 130, 134, 154, 156, 179; city-founder 138, 139, 141
Antiochos V, king 132, 162
Antiochos VI, king 157, 159, 161
Antiochos VII Sidetes, king 155, 161, 163–5, 166, 187
Antiochos VIII Grypos, king 168, 170, 171, 172
Antiochos IX Kyzikenos, king 170
Antiochos XIII, king 182 n, 191–5
Antiochos, Kommagenean king 191, 195
Antiochos Hierax, rebel 124
Antipater, Laodikeian leader 166
Antonius, M. 196
Apama, wife of Seleukos I 49

Apamea 10, 43, 50, 79, 81, 97, 112, 160–1, 168, 169, 185, 187, 188, 197, 198, 199; acropolis 61, 111; *asylos* 175–6; autonomy 195; communications 73, 80, 104–6; dependent towns 42–3, 106–7, 108, 130, 138; foundation 39, 48–9, 50; growth 126–8, 135; history 151, 159, 165, 171–2, 175; *kleroi* 114–15; military centre 59, 104, 120, 122, 126–7, 172; original name Pella 39; satrapy 41; settlement near 116–17; site 58–9, 69, 82–3, 85, 86, 87, 91–2, 95, 97; situation 69, 72–4

Apamea (suburb of Zeugma) 51, 75–7, 84, 92, 196

Apamene 42–3, 49

Apollonia 42–3, 107, 140

Apollophanes 122

Arabs 45, 132, 133, 183; archers 179; dynasties of 130, 131, 177–81, 191–8

arable farming, extent of 14–20

Arados 2, 16, 24, 27, 28, 30, 46, 68, 138, 150, 189, 197, 198; Alexander and 17, 27, 31, 144; Antarados and 94; communications 73, 105, 127; fleet 16, 27, 145, 192; history 144–7, 151; independence 65, 145–7, 151–2, 158, 163, 164, 165–6, 169, 170, 171, 176, 177, 195, 197; kingship 144; Marathos and 93–4, 128, 135, 159, 166; plain near, *see* Tartus, plain of; *peraia* 16, 17, 18, 30, 100–1, 104, 120, 128, 145–6, 166, 167, 169, 197; possible base of Demetrios 54, 144; revolution 167; Seleukos I and 58, 59, 68, 144, 154; site 92–3; situation 93–4; Syrian 182–3

archaeology, evidence for land-occupation from 14–22, 204–9

Archilochos, royal Friend 152

Arethusa 52, 59, 102, 103, 106, 107, 178n, 179, 181, 186, 196, 199

Aristodemos of Miletos, tedious messenger 38

Arjouné 116

Armenia 52, 196

Asia Minor 1, 3, 31, 32, 51, 54, 58, 61, 124, 143, 170, 196

Assur 7

Assyrian Empire 21, 22, 29, 80, 140

Atcharné 69, 73, 104, 106

Athens, Athenians 17, 95, 152

Augustus 109

autonomy, civic 142–3, 144–8, 171

Axios, name for Orontes 42

Ayin Dara 107–8, 110, 130

Azaz 185, 187

Azizos, Arab king 174, 181, 189, 191, 193, 194

Bab 18, 116

Babylon 7, 21–2, 29, 32, 46, 51

Babylonia 3, 17, 21–2, 51, 143, 170

Bagche, pass 9, 78, 80, 103

Baktria 32, 124

Balanaia 101, 117, 131, 145

Balkis Tepe 75

Bambyke 24, 26, 28, 30, 39, 112; *see also* Hierapolis, Membij

Bargylos, mountains 8, 9, 43, 60, 69, 71, 73, 104, 105, 183–4, 188, 192

Beilan, pass 9, 25, 104, 105

Beroia 23, 42, 60, 79, 81, 100, 102, 111, 129, 176, 199; acropolis 61; communications 76, 78, 80, 104–5, 182; history 132, 135, 196; independent principality 173–4, 181, 191, 196; origin of name 44; Seleukos I and 52, 53, 132; settlement near 115–16; site 69, 86, 87, 92, 95; situation 68, 69, 79–90

Berytos 161 n. 164

Biqaa valley 59, 104, 105, 126 n. 183

Birejik 25, 76, 80, 199

Bottia 34–5

Brochi 5

Byblos 28

Caecilius Metellus Nepos, Q. 190

Carchemish 19, 25, 27; *see also* Europos (Carchemish)

Catal Huyuk 118

Central Place Theory 120–1; application to Syria 121

Chalkidene 40–1, 49

Chalkidike 40

Chalkis 60, 78, 79, 100, 129, 169; acropolis 61; communications 73, 77, 80, 105–6; foundation 40–2; history 132, 135, 159, 161–2, 164, 177, 180, 185, 186; Seleukos I and 51–2; settlement near 116; site 69, 78, 87, 92; situation 68, 69, 77–8, 133

climate 8, 9–10; change 12–13

Clodius, P. 190, 191, 193, 194

Cossutius, architect 125
Cyprus 17, 54, 171

Damascus 20, 29, 73, 86, 104, 105, 126 n. 128, 172, 190
Dana, hills near 10
Daphne, parade 179
Dareios III, king 26, 31-2
Demetrios I Soter, king 118, 154-5, 156-7, 162
Demetrios II Kallinikos, king 132, 155, 157-61, 162, 163, 164-6, 168, 169, 187
Demetrios III, king 173-4
Demetrios Poliorketes, king 1, 37, 45, 47, 53, 144, 177, 182; rival of Seleukos I, 41, 49, 52-3, 54-5, 96
desert, boundary fluctuation of 12-14, 19-21, 177
Deve Huyuk 174
Diodotos, *see* Tryphon
Dion 45
Dionysios of Beroia 173-4, 191
Doliche 42, 43-4, 60, 80, 103, 107, 130, 175
Duluk 42
Dura, *see* Europos (Dura)

Edessa 45, 75
Edomites 20
Egypt 3, 31, 32, 45, 157, 164, 187
Ekbatana 29
Eleutheros, river, as Syrian boundary 2, 8; valley of 9, 17, 73, 104-5, 106, 166
Emathia 34-5, 42
Emesa 59, 106, 130, 131, 133, 178-83, 184, 185, 186, 197, 199; *see also* Homs
England, Norman settlement of 47
Ephesos 122
Epiphaneia 23, 106, 107, 130, 131, 140, 141; settlement of 138-9; *see also* Hama
Epiphaneia-on-Euphrates 138
Epiphaneia, suburb of Antioch 125, 128, 141
epistates 62-3, 151-3, 157, 167
Eumenes of Kardia 32, 46
Euphrates, river 10, 17, 19, 41, 43, 81, 104, 181; as Syrian boundary 2, 8; bridge 25-6, 31, 46, 50-1, 75-7; valley of 11, 19, 25, 115
Europos (Carchemish) 46, 64, 102, 103, 139; Seleukos I and 52, 60

Europos (Dura) 45, 86; founded by Seleukos 46
Europos (Macedonia) 65
evidence, paucity of, for Syria 3; archaeological 14-22, 82, 115-18, 204-9; linguistic 23-4; numismatic 49-50, 144-5, 151, 170-1; place-name 39-46, 137-40; written sources 48-9, 52
Ezra 22

Fertile Crescent, settlement in 20-2

Gabala 101, 117, 145-6, 166, 183; growth 129, 131
Gabeni 184-5, 187, 197
garrisons, in Syria 32-3
Gaugamela, battle of 30, 32
Gaza 32
Gazetae 185, 187, 189
Gaziantep 80
geography of Syria 8-12
Gerrha 59
Ghab, marsh 59, 72, 73, 106, 184
Gindareni 184-5
Gindaros 105, 108, 130, 174-5, 184, 187
Greece 3, 64, 167
Greeks, settlement of, in Syria 17, 46-7, 60-1, 98; conciliation of, by Seleukos I 56-7

Hama 20, 27, 59, 106, 116; *see also* Epiphaneia
Harpalos 16
Hemeseni 184
Herakleia (near Beroia) 103, 140, 173, 191
Herakleia-ad-Mare 109-10, 129, 140
Herakleon of Beroia 172-4, 196
Herod the Great, king 86
Hierapolis 60, 120; and Seleukos I 26, 53, 57, 137; communications 81, 182; history 134, 135, 173, 191, 196; lack of growth 102, 134; modern condition 81; settlement near 115-16; site 81; situation 68, 69, 81; temple 26, 102, 134; *see also* Bambyke, Membij
Hierax, Ptolemaic agent 157-8, 162
Homs 24 n. 199; *see also* Emesa; Lake of 20, 116
Horum Huyuk 138
Huarté 116

Iamblichos, Arab chief 157, 159, 161, 177–8, 180, 186
Ichnai 45, 46
India, British rule in 62
insulae, size of 48, 50
Iopolis 34
Ipsos, battle 1, 47, 51, 57, 60, 144
irrigation 11, 12
Iskenderun 16, 24; plain 8, 108, 116–17
Islahiyé, *see* Nikopolis
Issos, battle of 24, 31, 35–6, 36–7
Ituraeans, Arab tribe 183, 184

Jabboul, lake and salt marsh 11, 181; settlement near 19, 115–16
Jebel Zawiyé, hills 10, 72
Jerusalem 22, 28, 132
Jisr esh-Shogour 73, 105, 138
Jordan, river 20
Judaea, Maccabee revolt in 158, 163, 168
Julius Caesar, C. 195

Kappadokia 51
Kara, river 10, 35, 38, 52, 80, 103, 105
Kassandros, king 1, 39–40, 51, 54
Khan Sheikhoun 73 n.
Kilikia 1, 22 n., 23 n., 28, 29, 32, 45, 46, 60, 71, 129, 190, 191, 196; acquired by Seleukos I 41, 58, 109; ruled by Demetrios 109; ruled by Pleistachos 54, 109
Kilikian Gates, pass 51
Kirikhan 80
Kleopatra Thea 159, 161, 163
Kleopatra Selene 178 n.
kleros 112–15, 119
Klonios, Laodikeian leader 166
Kommagene, Assyrian deportations from 22 n; kingdom 43, 78, 170, 173, 175, 176, 185, 190, 191–2, 195–6, 199
Korupedion, battle 58
Kurd Dagh, mountains 10, 35, 80
Kyros the Younger, Persian pretender 16, 18, 24–5
Kyrrhestike 40–1; confrontation in 41; satrapy 41, 49
Kyrrhos 44, 60, 102, 108, 128, 185, 186; acropolis 61; communications 80, 105, 182; foundation 40–2, 50–1, 134; history 134–5, 174–5, 196; modern condition 78, 79, 81; population 95–7; site 61, 69, 83–4, 85, 86, 87, 92, 97; situation 69, 78–9

Laodike, Seleukeian tribe 152
Laodikeia-ad-Libanum 64, 104, 106, 107, 130, 131, 139, 140, 161–2, 178 n., 186; *see also* Tell Nebi Mend
Laodikeia-ad-Mare 110, 117, 168, 169, 183, 192, 199; autonomy 175–6, 195; coinage 50; communications 105, 127, 184; foundation 48–9, 111; government 66, 152–3; growth 127–8, 135; history 152–3, 160, 166–7, 168, 171–2, 175–6, 188, 197–8; modern condition 71, 79, 81; settlement near 117; site 58, 84–5, 86, 91–2, 95
Laodikeia-in-Media, *epistates* of 62
Larissa 103, 104, 106, 160, 168, 169; dependent on Apamea 42–3, 130, 161; foundation 39–40, 42, 44, 52, 73, 107, 153, 159; growth 130, 131
Lattakia, plain 8; occupation 16, 17
Lebanon, mountains 8, 9, 183, 184
Licinius Lucullus, L. 176, 190, 191, 192, 193, 194
Lollius, L. 190
Lysias, brigand base 180, 192
Lysias, Seleukid regent 105, 154, 156
Lysimachos, king 1, 51, 54, 55, 57, 61

Maarra 42
Maccabees, revolt of 155, 158, 170, 183
Macedonia 42, 58, 61, 65–6, 95
Macedonians 7, 31–2; settlement of, in Syria 44–5, 47
Madkh, lake and salt marsh 11, 19, 77, 115, 133
Magarataricha, *see* Megara
Magnesia, battle 141, 179
Malkhos, *see* Iamblichos
Mallos 28
Marash 80
Marathos 16, 24, 27, 33, 39, 120; Alexander at 17, 27; Arados and 93–4, 128, 144–7, 159, 166; autonomy 146–7; communications 105; decline 117; possible garrison at 32 n.; site and situation 93–4; stadium 85–6; succeeded by Antarados 94; temple 27
Marcius Rex, Q. 190, 191, 193, 194
Mariamme 18, 30, 104, 105, 106, 131, 184, 187
Mariamnitai 184–5, 187, 197
Maroneia 43
Marrat en-Noman 73 n.
Masyaf 106
Mazabda 16, 111

Media 46
Mediterranean sea 43, 54, 58
Megara 42, 108; dependent on Apamea
59
Membij 18; survey near 115–16; *see also*
Hierapolis
Menes, satrap of Syria 32
Menon, satrap of Syria 25 n.
Mesopotamia 1, 28, 31, 45, 51, 105, 133,
170, 176, 196
Mesta Blouné, *see* Apollonia
Miletos 100
al Mina-Sabouni 16, 71, 111, 113, 117;
Greeks at 17, 33, 35, 39
Minet el-Beida 33
el-Mishrifé 20, 116
Mithridates, king of Pontos 188, 189, 192
Mopsuestia 28
mountains of Syria 9, 10
Myriandros 16, 24–5, 28, 30, 39; termed
a *polis* 63

Nabataeans 20, 45, 177
Nahr el-Kebir, *see* Eleutheros
Nazerini, tetrarchy 184, 185, 186, 192
Nebi Is, *see* Chalkis
Nehemiah 22
Neirab 19
Neo-Babylonian Empire 21–2, 29
Nikopolis 60, 103, 120; communications
78, 80; history 134, 135, 196; Seleukos
I and 52–3, 137; site 69; situation 68,
80–1; supposed foundation by
Alexander 35–6
Nineveh 29
Niya 111
nomads 11, 14, 45, 58, 178;
encroachment into settled land 29,
177
Nosairi 184

occupation of land 13–21, 115–18, 131,
204–9
Olympios, Seleukeian deme 152
Orontes, river 8, 9, 38, 69, 71, 74, 104,
181; named Axios 42; valley of 9, 10,
17, 19, 73, 104–5
Orthosia 105
Osrhoene, kingdom 170, 173, 196

Palestine 1, 3, 22, 28, 29, 45, 54, 73, 126,
130, 155, 158, 168
Palmyra 181–3, 189
Paltos 16, 101, 117, 145

Parthia, Parthians 38, 75–6, 105, 132,
155, 163, 164–5, 170, 174, 175, 187,
188, 189–90, 193, 196, 198
Pella, early name of Apamea 39, 42, 44,
49
Pella, Transjordan 45
Perdikkas 45
Persepolis 7, 29
Persian rule in Syria 22–3, 29
Philip I, king 132, 175
Philip II, king 178 n., 191, 192, 194
Philip II, Macedonian king 66
Philip, Seleukid regent 104, 154, 156
Phoenicia 1, 28, 29, 54, 126, 130, 144,
146, 161, 163
Pleistarchos 54
polis, applicability of term 63–5, 152
Pompeius Magnus, Q. 172, 173, 179–80,
187, 189, 190–8
Pontos 192
Poseidonia 129
pottery, Greek 17; Persian 18
province, Syria as Roman 2
Ptolemaic dynasty 188
Ptolemais-Ake 156, 162, 176, 189
Ptolemy I Soter, king 58, 60; boundary
of lands of 59; seizes Palestine and
Phoenicia 1, 51, 54
Ptolemy II 149
Ptolemy III, invasion of Syria 84, 123,
142, 145, 150–1, 152
Ptolemy VI 155, 157–8
Ptolemy Keraunos 143, 149

Qalat al-Mudiq 72, 73, 199; *see also*
Apamea
Qinnesrin, *see* Chalkis
Qoueiq, river 10, 77, 79, 115, 133

rainfall 9–10, 11–12
Ramitha 16, 111
Raphanaia 107, 131
Raphia, battle 179
al-Raqqa 11 n., 25
Ras el-Basit 16, 72, 110, 117, 129, 131;
Greeks at 17, 33
Ras Ibn Hani 16, 110, 117, 127, 129
Ras Shamra 16, 33, 72, 117
Rhambaei, Arab tribe 181
Rhodes 17
Rhosos 16, 24, 108–9
Rome, Roman Empire 1, 100, 141, 154–
5, 163, 173, 175, 185, 188, 189–98
Rum Kalé 138

Sabouni, *see* al Mina-Sabouni
Sajur, river 10, 11
Salamis, battle of 37
Salukiyé, *see* Seleukobelos
Samal 80–1
Samandag 71
Samaria 32, 45
Samsigeramos, Arab king 178, 179–81,
    186, 189, 191, 193, 194, 195, 196–7
Seleukeia-in-Pieria 18, 104, 111, 117,
    152–3, 160, 191, 198, 199; acropolis
    61; as a capital 122–3; *asylos* 162;
    autonomy 195; coins 49, 154, 157;
    communications 105; *epistates* 152;
    foundation 48–9, 57, 117, 152; history
    126, 135, 159–60, 161, 171, 176, 192;
    kleroi 113–14; modern condition 70,
    79, 81; population 95–7, 99; Ptolemaic
    rule 84, 96, 124, 127, 142, 146, 148,
    150–1, 152; settlers 98; site 56, 58, 84,
    85, 86, 87, 91–2, 95, 97; situation 68–
    9, 70–1, 109
Seleukeia-on-the-Tigris 49, 96, 135, 153
Seleukeia-Zeugma, *see* Zeugma
Seleukid dynasty 2, 137, 142–69, 170
'Seleukis' 41, 49, 142
Seleukobelos 107, 131, 138; dependent
    on Apamea 59
Seleukos I Nikator, king 1, 46; acquires
    Kilikia 41; acquires Syria 7, 32–3, 47,
    144; as city-founder 2, 39, 47–55, 56–
    62, 91, 100, 106, 109, 121, 134, 140,
    141, 200; at Ipsos 57, 61; bridge-
    builder 51, 104; coinage 50;
    conciliates subjects 53, 56–7, 112;
    death 142, 143, 149; destroys
    Antigoneia 37, 47–8, 55–6, 96; *epistates*
    62; instruments of control 61–3, 154,
    169; marriage with Stratonike 55;
    organizer of Syrian satrapies 41, 49;
    origin 65; planning of 58–62, 67, 86–7;
    possible founder of Alexandria-by-
    Issos 36; problems of, in Syria 54–8,
    112; quarrel with Ptolemy 53; rivalry
    with Demetrios Poliorketes 41, 52–3,
    54–5; settles Greeks and Macedonians
    in Syria 44–5, 47–55, 60–1, 98;
    supposed founder of cities 46; war
    with Antigonos 51
Seleukos II Kallinikos, king 123–4, 141,
    142, 143, 145–6, 150–1
Seleukos III Soter, king 101
Seleukos IV Philopator, king 62

Sermeda, hills near 10
Sheikh Zenad 16
Sicily 167, 168 n.
Sidon 28
Silas, brigand 180, 192
Silpion, Mount 34–5, 95, 122, 125
Simyra 117, 146, 166
Sqalbiyé 73
Strato of Beroia 173–4, 181, 188
Stratonike, wife of Seleukos I and
    Antiochos I 49; patron of Hierapolis
    53, 112
Stratonike, rebel 124, 142
Syria, acquired by Seleukos I, 7, 30, 32–
    3; Alexander and 24–8, 30, 31–3, 34–
    7, 47; Antigonos and 45–7, 51;
    Assyrian policies in 22; boundaries 1–
    2, 8; cavalry of, at Gaugamela 30;
    climate 8, 9–10, 12–13; coast 8;
    condition 7, 30; communications 58–
    9, 67, 75–7, 103–7, 181–2; garrisons
    32–3; geography 8–12, 67; importance
    3, 31; in Neo-Babylonian Empire 22;
    Mamluk policy 29–30; military
    campaigns in 23 and n., 30, 32, 52–3;
    occupation of land 13–20, 177, 204–9;
    Persian 18, 22–3, 24–9, 31–2; Roman
    province 2, 67, 185, 194–9; satrapy/ies
    32, 49; Seleukid rule 1, 41, 54, 170;
    settlement of Greeks in 17, 32–47, 100,
    125, 141; small towns 101–10;
    supposed foundations of Alexander
    34–7; villages 110–11, 187
Syrians, alienation 119, 148, 158, 176–8,
    186, 199; conciliated by Seleukos 53,
    56–7, 112

Tabbat el-Hammam 117
Tardytenses 184–5, 187, 189, 197
Tarutia 185, 187
Taurus, mountains, as Syrian boundary
    2, 8, 51; Seleukos' boundary 41, 109,
    129
taxation 29, 119
Tell el-Abd 19
Tell Abu Danné 19
Tell Afis 19
Tell Durak 16, 117
Tell Hana 20
Tell Mardikh 19
Tell Mastuma 19
Tell en-Naam 19

Tell Nebi Mend 20, 27, 116; *see also*
  Laodikeia-ad-Libanum
Tell Qarqur 116, 140
Tell Rifaat 27, 108, 110, 130
Tell Sukas 16, 17, 33, 39, 117
Tell et-Tin 116
Tell Tuqun 19, 116
Teos 152–3
terror, as a method of government 21–2
Thapsakos 17, 24, 25–6, 28, 30, 31, 35,
  39, 50–1, 104; probable garrison 32;
  termed a *polis* 63
Thessaly 30–40
Thrace 43
Tigranes, Armenian king 175–6, 179,
  188–90, 192, 196
Tigris, river 28
Timarchos, rebel 155, 162
Transjordan 45, 177
Tripolis 28, 162
Tryphon, king 105, 132–3, 155, 157–8,
  159–61, 162, 169, 177
Tyre 26, 28, 31–2, 54, 104

Umm el-Mara 19
Urima 138

Vespasian, Roman emperor 179
villages 110–11

warfare, effects on Syria 23, 30, 155–6,
  162–3, 168–9, 171
Wars, Syrian 1, 146, 149–50, 155

Zawiyé, Jebel, *see* Jebel Zawiyé
Zeugma 25, 44, 53, 122, 128, 199;
  communications 75, 78, 80, 104–5,
  181–2; foundation 50–1, 52; history
  133–4, 135, 174, 175, 176, 195–6;
  modern condition 76, 79; settlement
  near 116; site 69, 85, 92; situation 75–
  7, 133; suburb of Apamea 51, 92, 196
Zeus 34, 56
Zinjirli, *see* Samal
'Zizon', *see* Azizos